D0927970

INQUIRY AND REFLECTION

SUNY Series, Teacher Empowerment and School Reform
Henry A. Giroux and Peter L. McLaren, Editors

INQUIRY AND REFLECTION

Framing Narrative Practice in Education

DIANE DUBOSE BRUNNER

Foreword by Maxine Greene

State University
of New York
Press

Published by
State University of New York Press, Albany

Production by Susan Geraghty
Marketing by Fran Keneston

Printed in the United States of America

For information, address State University of New York Press,
State University Plaza, Albany, N.Y., 12246

Library of Congress Cataloging-in-Publication Data

Brunner, Diane DuBose, 1949–
        Inquiry and reflection : framing narrative practice in education /
Diane DuBose Brunner.
            p.   cm. — (Teacher empowerment and school reform)
        Includes bibliographical references.
        ISBN 0–7914–1869–3
        1. Critical pedagogy.   2. Narrative (Rhetoric)   3. Education-
-Experimental methods.   I. Title.   II. Series.
LC196.B78   1994
371.1'02—dc20   93–17270
                                                                                    CIP

10 9 8 7 6 5 4 3 2 1

Some of the ideas in this book are published in the folowing essays:

Brunner, Diane D. "Opening Spaces for Confrontive Encounters with Literature." *ERIC* (Microfiche Doc. #ED322514), February, 1991.

――――. "Stories of Schooling in Films and Television: A Cultural Studies Approach to Teacher Education." *ERIC* (Microfiche Doc. #ED 335330), December, 1991.

――――. "Crossing Boundaries: Teaching about Cultural Stereotypes," in *Vital Signs 3: Restructuring the English Classroom,* James L. Collins, ed. (Portsmouth, NH: Heinemann, Boynton/Cook, 1992), 60–73.

――――. "Teacher Resistance and the Construction of More Educative Texts," *Teaching Education,* 4 (1992): 97–106.

――――. "Dislocating Boundaries in Our Classrooms," *The Feminist Teacher,* 6 (1992): 18–24.

For my mother and father, Edna and Homer DuBose, whose stories taught me the value of narrative.

CONTENTS

FOREWORD

This is a book that beckons and provokes. Beginning with accounts of personal narratives, it moves on to narratives of schooling, of created worlds, and of the culture in its multiple modes or presentation. Diane Brunner is intent on moving readers to more reflective, more self-critical practice; and she does so by turning her varied lenses on roads not usually taken, on domains not commonly explored. Among these are the roads and domains of imaginative literature and the several media. Applying unusual critical and appreciative capacities, Brunner opens new possibility for textual study in relation to teaching. Her idea is to enrich, complement, and undergird discursive accounts of classroom practice with the kinds of works that involve readers, not only with visions of the possible, but also with the consciousness of contradiction and incompleteness that moves people to pose significant questions about their lived worlds and their work.

Like other critical writers in these times, Brunner is concerned for freeing learners to take their own initiatives in the face of social limitations and the pervasive play of power. Like others, too, she confronts the temptation to substitute a fresh new (presumably more humane and emancipatory) orthodoxy for one that is clearly oppressive, manipulative, and banal. Few readers will remain unconcerned when they consider her examination of the university professor "authorizing" what classroom teachers do when they turn, even critically, to practice. She writes about the complicity involved in the giving of "recipes" and the quashing of questions. Any adequate program of teacher education or teacher research must begin, this writer believes, with hard questions arising out of "a raced, classed, and gendered self-critical, self-conscious awareness" and extending "to wider political contexts that include always questions about knowledge, power, voices, and position." To move from the private to the political in this fashion requires an opportunity to look through one's own perspective, to problematize that perspective, to see it in the light of constructed knowledge. Nothing can work toward that end more effectively than informed engagements with works of art—ranging, in this text, from *The Dead Poets' Society* to *Catch-22,* from *Boyz N the Hood* to *A Room of One's Own.* All of these, and many more, are presented in rich interplay with texts by critical theorists, sociologists, psychologists, philosophers in the interest of allowing "multiple voices" to be heard.

Because Diane Brunner is convinced there can be no final answers to the hard questions and that no project can ever be complete, her book launches her readers on their own persisting quests. On the way, they will find instances of what it means to write in response to a significant reading, what dialogue can mean in the shaping of a vision and the constructing of the "real," what it means for teachers to break with determinism and embeddedness in the choices they make of themselves. This is a book that gleams with insights; it may be a book that opens readers to themselves. As it extends the spaces for imagining and acting, it may lay the ground for a new mode of community in which increasing numbers of voices can be heard and understood, in which the possible comes closer to being the achieved.

Maxine Greene
Teachers College
Columbia University

PREFACE

When I was three or four, I'd follow my mother from room to room listening to stories. She entertained me while she washed dishes, made the beds, ironed clothes, and so forth. She told stories that were home-rendered versions of some of my favorite books like *Henny Penny*, for example, and together we'd join in a sing-song verse of "the sky is falling, the sky is falling." And sometimes she told stories of her childhood, growing up in the backwoods of Alabama—stories that to some would qualify as tall tales but to my mother were true. For example, there was the story about the light on the hill that moved by itself and could only be seen certain nights of the year. Rich with color and detail, mother would weave together different aspects of her story each time, partly to keep me fascinated and partly, I expect, because she wouldn't remember from time to time what she had said previously. With each change, each nuance, mother became more animated, and then one story would lead to another so that if I were lucky, the stories would continue the entire day.

By the time I was ten, I knew every possible version of the story about the ghost of a young woman who stopped every year on the anniversary of her death to ask if she might pick a rose from mother's prize rose bush, which mother said grew larger and fuller each year. Or I'd heard my father tell, more times than I could count, about the half-boy/half-dog who appeared to come out of a creek my father fished in and who proceeded to follow him home crying, "wait for Dicey, wait for Dicey." "Used to be a damn good fishing hole," my father would say in the end.

Approach either of them in the right spirit and they'd break into story. Their stories were engaging; they drew me in. Inside this world I could see other worlds, and I could begin to see what connected one world to the other. Me to them and them to their people. And the truly marvelous thing about this story world was that things never seemed to look the same way twice. Like the rose bush that grew larger each year, stories grew; they seemed to take on a life of their own and all at the same time exist solely because my mother or father told them. For example, I could not tell the same story they told because in my telling, it became a different story, and I learned to value that difference. In other words, there was no fixed script. No matter how many times I heard a story, it changed in my telling as if it had a will of its own. Just as the rough next to smooth textures of a crazy quilt or the billowy shapes we see in clouds that change before our eyes, stories and the worlds they told of were alive—experiences dignified with each telling. I could write them down, try to fix them forever, but the memory of how they sounded and the various images they invoked each time they were told and changed kept those stories alive. Through story (and not just theirs) I learned about uncertainty, and I learned to do more than just tolerate the ambiguities that seemed so much a part of my world; I learned to take up those ambiguities or conflicts and work them over and over in my mind struggling to find meaning. Through story I came to understand ideas that were often abstract by connecting those ideas to my own lived experiences. Through the stories that dignified my mother's and father's experiences, I came to appreciate the value of narrative. (I am including books and other forms of aesthetic materials here with respect to valuing narrative.) And I especially grew to understand that the kind of autobiographical digging that took place each time they remembered and reconstructed their experiences through story was not only valuable for them but for me also. Their practice had created in me the habit of imagining, of digging deep, of remembering, of listening for stories, of assessing, of reconstructing, of questioning a particular construction, and of constructing again.

From the spirit world of the young woman who had a fascination for my mother's roses to the legend of a holy burial ground where native Americans were said to have kept vigil by torch-light long after their loved ones were with the spirit warrior to the everyday life of a fisherman whose invention muddied his fishing waters, their stories combined the religious, social, and aesthetic aspects of their lives. In "The Path of the Red and Black Ink," Gloria Anzaldua describes the "ethno-poetics" of her people. She says, "My people did not split the artistic from the functional, the sacred from the secular, art from everyday life." Nor did mine. No less than an Aztecan tribal dance, my parents' stories transformed both the teller and the listener "into something or someone else" through a power invoked in the performance. Anzaldua compares this living art or "invoked art" to Western art or to "art typical of Western European cultures." What Western art is missing, she says, is the performance ritual. "It has become a conquered thing, a dead thing separated from nature" like the Indian mask taken out of its culture and transported to an alien art museum away from the ritual and the power that such ritual can invoke. Invoked art, on the other hand, says Anzaldua, "is dedicated to the validation of humans"; whereas Western art "is dedicted to the validation of itself." "Invoked art is communal and speaks of everyday life"; it depends on community and experience for its expression.[1]

Like "ethno-poetic" or invoked art, writing that breaks forms that have been institutionalized by tradition and privilege suggests a contradictory practice; it suggests practice that arises from the human body like Aztecan blood sacrifices. Writing that infuses the blood and bones of the writer's life with what she or he is writing reconceptualizes the notion of text as invoked art reconceptualizes the purpose of art.[2] Therefore, as I struggle with the tensions created by my own contradictory practice of writing that includes personal stories, I ask for your indulgence and, perhaps, even for your acceptance of writing that blends public and private forms—understanding that acceptance of a nontraditional form of writing, in this instance, is also counterhegemonic because it questions textual authority and patriarchal tradition.

But even as I suggest comparing patriarchal forms of writing with Western art and writing that blurs distinctions between personal and public with invoked art, I want to make clear what I am about here. That is, I am not suggesting we formalize public/private writings. If that were to happen, we'd risk this work and others like it becoming a dead object rather than a practice—something that resembles Westernization rather than anything invoked. For as Anzaldua suggests, my practice is simultaneously full of "numerous overlays of paint, rough surfaces, smooth surfaces . . . a hybridization of metaphor, [with] different species of ideas popping up here, popping up there, full of variations and seeming contradictions."[3]

Therefore, I situate this notion of invoked art as writing/contradictory practice much like Anzaldua does, in the particular practice of writing for which she claims is but "putting stories on paper"—stories that explain theory, stories that explain practice.

She says this about her own practice: "writing produces anxiety. Looking inside myself and my experience, looking at my conflicts, engenders anxiety in me. [Writing] feels very much like . . . a lot of squirming, coming up against all sorts of walls. Or its opposite: nothing defined or definite."[4]

What I have attempted in this book and am attempting to explain here is that blending personal stories with public information both in order to help me make sense of things and to help me express my thoughts as clearly as possible is grounded in what Clare Juncker suggested as the deconstruction of boundaries like public/private, self/other, and so forth.[5] Therefore, like Anzaldua's conception of invoked art—art that combines rather than divides, art that is both/and—I hope my writing continues a both/and argument by encouraging contradictory writing practices. Also like Juncker, Dale Bauer says this about public and private writing: "Rather than opposing the public and private voices . . . , we need to see how to negotiate [them] in order to speak a multiplicity of voices into the cultural dialogue."[6]

Like Juncker and Bauer I suggest both/and constructions rather than either/or, for I believe, particularly in writing, such a construction speaks of shuttling back and forth between public and private worlds, between subjectivity and objectivity, between experience and narration—the way we actually tend to live our lives. In other words, when we negotiate positions bereft of extremes (i.e., when we're not satisfied to express ourselves in one way *or* the other, but in many ways, all of which acknowledge our identities), we may begin to dislocate positions that privilege tradition and the dominant culture. Therefore, pushing back the boundaries of acceptable discourse here can be seen in terms of both the form and the content of our language. That is, we challenge acceptable writing practices/textual authority when the form of our writing is contradictory—when we infuse our language with a personal voice, a presence of persons as Roland Barthes suggests.[7] And we also challenge or question patriarchal tradition (what is taken as a given— fixed meanings, fixed social codes, fixed relations of power that beget fixed knowledge, and so on) when the content of our writing identifies us with counterhegemonic ideologies or positions that counter dominant perspectives and shows the incomplete nature of any particular discourse.

My advocacy then is toward a dislocation of boundaries—a blurring of genres—in order to move away from either/or extremes that limit voice and tend to produce totalitarian discourse. Therefore, my practice is not limited to critique; it is also about surfacing possibility. Although I make various and often diverse theoretical and interpetive choices, I nonetheless regard multiple meanings/interpretations as central to theorizing both/and. I draw on multiple aesthetic forms and conversations because I assume the imagination is central in seeing/theorizing other ways of thinking, acting, being in the world. And I often read/critique these literatures along seemingly contradictory lines because I want to show the partiality of any single discourse or theory to explain the range of human potential/possibility. In a much more general sense, I argue for a lack of certainty so that other discussions are possible. And it seems to me that if we are going to argue such a position, our writing ought to reflect/model that.

This lack of "certainty" to which I refer suggests what Barbara Eckstein in *The Language of Fiction in a World of Pain* says is needed in order to confront dualism. She says that by rejecting the notion of certainty we reject its "fact" and its method. In other words, Eckstein is claiming that certainty seems to lead to bipolarization whether or not what we are certain about contradicts power and authority. And this may occur because certainty seems to be based in a kind of problem-solving rather than problem-raising or questioning attitude that leads us to leap ahead to conclusions—to ends.[8]

Most importantly, perhaps, a position of uncertainty seems to suggest the lack of a totalizing assignment of meaning. It implies a willingness, as Barbara Johnson suggests, to question interpretations or at the minimum to question the kind of interpretation we thought we might make.[9] Though Eckstein notes the possibilities for infinite regression within the practice of deconstruction, such practice, she reminds us, does tend to promote questioning, self-consciousness, and lack of certainty.[10] Lack of certainty or deferring absolute interpretation then is at least part of the notion implied by Jacques Derrida's use of the word *differance* within the context of his work in deconstruction. Yet we are reminded in Derrida's work that lack of absolute meaning does not prevent the function of absolutes within society—within the political systems of power that we attempt to work our way out of.[11] So, though the attempted dislocation of accepted forms of discourse makes this writing a possible medium for recasting problems of knowledge and value, we may not expect such writings to act as solutions that rupture the power/powerless dichotomy. We may only expect such practices to question the powerful effect of dualisms already at work.[12]

With Janet Miller, then, I refer to this book as a contradictory practice, for it is both contrary and full of contradictions. In other words, part of the contradiction lies in advocating a contrary position—a position that suggests my own complicity with the will to or desire for certainty about that with which I am in contradiction.[13] Yet lack of taking up a contradictory position makes me no less complicit in the systems of power I rail against. For as Eckstein writes of uncertainty in the conclusion of her book, "No authority does not mean no responsibility. . . . [What] the world requires arises from wounds born of identity with victims and complicity with victimizers. While shame hangs its head and guilt seeks forgiveness, complicity acts to undo what it has done."[14]

Thus, my contradictory practice here in this book also becomes a *search* for "authenticity," to use Eckstein's words, "in a self whose goal is not power over the other"[15] but the desire to understand and to invoke complicity. Yet even in this desire, as Eckstein writes, "a text or interpretation weaves a web of complicity entangling its author and its readers."[16] Moreover, it is through this same search for authenticity that I approach my teaching—the same practice that helps me have the courage (much to the chagrin of my family) to tell personal stories (and sometimes very difficult ones) in order to help students think through particular theoretical constructs. Yet, inevitably, this practice shows my own complicity in privileging theory. Still, searching for authenticity or sense of *self with others* may be the way many of us imagine the possible and analyze the stories of our lives all the time—not something that seems very contradictory. Yet Eckstein suggests that it is through a search for authenticity and selfhood that we gain, perhaps, the deepest understanding of others. She writes, "One's changing perceptions of the other provide the changing definitions of the self. One is in continuous dialogue with what is different and what is the same. [The self is] not separate from history."[17] Therefore, any notion of self with other, with history, seems to also suggest a kind of necessary complicity with the social, cultural, and political systems to which individuals belong either by choice or by default.

Finally, it is in suggesting the link of self with history to Anzaldua's[18] notion of art that is not separate from everyday life and the artist who is not separate from her or his community that makes this work seem, perhaps, most contradictory. Many of us are not accustomed to thinking of our private selves and our public selves as cohabitating the same spaces. We seem to be more comfortable separating the intellectual from the political and each from the emotional. Yet this knowledge of self and other to which Eckstein refers is, as Jo Anne Pagano suggests, "a *search* for . . . finding and forming oneself in the representations with which our world is written"[19]—public and private, intellectual and political, and so forth. This book then is part of that search.

ACKNOWLEDGMENTS

If language is a collective creation, then this text and every text represented here are collaboratively interwoven to shout my concerns over the nature of schooling and both the limits and the possibilities of teaching and learning in schools. This work not only reflects a wider ongoing debate, but it also reflects the richness of conversations with students and teachers whose concerns mix with my own to offer balance and to challenge my thinking.

I have many to thank and many whom I wish I had already thanked. In part the writing of this book has been an opportunity to reflect on those important teachers in my life: My parents, Edna and Homer DuBose and other members of my family (all of whose stories taught me so much about narrative), my husband, Roger, and children, Chris and Tiffany (whose love, quick wit, and untiring patience helped keep me "real" and gave me a sense of perspective about this work), my other mom and dad, Eileen and Ed Brunner (who have loved, supported, and encouraged me like a daughter), teachers from grade school through graduate school (some of whose names are revealed through stories in this book and many whose names are not), students from early high school teaching experiences to present, and friends and colleagues (especially Tess Tavormina, Ellen Pollak, and Victor Paananen who offered me early encouragement to go forward with the project, Kitty Geissler who kept me from going crazy, and Jim Collins and Susan Luks who read and listened to drafts, gave feedback, and kept asking when the book would be finished). Each has taught me valuable lessons; each is responsible in her or his own way for my intellectual journey of which this book is a part.

I especially wish to thank Lois Patton for always believing in me and for the many long conversations we had that came just at the moment when I needed encouragement. No editor could have been more supportive in addition to offering useful advice and valuable insights. I also want to thank the series editors, Henry Giroux and Peter McLaren, for valuable conversations during the preparation of this manuscript. The students of TE326 (Fall, 1990) played a major role in the development of this work. I owe all thirty-one students (now teachers) a huge debt of gratitude for their willingness to share personal stories and to respond on tape to the books and films discussed here. A special thank you TE326, Fall 1990 class. Finally, I want to express appreciation to my research assistant and friend, Rashidah Muhammad, who taped and transcribed all conversations in TE326 for an entire quarter and who read numerous drafts of this work in manuscript. Without her help, I am convinced, I would still be writing this book. Rashidah was by far my toughest critic, and I think now it was our conversations that kept me reflexive. She worked far beyond my ability to pay her and no simple thanks seems sufficient.

CHAPTER 1

Introduction: Narrative Frames

Rosemary is learning to read. An arthritic, Rosemary has frequently been confined to her bed. To compensate, her mother reads marvelous adventure stories, practically around the clock. Some of Rosemary's favorites are *Puck of Pook's Hill, The Eagle of the Ninth, The Gladiators,* and *Last Days of Pompeii.* When Rosemary's mother wants to teach her to read she sits her down with a book about a rosy-faced family who lives next door and has cats that sit on mats. Rosemary hates this book and decides she will never learn to read. But Rosemary does learn to read while in Miss Beck's first-grade classroom. Miss Beck is a wonderful teacher who values literature as much as Rosemary. Rosemary learns to read from an old volume of Grimm's *Fairy Tales,* though she doesn't know quite how or when. She only knows that when she entered Miss Beck's Academy she could not read, and by the end of the first term, without any apparent transition, she is reading everything.

Benjie is thirteen years old, African American, poor, a seventh-grader. He attends a tough school in the heart of Harlem. He's a street-wise junkie who hates school and teachers. Benjie says teachers say one thing with their mouths while their eyes are screaming something else. He says teachers call on the poorest readers to read aloud so they can make fools of them.

Jerry attends Trinity High School. He plays football and tries to stay out of trouble. Though Jerry is no trouble-maker himself, he is often perceived as one. Jerry meets trouble head on when he accepts the challenge of one of the school's gangs and refuses to participate in Trinity's annual fund raiser.

Trinity is a private school dedicated to preparing middle-class males for college. Like many high schools, Trinity has its gangs.

And like many schools, Trinity allows them to function by ignoring their presence. It particularly ignores the presence of the Vigils.

And teachers at Trinity do their part. Especially Brother Leon. Jerry says that Brother Leon will as soon strike a student with his blackboard pointer as look at them. He also humiliates his students. For instance, in class one day, Jerry says Brother Leon made fun of Bailey and accused him of cheating because he's a straight A student. Leon told Bailey that only a genius could make all A's. And while awaiting laughter from the class, Brother Leon went on making fun, telling Bailey that he looked like a genius with his glasses, pointed chin, and wild hair.

Archer Sloane is an English professor in his fifties. He comes to his task of teaching literature with seeming disdain. He is disliked and feared by most students, and he responds with a detached and ironic amusement. While he lectures, he impatiently runs his fingers through his gray, curling hair. His voice is flat and dry, without expression or intonation.

Profiles of students and teachers? Brief glimpses of life in any school? No. Instead they are vignettes from literature, from stories of schooling, that portray with all the realism and drama the everyday lived culture of schools. Rosemary is Rosemary Sutcliff in her autobiography *Blue Remembered Hills*; Benjie is from *A Hero Ain't Nothing but a Sandwich*; Jerry is the central protagonist in *The Chocolate War*; and Archer Sloane is the teacher William Stoner most remembers in the novel, *Stoner*.[1] I was always drawn to these stories when selecting books to use in my literature methods courses. I was drawn to them long before I realized why. Students read these and other stories with eagerness, and as we began to discuss these realistic but highly imaginative books I noticed a pattern. Discussion nearly always began with students relating their personal schooling stories, either pleasant or terrible memories of situations they had encountered as students or as prospective teachers during field experience.

Rounds of storytelling then became our discussion, and it seemed that their stories were a vehicle for extending both the imaginative text and the more methodological textbook—for making meaning, often for articulating that which had not heretofore been considered, and for expanding their concepts of teaching and learning. Eventually with questions from peers about individual experiences and with a little nudging on my part in the form of questions that might draw out deeper issues, storytelling worked its way into dealing with teaching/learning issues that began to get at how various aspects of school, in general, and the lessons we plan, in particular, are taken up by students. Reading imaginative texts alongside professional texts seemed to open up both discussion about schooling and discussion related to the teaching of literature.

Questions about expanding traditional literature curricula to include trade books (children's and young adult literature) launched my thinking about more critical pieces to add to their reading—readings that might say something about the privileging of particular texts (surrounding the most commonly discussed issue in my English department—canonicity). It was not until much later that everything seemed to come together to form the research on which this book is based.

As I continued to think about the connections students were making, I wondered what connections there were between the kinds of stories I asked students to read, even those that did not relate to schooling, and the kinds of stories they told. I played with the arrangement. I used different books for a term, trade books they might teach to adolescent readers that had little if anything to do with school but that nonetheless had teenage protagonists. Even when there were no teachers and no schools in the books we read, students still related teenage life and teenage problems to some aspect of schooling. As teachers-to-be, my students saw the potential for schooling relationships in nearly everything we read, at least in terms of the broader context that often related to effects of schooling experiences. I could bring in newspaper clippings or magazine stories and the responses were similar. When I asked students if they could speak to this reaction, their reply was simply that they were usually inundated with more standard educational texts as well as the lecture format in other classes. Students eagerly confessed that "stories," whether from literature, film, or simply the newspaper, provided something they missed when faced with only professional readings. Stories provided a more realistic experience (and if about schooling then referential to teaching) and because the literature was imaginative, students said they tended to fantasize (if about schooling then about different situations related to school). Imagination in this case seemed directly related to reflection (albeit, perhaps, uncritical)—to the kind of wondering about or puzzling out situations they encountered in the books we read.

Lacking a kind of situational exploration of teaching and learning, students felt their textbooks were often one-sided presenting a more monolithic approach. Student often complained that ideas were presented as if all students responded the same way to school, but experience had already taught them that neither teaching nor learning was easy given the variety of baggage both teachers and learners often bring. Textbooks that taught various aspects of the English curriculum like reading and writing processes and the study of language/grammar and literature focused only on the positive. Reporting only success stories had a way of making students feel uncomfortable given what they remembered from their own experiences. They wanted to know what teachers did when things went wrong. Many had already had the experience, in their field placements, of trying something according to a textbook and finding the lesson fraught with problems they couldn't quite handle. Often the young adult literature we read explored some of those difficulties, albeit often in somewhat harsh but, perhaps, more honest detail. Imaginative literature then became a window onto what students sought for affirmation—that not all lessons succeed, not all plans are perfect, some ideas work with some students and other ideas do not. Especially when that imaginative literature dramatized the classroom, students seemed more capable of seeing the complexities of teacherwork. When they had begun to sense that they were failures if a lesson didn't work in their particular field experiences, through the reading of stories that illuminated various schooling situations, students seemed to begin to see more systemic reasons for their difficulties and they began to pose a range of possibilities for some situations. That is, with a more open-ended curriculum, students seemed more capable of articulating alternative arrangements for teachers and students, and they seemed to begin to see school within a broader social framework.

Stories then tended to help them make connections that seemed to lie somewhere between expectations predicated on future scenario planning and their experiences, both past and present. And these stories, often conceived of only at the point of utterance, seemed to suggest a kind of active theorizing about schools and curricula, teachers and teaching, and their positions within that multidimensional structure. For example, after reading *The Chocolate War* and discussing the cruel nature of Brother Leon in this book,[2] Mary, a junior recently admitted to the teacher education program, remembered a teacher she'd had who frightened her and she shared that experience with the class:

> I had this teacher once that told us how mean he was and that he was a great fan of Edgar Allen Poe. Then he went on to describe some of the torture treatments in Poe's books like sewing live rats in someone's stomach. I mean it was just awful; you didn't want to breathe in that class.

Discussion then turned to the significance of Mary's personal story and what meanings she had made of that experience. One student asked how that had "affect[ed her] learning in that class" and if she ever felt "free to contribute to discussion after that?" Another student asked if she really "believe[d] the teacher or did [she] ever think he might have just been trying to scare the class?"

After these questions from students, I asked if we thought Brother Leon was just trying to scare students and if so why? What would behavior like Brother Leon and Mary's teacher have suggested about the role these teachers perceived they had? What might Mary's teacher's behavior have suggested about how he perceived literature or the teaching of it? What occurs when teachers strike fear in the hearts of students? What does it mean for the teacher; what does it mean for the student? And how important are learning environments to students abilities to learn, particularly respective to reading and learning from literature?

I thought about Mary's story and what her telling might have suggested. First, she chose to tell this story; it was not written in her response journal (a journal for reactions, questions, and comments to class readings). Did vocalizing this experience signal something important? I wondered whether she truly believed this teacher would harm her class and how her seeming anxiety suggested by this response had effected her abilities to respond to literature thereafter. Did she perceive literature as having only "correct responses" or would she have risked connecting that literature to any lived experience the way one of our other course texts suggested?[3] Or had she simply buried that experience after class that day? The fact that our reading made her recall on this day suggested something, but what? That it had affected much of her schooling or that it had been repressed until now? What would she do with this memory now? How would it affect her as a teacher?

Or would she even remember this day? Reflection on the subject, not just a response soon forgotten, seemed important. Not so much how to evoke such reflection but how to sustain it for a period and work through it making sense of all its implications would be more difficult to achieve. And how to make more critical student's reflections that seemed to automatically occur when they read imaginative texts and professional texts would, perhaps, be even more difficult given the critical theoretical texts I would want to include to help them pose even harder questions. I wondered for several months about Mary's story and others' shared both through class discussions and often in journals.

The project I worked on over the summer months had to do with double-entry journals, something I had read about as a graduate student and was reminded of again when I attended a workshop sponsored by our Literacy Coalition. Our speaker, Ann Berthoff, focused her presentation on the uses of what she called a "dialectical notebook" for helping students make connections through reflection.[4] Berthoff used the word dialectical in this sense to mean the tension between language and thought. She described the journal as a place to record responses to readings or class discussions, take notes and so forth, and then after reflection, write a response to earlier responses, making personal connections. I believed this journal form might have the potential to promote a more critical reflection: the kind of thinking necessary for questioning assumptions and for reviewing, revising, and extending responses toward some deeper more meaningful learning experience. Consequently, I began to work on ways to use it and to determine whether a response to a response, as the double-entry notebook format suggested, would have any effect on the critical nature of reflection I might help students work toward.

In the fall I prepared and delivered a paper at a curriculum conference, raising some questions about critical inquiry and reflection, dialogue, and the dialectic that this journal format seemed to produce. At the conference several presentations legitimated my thoughts about the importance of critical reflection and the importance of teachers connecting teaching experiences to their personal lives—to understanding the relationship between one's private self and one's public teaching self. My thoughts returned to the stories of schooling and to how reflective my students had seemed sharing their stories. Flo Krall's growing up story and her readings from Rachel Carson's *Silent Spring* particularly resonated with what I had been thinking.[5]

Other presentations clicked for me as well. Ann Trousdale with Ken Kantor, Sue Jungck, Ann Bennison, and Dan Marshall gave a readers' theater performance in which they shared schooling narratives from literature while video monitors showed clips from sitcoms about teachers in classroom situations.[6] Later, Delese Wear, who teaches in a medical humanities program, gave a presentation about using literature in parity with textbooks to dramatize the emotional, indeed, more human side of any profession.[7] She pointed out that although textbooks often *name problems* and *suggest solutions*, literature *illumines the situation by calling forth an emotional response* from readers.

And then I began to understand much of what I had wondered about previously respective to the way students responded when we read literature. Though I had practiced a response-based approach to teaching, students had gone beyond Louise Rosenblatt's transactional theory that readers who vicariously experience a text will through personal connections create their own text or "poem."[8] Students had, it seemed, begun to fashion critical responses based on personal, emotional connections to literature, perhaps, due to their textbooks leaving out problems or simply naming them. Literature illuminated and showed possibilities; textbooks named/defined and stated solutions.

They were in a teacher education course reading teacher education materials, and they appeared to do an "educational reading" on the literary texts we read. As I attempted to pose with them many of the critical social issues confronting students and teachers, students began actively theorizing in simple form a "deconstructionist" response—that is, they began questioning the basic assumptions about teachers and students and teaching and learning and about the gendered, classed, and raced roles each played in the drama of schooling. The schooling scenarios within the books we read posed for them difficult ethical and philosophical problems related to teaching and learning. To say, however, that their questioning process alone could have produced the kind of self-conscious awareness I saw this practice fostering may be limiting. In other words, although a reader who is practiced in beneath-the-surface examinations of texts may without benefit of a literary experience engage in the same process my students seemed to engage in with stories, it seems more likely that the human connection to educational questions evolved, perhaps, more naturally through the reading of literature—fiction and autobiography, in particular—along with other course materials.

Furthermore, though responses may vary when we consider what draws us to a good book, some responses nearly always given are that good books cause us to think or a good read puts us in a thoughtful or contemplative mood—all of which is to say we become reflective. This mood or state of thoughtfulness may then create the space to focus more critically on social, cultural, and political issues when those are raised in other texts we read.

Until now students had read about teaching approaches and had understood teaching in a more clinical manner because their textbooks did not seem to illuminate situations the way literature did. However, through imaginative texts, students can begin to balance that clinical approach with a more humane understanding of teaching and learning through what in literature is often situated in conflict and resolution. Keeping these two domains of reading separate is the usual fare for students—what is often the case when pedagogy is taught in education departments and literature is taught in English departments. Combining these forms and adding a critical dimension from theory (even small passages) opened worlds of new understandings and possibilities for both me and my students.

For example, against the backdrop of Sylvia Ashton-Warner's *Spinster*,[9] a novel based upon Ashton-Warner's teaching experiences in the Maori schools for seventeen years and *Teacher*,[10] her autobiography, students read Cynthia Brown's *Literacy in Thirty Hours*[11]—a more methodological explication of Paulo Freire's literacy work in Northeast Brazil—along with a selection from *Pedagogy of the Oppressed*[12] about nonhierarchical student-teacher relationships. The latter two books draw heavily on the problems Ashton-Warner encountered with respect to *ideological* differences around the teaching of reading—something not often dealt with in more typical reading instruction books.

Ashton-Warner argues for teaching children to read from the first words they utter by actually having them write their own books to read instead of learning to read from primers or basal readers. She makes a strong claim for children's books to match not only their language but also their color so that they learn to value their words and experiences. In *Spinster* one child writes about Whareparita, a sister, giving birth to twins while another writes about her mother getting punched in the face.[13] Through emotion-filled story narrative, Ashton-Warner illustrates the Freirean notion of reading and writing the word and the world and the importance of students' valuing their own words and experiences as she details her own struggle with school officials who would rather Maori children learn to read Maori literature from primers first.[14]

Cynthia Brown politicizes the act of learning to read by saying that the way students use their capabilities in reading will often depend on teachers' political agendas. In other words, if teachers want students to read critically then they will create an environment for that to happen. She writes:

> If nonreaders learn to read by writing and read their own words and opinions, then they learn that their perceptions of reality are valid to others and can influence even those in authority. If, on the other hand, their teachers require them to learn the words and ideas in a primer which is donated by those in power, then the learners must accept that experience as more valid than their own.[15]

When the children write their own books, sometimes it means they actually write stories and sometimes it means they rewrite stories by inserting personal experiences into the stories that Miss Vontop reads (teacher's name in *Spinster*). In the story of "Little Red Riding Hood," for example, when the mother tells Red Riding Hood to take the basket of goodies to grandmother, the children insert that it would be okay to stop and play with Wiki or Mark, but if "Wed Wideen Hook" should see the wolf, she must walk straight past. In the middle of this story, one child interrupts to say that she likes talking to the wolf because he says funny things.[16] This passages echoes another course text by Louise Rosenblatt, *The Reader, the Text, the Poem*. Rosenblatt's reader response theory is articulated in this text and illustrated in Ashton-Warner's books. That theory suggests that readers create a "poem" or their response when they interpret a book through personal "lived-through" experiences.[17]

An example of how students' responses reflect both their understanding of the texts read and tend to be drawn from their personal experiences can be seen in David's storylike interpretation or response. David is a senior English education major who is currently in a teacher preparation program that allows him to spend a substantial number of hours per week in field experience. In David's case that experience consists of helping his supervising teacher by tutoring students who need extra help. David's response occurs in a conversation related to the importance of validating children's own language. This conversation follows our reading of *Teacher*. In *Teacher* we see Ashton-Warner validating the language children bring to school by having the Maori children learn to read from the books they've written and also by allowing children to name the key vocabulary for each day—words they've heard and are curious about.[18] Students in my class seem immediately struck by the importance of learning to read one's own words first and by their memories of how they learned vocabulary (and are perhaps even beginning to perpetuate this method in their own field experiences). David's two brief responses addressing issues of vocabulary and writing center on the larger focus of our discussion—that is, the value of learning from children. He says:

> 1.   I remember a teacher I had in fourth grade who . . . had some very old-fashioned ways of thinking about schooling. She had long vocabulary lists that we had to memorize. I mean English is so vast; how do you hope to do it with vocabulary lists? And she also had very quiet classrooms—you could hear the hum of a beehive. She said you have to memorize these things and not a care in the world was given to whether or not we understood what we had to memorize.

> 2.   But the high school I went to had a fairly whole language emphasis. So I didn't see a lot of rote memorization there. I can see it now in my field experience though. The instructor had a student who was having problems with commas—probably didn't notice what she had written—so she called me over, and said, "David is an English major; he can explain where commas go." She wanted me to go over the grammar rules of commas. I waited until the instructor went away, then I told the student to read the sentence out loud. She did. So then I said, "Do you remember where the spaces were when you spoke?" She said, "Yes." I said, "Put the commas there."

On the value of learning from students, Ashton-Warner often notes that at such times when children write passionately of their lived experiences, they become her "ardent" teachers, teaching her about their lives and their abilities to communicate through reading and writing.[19] From this point, students return to Freire's own words about student-teacher relationships—a partnership in teaching and learning as expressed in *Pedagogy of the Oppressed*.[20]

Through such reading experiences, students may come to understand connections between what Freire suggests about pedagogy and what Rosenblatt suggests about reading. Then, of course, playing what they learn from their experiences against what I learned from watching them engage in those experiences, we all more fully understand what Robert Scholes means in the statement, "Our job is not to produce 'readings' for our students but to give them the tools for producing their own."[21] Thus, my goals as I understood them then were that I wanted my students to begin to question the structures of schooling that they saw dramatized in the literature we read and to do that against their own backgrounds of experience, whatever that experience may have been. Though David, for example, seemed to recognize that the student writer knew more than the teacher gave her credit for knowing and that there might have been other vocabulary worth learning in fourth grade, he had not moved to a place where he could begin to problematize his teachers' circumstances within schooling institutions. That is, although David named what he saw as problematic, it was not obvious to me that he had begun to question the structures of schooling that might have contributed to the particular behaviors he named. Yet literature and other aesthetic materials paired with critical educational readings still seemed to offer possibilities for that kind of knowing, questioning, theorizing.

COLLECTING AND CODING STORIES OF SCHOOLING

During a sabbatical term I began collecting all the materials I could find, both literary and critical, that students might read as sites of contestation. My search included stories of schooling in books, films, television, songs, and so forth. A large corpus includes formal schooling narratives in literature, films, television, songs, and informal schooling stories in autobiographies (i.e., growing up stories about early experiences with reading and writing or students learning about themselves and their world in nontraditional settings). See the annotated bibliography for a complete list of the books used in this project.[22]

Beyond identifying narratives, I coded stories for ideological centers through which meanings related to both form and content might be produced (i.e., centers of caring and connectedness, student-teacher relations, themes of resistance related to domination/subordination along class, race, and gender lines, hidden curriculum, and the knowledge question).[23] These centers are also commonly noted in the literature on feminist pedagogy and critical social/educational theory.[24] Also within particular cultural and ideological frames of reference, I coded passages that dealt especially with language arts *contents and processes* in critical ways.

In the professional literature from which these codes are drawn, *caring,* for example, is defined as follows: Nel Noddings refers to caring as a philosophical approach to feminine ethics and moral education. She writes, "Caring preserves both the group and the individual . . . [and] limits our obligation so that it may be realistically met. It will not allow us to be distracted by visions of universal love, perfect justice, or a world unified under principle."[25] In other words, according to Noddings' definition, caring seems to allow us to look through the blind spots making problematic situations of inequality without pretending that they do not exist. Noddings's principle depends on a desire to be in a "caring relation" with others.

Codes that relate to student-teacher or teacher-learner relationships are those most commonly discussed by Freire, Giroux, Apple, Pagano, and Miller and similarly defined by each.[26] That is, in each instance, these relations refer to power differentials grounded in patriarchal practices and institutionalized by tradition. For example, critical social theory politicizes dissension related to power as it is reflected in structural hierarchies like student/teacher/administrator and related to pedagogical practice like authoritarian teacher roles indicated by methods and instructional materials.[27] Although much conflict in schools arise out of the larger social context of schooling, some confrontations between people seem to be related to competitiveness among individuals.[28]

In examining the effects of structural power or domination, resistance that is a natural by-product of power is seen as political when it becomes a struggle "directed toward putting an end to relations of domination," according to Apple.[29] On the other hand, Henry Giroux defines resistance that is not a part of the political project of creating alternative public spheres as the "personal space in which the logic and force of domination is contested by the power of subjective agency to subvert the process of socialization.[30] And in *Creating Spaces and Finding Voices*, Miller defines that resistance (hers and five teachers) in terms of collaboration as she describes the constant struggle for voice in their collective efforts to challenge conventional modes of research.[31]

With respect to teachers' roles reflected in practice and selected teaching materials, Freire describes a teaching/learning relationship that is either closely tied to domination and insists on knowledge transfer rather than thinking, or he describes teachers and learners as coinvestigators.[32] The former model insists that teachers deposit information into a passive student.

And finally, other codes describe what has been called the hidden curriculum or social dynamics in the classroom that tends to structure inequality; that is, the hidden curriculum is what students learn from the form or style of teaching, which frequently overrides or even causes resistance to content learning.[33] It often relates more to what is withheld than to what is taught, and it includes the knowledge question. That is, what counts for legitimate knowledge and who decides what counts? Questions of knowledge fundamental to issues of power and control, then, are central to this book.[34]

Moreover, here, I want to bring into discussion some "possible ways forward" as Raymond Williams writes in the last paragraph of *The Long Revolution*. With Williams, I want to "open discussion, extend relationships, [and focus upon] the practical shaping of institutions."[35] This book then is about *reform*ulating but not *form*alizing the language of the classroom—both in teacher education programs and in schools by grounding all teaching within experiential contexts and by using narrative as the pivotal frame of reference. It is about seeing both arenas—teacher education and public schools—as sites of contestation: oppositional, full of contradictions and ambiguities.[36] But it is not intended as a totalizing structure for the reformulation of teacher education. That is, as Williams suggests, these are but some "possible ways forward."[37]

Finally, this book is about finding ways of helping students make connections by anchoring our lessons to the things they know and can know with whatever limitations exist. It is about not teaching in abstractions that tend to elevate and mystify that which we cannot find words to explain. It is about connecting our words to things we know from experience and can make known to others through experience as Pagano suggests.[38] Although I agree here with Pagano's assumption that we can make our language and our theories concrete within the frame of our experiences, and students can do this within their own experiential realm, I do not assume that the meanings of the words we use have fixed referents. In other words, for me the signification of meaning is not only relational/referential but it is also cultural. Therefore, my voicing of meanings—my own attempts to be concrete and referential—is not without problems even though my unpacking of particularly difficult theories may ease students' minds somewhat. When we build contexts for learners, then, we need to keep in mind the cultural embeddedness of language as well. Although we may build contexts for learning that attempt to speak to particular individuals with particular experiences in particular historical moments, we need to realize also that our attempts may not provide a perfect match for students—it may, on the other hand provide a fit. Thus the variance between match and fit may account for the diversity in meanings that students and teachers understand from vast experiences that range the personal to intellectual and the sociopolitical to cultural. Yet telling our own stories and creating spaces for students to tell theirs is to understand somehow that stories provide links and that all our stories are ways of anchoring the world, of attaching meaning to words, and of knowing/articulating what we know.

I have interspersed stories throughout this text in order to illustrate how I have used schooling narratives (drawn from books, films, television, etc.) paired with critical readings to draw out students own understandings of schooling experiences—to help provide links. Occasionally, students' stories join these pairings to offer yet another layer of meaning, discussion, and debate. Their stories, however, are not intended to make the case that narrative practice necessarily engenders reflection. I mean instead to pose questions here about the possibilities for reflective practice. In other words, I wish to invite discussion, not to suggest methods or to pronounce solutions to the complex problems of educational reform.

ENTERING A WIDER DEBATE

Complex problems do not have simple solutions, and all research is not meant to provide answers. In fact, as Miller and others suggest, much research is meant to illuminate complexities and that illumination may simply provoke thought.[39] See, for example, Jesse Goodman's book *Elementary Schooling for Critical Democracy* also in the "Teacher Empowerment and School Reform" series.[40]

In particular, Goodman's book illuminates the complexities around the notion of educating a democratic citizenry beginning with elementary school. His contribution to this series does much to illustrate the current popularization and oversimplification of the word empowerment, and it suggests as I do here that teachers—individuals operating as a collective—are integral to any school reform project that is based on principles of educating for freedom.

Another important contribution to this series and to the school reform literature, in general, is the Schwoch, White, and Reilly text entitled *Media Knowledge*.[41] Their voices, as do the voices in this text, remind that our students experience an almost overwhelming amount of popular culture through media, which, therefore, makes popular media (e.g., television, radio, film, recorded music, magazines, news, and advertising) an important pedagogical site. Their questions challenge us to consider how consumers of media texts learn and how that learning either supports or undermines American education.

Giroux, Simon, and contributors raise similar questions about the relation between popular culture and pedagogy in a collection entitled *Popular Culture, Schooling and Everyday Life* (e.g., how students become self-reflective in the process of learning vis-à-vie popular culture, etc.).[42] In support of texts that recognize and affirm the role popular media plays in the process of learning and in the production of knowledge of both teachers-to-be and of other students, in *Work Time* Evan Watkins suggests that little of what we do in our classrooms can overcome the powerful affects of popular culture unless we in some way decide to make use of that ready resource.[43] He critiques, in particular, the work of English departments and of those who would see their role as substantial in the acculturation process of students. Therefore, what needs to be remembered here and in other texts that offer possibilities for reform is that these are possibilities—"possible ways forward"; the larger our pool of resources, the more capable our teaching will be in this rapidly changing technological society.

My work then is situated within these other discourses, but it is grounded in the particular research and practice that names my teaching project, the essence of which questions how we make sense of our public and private lives and what role narrative plays in that meaning making process. (Again, narrative is both the literatures we read—including films we watch/read and songs we hear/read—and the stories we tell as we read the world.) As I have reflected on my own experiences, I have wondered about the potential of aesthetic texts[44] to invoke reflection, to keep us questioning longer, and to keep uncertain that which is often claimed a certainty. In other words, I have wondered if a habit of reflectivity is possible, and if it is, can we link it to practices that are grounded in narrative activity? I have also considered the importance of self-reflection or reflexivity within the larger questions of reflective thinking and practice. This book then represents much of that wondering. In many ways it is a reflection on reflective practice. Though I describe the use of books, movies, television, music, and advertising in parity with professional texts (often critical theoretical works), I do not mean to suggest methodology. Rather, my intent here is to describe one possibility for narrative practice and how such practice might lead to critical inquiry and reflection. It is more a frame of reference than a particular course of study, more a surfacing of possibilities than a statement of probabilities. I do not wish to replace one orthodoxy with another; rather, I wish to offer a range of materials and some possible ways of thinking about the use of those materials that could potentially benefit any method of instruction or be adapted to any curriculum in which the goals of instruction are engagement with a subject, contemplation on both subject and experience, and meaning making. Not necessarily these particular materials but the kinds of materials these represent may illumine a possible unlit corner, thereby encouraging a wider political debate on school reform. Foremost, perhaps, is my desire to situate my teaching project among others who see teacher education as part of a larger social movement.

DISLOCATING THE BOUNDARIES OF THEORETICAL DISCOURSE

That movement, for me, is grounded in feminist principles and interpretations that suggest a move toward both/and constructs. Thus one goal here is to make a point about false dichotomies, either/or constructs, and extremes of any sort. Tensions exist within the pages of this book. They exist partly because theories, research, and practice do seem to be more contradictory than complementary and partly because I tend to be somewhat eclectic in both my theoretical and interpretive choices. Although I am somewhat eclectic, I am also intentional.

The various interpretive methods I have used here are a rather deliberate attempt to illustrate the sort of uncertainty that accompanies contradictory practice. They are also to illumine something of my understanding of embodied narrative—narrative that takes on the presence of persons engaged with and situated in the world in a variety of ways. Drawing on my own understanding of feminist principles and practices, then, I assume narrative can be construed as a blending of public/private because the private in this society has been made public and therefore political—for example, the various ways sexuality is regulated, the structural hierarchies that govern positions of dominance and subordination in the workplace as well as in the home, the social roles implicit and often explicit within gendered categories, even the ways in which male and female students tend to be treated differently in classrooms.

Therefore, with the body at its center, narrative becomes, in part at least, a process because humans change and both condition and are conditioned by that process. In other words, as any text tends to change with its reader, narrative, as I have experienced and observed it, tends not simply to change and remain changed or fixed but to grow, to fluctuate, to shuttle back or forth recursively—the way we tend to live our lives. Narrative may also be described as an interactive practice with all the give and take of conversation when it values a multiplicity of voices and perspectives.

Moreover, unbounded by linear forms, this rendering attempts to locate the sense of narrative not narrowly as representation only, not merely a telling of events or an ordering of one's life, and not even simply as a mode of "story" knowing or imaginative play that leads to making sense of the fictive world and vicariously of the lived world. All of these and none of these may capture in its entirety the sense of complexity and range of boundless possibilities within narrative. Embodied narrative seems to be much more than the articulation of what is understood, more than the framing and understanding of one's experiences, more than play with words. I believe this applies to narratives we read, narratives we write, and narratives we vocalize, and, indeed, even those we only think but never vocalize. Because I perceive that narrative is highly complex, it may be difficult to describe without lapsing into reductionism that limits as it defines. (What it may seem I am doing here.) If readers take this text as a model, narrative may be best characterized as expressed uncertainty; on the other hand, I would suggest no model exemplifies the range of narrative possibilities because no rendering of any such model can capture the infinite range of human possibilities.

Thus I have not chosen to remain within one theoretical framework or chosen one method of analysis because no such theory, philosophy, or method may provide the ultimate lens for making sense of this work, for writing this text, or for understanding anything today, tomorrow, or in the future. Instead I have drawn on philosophies, theories, and methods that have tended to provide the best fit within the multiple interpretations that stem from my own cultural positioning. As we each theorize our lives and understand theories against our lives, I perceive we write/read/voice/think and continually revise narratives and even meta-narratives of the gendered, raced, and classed identities our cultural positionings form and through which we forge new identities. Thus theorizing our worlds and experiences seems close to narrativizing our worlds, our experiences, and our identities.

For these reasons, then, at times I have sought to produce a class analysis on materialist culture,[45] and at times I have tended to be more psychoanalytic.[46] At other times I have examined relational contexts or cultural codes, an inquiry based in the science of signs or semiology, and sometimes I have drawn on phenomenological inquiry with an eye toward reconceptualizing.[47] Each approach works with and against the other and tends to broaden the lens on narrative through which I can make meaning. Yet I am not persuaded to deny the possibility that still other interpretations might make more sense. I defer meaning because I am uncertain and because a part of my project is to push on the boundaries of totalitarian discourses, particularly grand theory that claims some universal truth about the way the world works. The trouble with any single theory or method is its partiality.

For example, as political philosopher Michel Foucault has suggested, semiology as a study of communication tends to avoid the blood and guts of struggles/conflicts, and phenomenology seeks to locate a basis or genesis for a particular phenomenon that does not show that phenomenon as an open-ended process that both conditions and is conditioned by (e.g., as in the effects of power within what Foucault calls "regimes of discourse" or the production, accumulation, circulation, and functioning of a discourse).[48] Another way to explain this is to explore what may occur when we study our present and past experiences as a means of coming to know ourselves (what seems to be a common phenomenological endeavor). It's true; we may come to know something about ourselves, but we may not necessarily know ourselves entirely. Simply an examination of our beginnings (and even compared with present experiences and circumstances) may not necessarily take into account the various pushes and pulls of society or the ways in which we come to see ourselves with and against different social communities, positions, and relations of power. (It is because of these latter formations that knowing oneself and narrativizing one's existence through any social or psycholinguistic formulation becomes a political question.) We may examine the mirror reflection, in other words, without examining its underside or backside. Put another way, we may not see through the looking glass, and even if we do, who we see changes continually.

Yet phenomenological inquiry together with other methods may contribute much. That is, each theory and each method may contribute to an understanding of the complexities of any subject of study located with and in specific phenomena/relations. For example, each in its own way may contribute to an understanding of how the histories, forces, strategies, and mechanisms of particular phenomena/relations are connected, extended, displaced, and transformed.

Revealed then in my own desire to remain uncertain is my bent toward interrogating anything that gives the appearance of being certain. The deconstructive approach to which I refer, however, may be more analogous with an erasure than with complete dismantling. In other words, an erasure clouds the impression of something so that one can see what is/appears to be as well as what could be (the underside of the mirror, if you will) and also what is embedded that is not so easily seen.[49] I am especially interested in questioning the political nature of relationships of difference—written between the lines (the relation of student to teacher is but one example).

Interrogation, then, has not been so much for the purposes of unraveling to find myself at the beginning; rather, my questioning has been less a disentangling and more a continual flinging out and reeling in until I catch on something that makes some sense.[50] What may seem to be comfort with uncertainty is but a reflection of what I wish were true; what I am learning, however, may be called more appropriately a patience with uncertainty. And it is perhaps this patience that encourages me to take up various theoretical perspectives even those that seem opposed. For example, Derrida, to be specific, may have little need of a sign that signifies meaning. To Derrida there may be no signification of certain meaning, no relational context that assures one of the exact interpretation (or of choosing a single theoretical perspective that explains the complexities within a particular phenomenon). Nor is he in search of origins—beginnings shift; they change just as the experiences we live change the way we think of those experiences. In fact, Derrida says explicitly, ". . . I am very mistrustful whenever people . . . say, 'This begins here.'"[51] When trying to make sense of our own lives, then, our worlds—the personal and the public—why not think of what applies, why not fling out and reel in until something catches on?

Gloria Anzaldua makes this idea explicit for me when she writes:

> [We need theories] that cross borders, blur boundaries—new kinds of theories with new theorizing methods. We need theories that will point out ways to maneuver between our particular experiences and the necessity of forming our own categories and theoretical models for the patterns we uncover. We need theories that examine the implications of situations and look at what's behind them. And we need to find practical applications for those theories. . . . We need to give up the notion that there is a "correct" way to write theory.[52]

Yet this may be the greatest challenge we face.

For as a professional, I have not been taught that it's okay to be tentative, uncertain, nor have I always felt comfortable in situations that seem to require trying what works (because even what works seems relative or situationally and ethically dependent on many things). As a teacher, should I have the answers or pretend I do even if I do not? Or can I just admit that everything seems slippery, questionable, and uncertain? As a researcher, I have often looked for solutions, answers, tried to do what seemed rational, logical, even sometimes tried to follow a linear path, but then something always nagged at me, some question popped into my head that I could not get rid of and I'd be back where I began, asking more questions, having few if any answers. Sure, I fear not being taken seriously if I admit to such circular thinking, yet that is how thinking often is. Thinking is not an exact science; it's messy. So is theorizing. Comfortable with uncertainty? Not yet. Patient? Most of the time.

Permission to be uncertain, then, largely drawn from principles of deconstruction and feminist criticism, propels this book. The theories, philosophies, and methodologies I have relied on most assume prevailing social constructionist perspectives that suggest not only language but also communities generating that language are socially construed and that knowledges like other facts, texts, rules (including rules for social orders) are community generated. Foucault notes, however, that there is also a political economy involved in the generation of facts, texts, rules, and so on and that "the problem is not one of changing people's 'consciousness' or what's in their heads; but the political, economic, institutional regime of the production of truth."[53] Therefore, because as Michael Ryan states, "philosophy cannot be apolitical and politics often rests on philosophic,"[54] my decision to remain eclectic is largely political and has much to do with an understanding of feminism that suggests, even promotes, border crossings.[55]

Perhaps, Barbara Eckstein's description of deconstructive practice is most apt for my purposes here because it seems integrally tied to a notion that feminist inquiry seeks to reveal the political order within relationships that perpetuate oppression. She sees the process more in terms of examining the "tain of the mirror, the underside, the inside of political structures housed in private homes and public buildings."[56] Thus by focusing on differences *within* rather than differences *between*, internal differences, Barbara Johnson suggests one may begin to disclose sources of struggle for power that seem dependent on the desire for certainty—the desire for certain difference.[57] And Gayatri Spivak suggests questioning that discloses contradictions, or what she calls *complicities,* may actually work against the *will* to certainty, which creates only more oppositions.[58] Here I do not intend to suggest bipolarization necessarily by suggesting relations of difference though they do seem oppositionally positioned (e.g., mother to child, student to teacher, employee to employer, woman to man). What I do wish to suggest, however, is that it may not be the nature of opposition per se but the nature of political codes that are culturally embedded within our language that tends to set one against the other.

Julia Kristeva's work provides some understanding here respective to the oppositional positioning of "otherness" established within semiological codes—cultural codes that help us read and categorize various (including political) ways of being in the world.[59] What Kristeva calls *otherness,* she seems to suggest may be a notion or concept of difference that could be radically altered if issues of power were not at the center of the relationship "driving" it then necessarily into certain difference rather than difference in question. She suggests it may be the political code or order—the way we see and come to mean or know in relation to power—that needs to be changed. Her use of *otherness* then suggests an*other* way of viewing cultural codes—codes of powers, codes that signify value, codes that signify place and identity, how knowledges are invented, and so forth, indeed, a blurring of boundaries between margin and center. Here Kristeva suggests that a rupture or "scission" of the symbolic or what marks a threshold between opposing ("heterogeneous") realms, a "unity divided into signifier and signified," is always possible because of the ambiguity of language.[60] Gloria Anzaldua describes this rupture as "explod[ing] the neat boundaries of the half dozen categories of marginality that define us and . . . bring us [face to face] with our own [histories]."[61] In describing the break between signifier and the signified, Kristeva is also describing a break that represents a vision of new possibilities, turning the inside out, reversing or inverting the order of things. Her analysis of otherness suggests the need for different understandings of what particular signs signify, indeed, of what they are capable of signifying.

Kristeva's description of other or otherness is not unlike Simone de Beauvoir's description of her own otherness in the service of seeking a more authentic self—an otherness that became vulgarity to her family when she denounced her father's bourgeois ideals and took a position against the status quo.[62] For though Kristeva's "other" is often defined in Lacanian terms[63] as the "place of the signifier," she suggests signification is more a process and the "place" to which Lacan refers more a boundary with social implications than a base—a kind of "social censorship"—positioning the other away from whatever symbolizes the status quo. The "split unification" symbolized by the mother/child—an embodied both/and construct—is "always produced by a rupture and is impossible without it. . . . Not only is . . . this division . . . the result of a break [in cognitive psychological processes] . . . *preceding meaning and signification* [emphasis mine] . . . [it is] already regulated [by] drives. . . . That language is a defensive construction reveals its ambiguity."[64]

An example from Frederich Nietzche's study of the evolution of morals may help to explain Kristeva's concern over what seems in social practice to be a kind of fixed cultural encoding. In his historical account, Nietzche wrote that words like *noble* and *good* could be traced to aristocratic origins; thus, words like *common* and *plebeian* and *low* were translated into the concept of bad.[65] But Kristeva's notion of scission suggests breaking with a fixed referent or signification so that, for example, words such as *low* or *common* no longer refer to a particular concept, and otherness is open to multiple interpretations—in other words, an epistemological break, a rupture that inverts meaning. And to this notion Derrida extends writing as a specific case in which language escapes signification.[66] Kristeva's "drives" that function beneath the surface of the semiotic (what in my reading extends the semiotic beyond structural linguistics) may then account both for her notion of rupture as well as for Derrida's sense in which writing escapes signification, because as Kristeva claims, social practices inscribe notions of sameness and difference and writing is but expressed social practice.[67]

Kristeva's work provides links with poststructuralists', deconstructionists', and French feminists' perspectives and suggests that social practices that regulate language (and also mark its ambiguity) are both united and split at the threshold of desire—on the one hand, desire for power (e.g., power to prevent change); on the other hand, desire for change (e.g., change that emasculates power). That is, language itself does not seem to prevent progress; rather, social practices (based in desire) are responsible for concepts like otherness referring to that which is outside the mainstream, the dominant culture, the norm—that is, other than white male privilege, other than heterosexual, other than politically right, other than teaching that which upholds patriarchy and tradition, and so forth.

In addition to those scholars who have informed my understanding of feminists' methods of inquiry and those who have offered various lenses for reading and interrogating words and worlds are the scholars whose philosophies and theories have served as underpinnings for this project on embodied/imaginative narrative as a linguistic act of knowing and way of framing educational inquiry. For example, as regards the constitutive nature of language for purposes of world making, Alfred Schutz's philosophy of multiple interpretations of reality has particularly guided my thinking.[68] His notion of "wide-awakeness"—that is, to be deliberate and open to possibilities—describes for me the necessary prerequisite to understanding and accepting multiple interpretations. Maxine Greene's work also references notions of wide-awakeness as "committed rationality," deliberate action, and surfacing possibilities especially through the study of imaginative literatures and in dialogue with others.[69]

Additionally and with respect to linguistically constructed multiple realities, I follow Mikhail Bakhtin's notion of dialogical processes that suggests that multiple voices—that is, discourse communities and individual speakers and writers—act on and contribute meanings/understandings that construct discursive practices.[70] A distinction is made in this text between dialectical processes and dialogical processes primarily because of Bakhtin's emphasis on multiplicity. Yet I admit this sets up a somewhat false dichotomy because opposition/tension seen in traditional dialectics no doubt arises in any dialogue that is based on difference and multiplicity. In traditional dialectics, for every thesis there is its opposite, a radical antithesis, an alternative thesis standing in opposition—thesis and antithesis at polarized extremes. But dialogical processes suggest multiple meanings/possibilities arising from multiple voicings (with self and others), which create tensions that may be entertained, taken up, considered, and multiple paths chosen rather than a singular path. Though Raymond Williams offers what may appear to suggest a kind of thesis/antithesis interplay, his notion of emergent meanings and practices that combine and extend traditional (residual) meanings suggests, perhaps, not replacement of one idea or way of being for another but an opening up of possibilities integrating old with new.[71] Or as Foucault suggests, a kind of reassembling of "the sets of transformations in the regime of discourse necessary and sufficient for people to use [different] words . . . for people to be able to look at things from such and such an angle and not [just] *one* [angle]."[72]—a dynamic process suggesting a wide range of possibilities rather than a fixed entity and instead of "one" alternative, what seems closer to both/and.

It is with respect to multiplicity then that Alice Jardine argues against dialectical processes in favor of those which do not rely on bipolar opposites.[73] Yet by taking up Jardine's argument and referring to dialogical processes here, I do not mean to suggest that dialectical tensions between language and thought do not exist within the dialogic as Bakhtin describes it (again, inner dialogue and dialogue with others). That is, it may not be necessary that oppositional constructs negate one another simply because they oppose; instead, they may act as tensions, contradictions, to be dealt with but not necessarily taken up, examined, and rejected in favor of one or the other. When I use phrases like both/and, contradictory practice, and dialogical processes, then, I am not so much arguing against a dialectic of oppositions for such is often the basis of critique (especially in the materialist sense—power/powerlessness, bourgeois/working class, etc.). Rather, I am arguing for multiple ways of knowing and being instead of polarized extremes and for tensions that are a part of the dynamic interplay in any discursive practice. Tensions do not need to carry a qualitative good/bad label; they do not have to be seen as something to be free of. For in ridding ourselves of tensions and dilemmas, we rid ourselves of difference that is marked by/based in struggle, and consequently, we rid ourselves of multiplicity. Or as Foucault put it, ". . . the dialectic, as logic of contradictions, [cannot] account for the intrinsic intelligibility of conflicts. 'Dialectic' is a way of evading the always open and hazardous reality of conflict by reducing it to a Hegelian skeleton . . . "[74] It may be then that the reductive categories inscribed by traditional dialectics is what tends also not to allow for the full range of possibilities humans are capable of.

Bakhtin's notion of heteroglossia seems to make this more concrete. For as Bakhtin describes heteroglossic communities of difference, he describes not only the tension around the creation of a common or unofficial language with which to speak to one another but also the tendency on the part of members of any community to assimilate the category inscribed as official—"words of the father, adult, teacher"—what he calls integrating a discourse of power into one's own language.[75] Therefore, by suggesting that language is created both with and in the language user and with/in others in a particular discourse community and by suggesting the constant tension to create an *inclusive* language that lies *outside* authoritative discourses (not unlike Kristeva's notion of split unification necessary for rupture[76]), Bakhtin seems to suggest a both/and construct not only respective to the nature of difference and possibility but also to the psychological and sociological characteristics of language.

These perspectives represent a way of theorizing that suggests both critique and possibility—that interrogates relations of power and notions of taken-for-grantedness and at the same time offers possibilities for effective change practices. Therefore, such theories seem particularly important when we consider narrative acts as socially discursive practices and when we consider the narrativization of experience in all its forms as aesthetic acts that allow us to interrupt a totalizing assignment of meaning and to imagine the possible. For a further perspective on narrative as a socially constructive, discursive practice of making meaning, Roland Barthes makes this explicit:

> The function of narrative is not to "represent," it is to constitute a spectacle still very enigmatic for us. . . . It may be that men [and women] ceaselessly re-inject into narrative what they have known, what they have experienced; but if they do, at least it is in a form which has vanquished repetition and instituted the model of a process of becoming. Narrative does not show, does not imitate; the passion which may excite us in reading a novel is not that of a "vision." Rather it is that of meaning . . . ; "what happens" is language alone, the adventure of language, the unceasing celebration of its coming.[77]

And I reiterate that what can also excite us in the reading of a novel, in the adventure of language is the use of imagination, both literary and social, and with it the capacity to see other possible ways of being in the world.

I also look to Jerome Bruner, whose work references narrative as an act of world making, and Kenneth Bruffee, whose discussion of social constructionism posits both the collective and constitutive nature of language.[78] It seems then that in the discursive practice of narration or storytelling as an act of world making or meaning making we find further evidence that language itself may be to use Stephen Greenblatt's words "the supreme instance of a collective creation"[79] capable of constructing different realities.

These theories, therefore, seem to link with Bakhtin's questions respective to the ontological nature of reality and find further overlap with the more political post-Marxist writings of Foucault. Foucault's work poses questions about what counts for knowledge and who decides what counts, political questions that are necessarily embedded within notions of the effects of powerful arrangements within discursive practices—practices that lead to narrating and legitimating personal experience (what may be thought of as ethno-poetic narration) and thus personal knowledge. In other words, Foucault's political analysis of the very nature of knowledge or "truth" revolves around an "analytic of power" or "the cluster of relations . . . which makes possible an analytic of relations of power."[80] These "regimes," as Foucault put it, then lend themselves to questions of class, culture, and positioning (connections that seem necessary for framing narrative practice, i.e., whose story counts, what literatures are most valued and why, who stands to gain the most and who will be disenfranchised?—all questions of who knows and how what is known is valued) and therefore lead me back to Marxism and to the sort of neo-Marxist critique I draw not only from Foucault and Bakhtin but also from the writings of Raymond Williams, Terry Eagleton, and Antonio Gramsci.[81] Their critiques of social class and culture especially respective to interrogating relations of power seem particularly useful because, for me, critique stands not in opposition to imagination but becomes a necessary aspect of wider vision.

As Paulo Freire's work suggests, first we need to know and understand (to have examined) powerful arrangements before we can imagine other arrangements and work toward change practices.[82] Thus it is my argument that both experienced teachers and prospective teachers as well as students need to recognize the particular world views from which they operate. The underpinnings of the work they do might suggest particular theories that inform their practice or lead them to theorize their practice against understood ideological frameworks. (Although it is often assumed that such an understanding is in place, I often find in my own practice that when I ask an experienced teacher or a prospective teacher to tell me about the learning benefits associated with a particular curriculum or how he or she has come to practice in such a way, their responses often do not warrant such an assumption.) And again, my angle on aesthetics/stories relates both to the help a story provides in connecting theory to practice as well as to the imaginative potential of embodied narrative (including but not limited to traditional literary narratives).

The wide variety of scholars then who inform and enrich this book seem to have for one reason or another shifted their own gaze away from a strict focus on the canonical literatures and philosophies of their respective fields of inquiry, looking now toward the discursive practices embodied within those ideas and literatures and to what Foucault calls the "effects of power peculiar to the play of statements [or language]."[83] Whether it be the literary canon in English literature or the particular body of knowledge espoused as the authoritative word in another field, those scholars mentioned here have questioned the textual authority of their particular fields by turning their gazes on the dynamic terrains in which language takes place in all its multiple forms. Much of this work, though widely arrayed, has a good deal of overlap—especially respective to the constitutive or world-making nature of language and narrative.

These widely diverse thinkers and others I have not named here contribute to a larger conversation that is also the conversation taken up in this book—that is, each contributes to a view of social constructionism and that view contributes to the work of feminism. As language is a collective creation, so is the project on which this book is based also a collective creation.

Therefore, I make no apologies for having chosen diversely among philosophies and interpretive methods. For if I can extend anything about meaning making here and about active theorizing—theorizing that grows out of practice/experience rather than theories into practice, it is that the ways in which each of us understands theory that already exists or theory that we generate seems to be through a lens that is particular to our experiences and is uniquely personal as it collides with and against others in this society. That is not to suggest, however, that personal concerns/agendas should override common concerns that exist in a wider context. It is merely to suggest, as I think Chandra Mohanty does, that when we join a wider political struggle, we join as persons with uniquely different classed, raced, and gendered backgrounds of experience—that is, our struggle is both personal and political, local and wide.[84] And we are each limited in what we can know because of our unique backgrounds. Therefore, personal meaning here suggests self with other, not self in isolation, and it suggests self that is continually made and changed and made again depending on experiences with others.

Important, generally, then to the tensions surrounding the

serving up of my life and the lives of some of my students as text here and, specifically, to the tensions surrounding personal meaning that is construed socially and is not unproblematic—how I read against my own experiences to interpret the world and its theories—is the writing self who is a white married woman, working mother, and researching teacher/teaching researcher with working-class roots. Therefore, my subject position not only affects my interpretations but the way I write about those interpretations in this text.

Gloria Anzaldua helps me understand how I am situated within this text and "situatedness" in general; she helps me understand my voice and "voice" in general. Anzaldua writes:

> A woman-of-color [I would add any woman] who writes poetry [or writes anything] or paints or dances or makes movies knows there is no escape from race or gender when she is writing or painting. She can't take off her color and sex and leave them at the door of her study or studio. Nor can she leave behind her history. Art is about identity, among other things, and her creativity is political. . . . [T]he soul speaks; the body acts. The hand is an extension of our will. The tongue mounts the hand and produces writing. When tongue and hand work together, they unite art and politics and attack the dominant ideology. . . . Creative acts are forms of political activism employing definite aesthetic strategies for resisting dominant cultural norms and are not merely aesthetic exercises.[85]

As I have attempted to make problematic the false dichotomies in our theories, philosophies, and methods of analysis in this chapter, in Chapter 2, I seek to make problematic the false dichotomies in our language that might impede possible ways forward. Discussing other practices makes little sense unless we consider the ways in which the language we use seems to undermine possible alternatives. Likewise, with respect to considering alternative arrangements for practice, I invite you to consider politicizing our research agendas and practices as well as what we consider research. In other words, what is the effect of some of our research on our participants, and are we still in the grips of positivism as we conduct critical, reflective inquiry? Finally, I invite close examination of the particular social orders of our profession before we can begin to consider creating spaces for critical inquiry, for reflective practice, and for thinking and acting as if things could be different.

Chapter 3 invites you to consider the meaning making potential of all texts, but specifically schooling narratives (here discussed as literary and other aesthetic media and the stories students tell relative to interacting with such materials). Embedded within this discussion is the larger issue of education as a liberal (/liberating) art. And Chapters 4 and 5 discuss the social constructs of power and knowledge, hidden curriculum, and intersections of class, race, and gender in stories of schooling. Specifically, Chapter 4 shows those portraits of schooling that illumine teacher work and Chapter 5 highlights texts that dramatize students' positioned reactions to teacher work. Chapter 5 examines, through literary images (in books, films, and television), some of the meanings students seem to make of schooling, resulting, perhaps, from a perception that their roles have been institutionalized by privilege and tradition.

Chapter 6 is as the title suggests: more stories, students' stories of schooling and my own. Just that. In other words, I purposefully have not categorized, nor analyzed these stories, and for a very important reason. Were I to categorize, I would have difficulty resisting the suggestion that some stories show more reflective responses than others to the texts we examined together. I have no desire to do that. Therefore, I invite you to analyze the student responses according to your own predilections and understandings of what counts for reflection. Occasionally throughout the book, I have interspersed students' responses when they illustrated a point I wished to make. However, neither in those instances nor in Chapter 6 should students' stories be read as evidence that the schooling narratives woven into this text will necessarily invoke critical inquiry and reflective practice if they are but used. Many things foster reflection as I have attempted to suggest through the writing of this book. These narratives may offer one more *possibility*. But again, the emphasis here is on possibility. Students' stories are offered simply as anecdotal records of one term when I systematically used the materials described here in an English education course. (With permission of the students, Rashidah Muhammad, my graduate assistant, tape-recorded each class and produced verbatim transcripts from the course. Student response segments are drawn from those transcripts.)

Chapter 7 can be read in part as a self-critique of particular practices that have employed measures of domination. In other words, I am concerned here with the reality that my attempts to produce transformative curricula may still, indeed, does marginalize some and privilege others—that is, while I rail against oppressive teaching, my own teacherly intentions may at times seem oppressive. For that reason, I need to continually remind myself that I am situated positionally with my students and that each of us has agendas. Grappling with my own complicity in this tradition by continually examining my own practices, my own meta-narratives if you will, may lead the way to reflexivity or self-critical practice that, finally, must be a part of what we mean when we frame practices for inquiry and reflection. And it is in this context that I discuss the relationship between reflective practice, teacher empowerment, and educational reform as I see it. I invite you to consider what inquiry that leads to reflection might look like if framed in narrative practice and what beliefs might limit and enhance that work.

In writing this book, I offer another lens for seeing issues of power, ideology, and culture by attempting to establish frames of references for narrative practice. But I bring only a portion of the story. For not one fixed frame of reference or perspective for the use of narratives in educational settings will do. Your stories, your frames, the possibilities you see for your classrooms are equally important. Together we may be capable of illuminating our pasts by telling the stories of our educational experiences and listening to the stories others tell. Together our stories may begin a process of unearthing assumptions that lead to rediscovering truths about ourselves and that lead to making culture, particularly in schools, which is relevant to our lives. Thus I invite you to continue this book by making those connections that only you can make.

CHAPTER 2

Reflection and Teaching

"Reflective thinking . . . involves a state of doubt, hesitation, perplexity, mental difficulty. . . . [Reflective] persons . . . weigh, ponder, [and] deliberate . . . a process of evaluating what occurs to them in order to decide upon its force and weight for their problem."
(from John Dewey, *How We Think)*[1]

The bird-watcher engaged in daily vigil grows tired of looking at a particular bird and learns she must study that bird in a new way in order to renew interest in it. She describes how carefully she examines the bird in which she has lost interest. She reverses its evolution and sees it as a lizard; she sees its feathers as lizard scales; she sees it stalking instead of flying. Then she reverses this process to see the bird once more.

I borrow this example on the value of seeing and seeing again from Annie Dillard's *Pilgrim at Tinker Creek*.[2] In this book Dillard shows us the *life full of wonder* as she sends a plea for the renewed spirit and wonder that accompanies making the familiar strange. In her chapter entitled "Spring," Dillard claims at last, this bird "might as well keep me awake out of wonder as rage."[3]

Reflective thinking involving doubt and hesitation—pitting one thing against something else in order to examine it more closely as Dewey suggests,[4] implies a state of renewal, as Dillard's bird metaphor also suggests,[5] because it requires seeing something in a new light. But before there can be renewal there needs to be a kind of unraveling that involves close examination, not, perhaps, a complete "break" but rather a "shift in scenery [that] takes as our starting point something else," as Foucault suggests.[6] Here Foucault is referring to what in psychoanalysis is called the "Freudian break" or "the radical break [from] which everything else has to be re-thought," but he describes it more in terms of simply turning something "inside out, like a glove,"[7] like Dillard's bird-watcher who sees the bird as a lizard.[8] Turning things over and seeing them in new ways. Making the familiar strange. Before we can see and name reflective thinking and practice, then, perhaps we need to see what impedes such practice.

RUPTURING THE CODES

Dillard's bird-watcher provides an apt metaphor to describe a reforming practice, if, that is, we seek reform that interrupts current practices—practices that seem to be rooted in dichotomous either/or extremes of right or wrong answers, yes or no, black or white with no middle ground or space to entertain the possibility of multiple meanings, multiple interpretations. For though Dillard is capable of seeing the bird in reverse evolution, she is also capable of returning to the bird. Dillard's bird-watcher is practiced in the art of seeing possibilities. She does not need to see either the lizard or the bird. She can see both the lizard and the bird.[9] Therefore, in suggesting this metaphor, I suggest a language of both/and instead of either/or.

In suggesting both/and, then, I am suggesting the need to develop a language of inclusion in the hopes that such language might lead the way toward inclusionary practices. Inclusion, however, if understood politically need not suggest equality that tends to blur differences. Rather, inclusionary practice as I perceive it might look more like a dialogic of difference that embraces multiplicity while it questions the effects of power within relations of difference or unequal relations.

My own leanings toward both/and then are drawn from those previously discussed feminist understandings of public/private and suggests that we accept or count as important not just what is public information or what has universal implications but we also count personal anecdotal ways of knowing as well. In other words, we do not have to reject one way of knowing for the other; rather, we can accept both as legitimate and viable. By working to create spaces then that include the private, we not only seek to make places for women's lives and works to be honored, but we also attempt to make spaces for students to connect school with community beyond the classroom and with home—with what often counts most to them and is meaningful in their lives—and we work to make spaces for teachers to connect what they know about teaching to private/personal experiences as learners. Inclusionary language and practice would count both public and private domains of experience and understanding. And as inclusionary practice acknowledged the private it would out of necessity entertain difference—from the complex struggles of students and teachers to the ways each makes sense of school and their lives as they affect and are affected by school.

Either/or language and practice excludes; it counts people out.[10] When we select one practice, one anything, over another, we automatically privilege one and marginalize the other. Attempting to problematize the language of inclusion and exclusion, however, can become a chicken and egg problem. Is it the language of exclusion that leads to exclusion, or do we naturally use exclusionary language because we in practice already exclude? When we learn to discriminate as children, to separate one thing from something else, we do so through our emerging language. Is it language then that helps us to learn how to separate, or do we find words to express that which we have already thought how to do?

Therefore, in making problematic much of the common language used in our profession to describe particular phenomena endemic to education, I want to suggest that our tendency to think in either/or dichotomies belongs, perhaps, to a paradigm of positivism. It is learned; therefore, it can be unlearned. What implies one right answer, one right approach, perpetuates what Adrienne Rich suggests is the worst kind of dichotomy, the power/powerless dichotomy.[11] In the phrase "rupturing the codes," then, I suggest the need to break up the practice of thinking that we must do or say or write or teach or act in *one way or another* that implies a "correct" way or it is wrong. In other words, I am suggesting here the possible need to break up certainty; indeed, reflection may occur through uncertainty. Yet Derrida himself reminds us that any lack of absolute interpretation (differance) does not mean such interpretation does not exist in society; for we know it exists within the political systems of power that we ourselves may attempt to work our way out of.[12] We know too how grounded our own interpretations of difference are. Sander Gilman suggests why: ". . . our own sense of . . . the world is built on the illusionary image of the world divided into two camps, 'us' and 'them.'"[13] Moreover Barbara Johnson suggests that our attempts to dislocate either/or (us/them) dichotomies may serve only as a possible medium for recasting the problems of power within our society. In other words, we may not expect our attempts to rupture the codes that foster dichotomies to completely annihilate them. Indeed, Johnson says we may expect only that such activities question the effects of powerful arrangements in and on discursive practices.[14]

Thus in this chapter and throughout the text, I intend to question the effects of power that impinge on our speaking, writing, teaching, acting, and so forth. In discussing particular schooling narratives, I have attempted to provide a context for questioning effects of power. The narratives selected (from literature and the several media as well as my own and students' narratives) tend to dramatize difficulties associated with breaking up tradition in order to create public spaces for personal reflection and critique.

Therefore, as we begin to question the false dichotomies in our language that impede progress toward new goals, toward renewal, I would caution not to think of the goal of reform simply for the sake of reform as a laudatory goal. To suggest one orthodoxy over another is not my intention here. In fact, if we were to reverse the evolution of the word *reform* as Dillard's bird-watcher metaphor suggests, we might see that form is the root of formalize and to formalize is to naturalize, institutionalize, and so forth—which, of course, leads to privileging. So to (re)form in one sense suggests to formalize anew, replacing one institutionalized form for another, one orthodoxy for another. (When I use parentheses around "re," however, I am suggesting a continual process of forming and reforming.) Still when viewed this way reform may suggest just another claptrap of false hopes, false agendas, false dichotomies. Thus our own complicity in perpetuating bipolar oppositional extremes is a part of what must be questioned here as the real work of reform. Suggesting, however, that the real work of reform may be located in questioning—in developing a kind of self-consciousness needed for reflection—may not seem like reform because we are used to thinking of reform as some sort of action. Yet, here and throughout this book, as I focus on particular linguistic constructs that deserve examination, I want to focus also on aspects of self-critical questioning and how self-critique can lead to action—action that is, in and of itself, a reformulation of the notion of reform.

But before I suggest what language I think is particularly at risk, I want to make problematic the notions of interruption and rupture—ideas that may be read quite differently if examined in a relational context. First, an interruption in the social order may create what Maxine Greene calls an opening onto what has not been before,[15] or what Derrida calls a "becoming space" for new thinking and imagining new practices.[16] However, historically in education we have seen the pendulum swing back and forth over decades of attempted reform—through, perhaps, many openings or interruptions in institutional order. Yet even in the midst of much new research and theory, still we are seeing a "conservative restoration" with "back to basics" campaigns.[17] As Harste, Woodward, and Burke remind us in *Language Stories and Literacy Lessons*, if the medical professions paid as little attention to research as the educational community seems to have paid with respect to language learning, then we would still be at the stage of blood letting.[18]

But I would suggest we go a step further than Harste, Woodward, and Burke here. In other words, if our research is not situated with respect to the wider political contexts of our lives, our workplaces, and those we serve, then with respect to putting research into practice, we may still suffer. Here I cannot resist the pain metaphor. What this suggests is the fact that our work and our lives are integrally related—that we embody our work and our work embodies us. The public is private and the intellectual is political as Bauer suggests.[19] Any theory or philosophy that attempts to suggest otherwise, suggests disembodiment. So, yes, pain and suffering are a part of our work, a human part that immediately suggests the complexity and, therefore, the impossibility of any totalizing discourse that would know outcomes or ends.

And, yet, the fact that I rely on metaphor here will, no doubt, seem like another contradiction—what for some may seem like reduction to simple metaphor. On the other hand, my point, so as not to be mistaken, is to suggest as Gloria Anzaldua does that the seeming contradiction of metaphors popping up here and there is but an indication of the complexity of the issues not of their simplicity, of *both* the rough *and* smooth textures laying side by side.[20]

Consider this: When research taps only the surface—with a claim that we need to make it practical for teachers, instead of digging deeper, asking harder theoretical questions—and is presented as a "how to" fixer-upper, then blood letting may be no worse an alternative. When what we have learned with respect to forms of instruction—such as attending to processes instead of products, for example, or to workshop arrangements that suggest cooperative or collaborative approaches—tend often to be practiced merely on the level of procedure, a tool for classroom management rather than a tool for addressing possibilities and limitations in the larger society (if attempted at all), then we may as well engage in blood letting. When in some instances useful instructional tools have become methods—methods that are methodical and suggest that mastering the steps is more important than the interaction that lies at the core, then we may as well use blood letting. When what, in composition, suggested an opportunity to focus on content sometimes does the reverse, when it offers a contentless curriculum where form becomes the entire subject—one that does not include unraveling and questioning, for example, the effects of power in the very classrooms in which these forms exist not to mention extending that discussion into wider political debate, then blood letting may be no worse. When finding one's voice does not mean voicing one's "inner pulsions," as Clare Juncker suggests,[21] but seems to mean finding a voice that the teacher approves of—a voice that will be acceptable for writing in school, then blood letting may work just as well. So, indeed, our notions of theory, research, and practice are all problematic, and all in need of continual (re)examination. In other words, (re)examination or examining and examining again and again in an ongoing process is one that, by virtue of its existence, may create an interruption.

On the other hand, an interruption in the social order of schools is, perhaps, not a strong enough word. For in that language alone, we tend to see interruptions as temporal—thus, our expectations are that nothing lasts. Perhaps, it is the most we can hope for. Or perhaps, it will be too dangerous to stop the pendulum from swinging at all. The fear that it will end on the very conservative side rather than hang in balance is a reasonable fear. For in our reform efforts, we do have agendas and we want our voices to be heard. And yet the agendas, the voices, of those whose interests represent dominant interests in society as in schools are those most often heard. For they speak the loudest, carry the most power, and seem never to be in favor of upsetting the status quo.

As when we were children and we played "giant steps and baby steps," much of our work seems to resemble those baby steps—steps we took when no one was looking. Yet as the Heisenberg principle suggests, when one tiny thing changes, everything is changed.

But if change occurs in great proportion or by degrees only, and ideologies remain the same, to what end is that change? Again a close examination of our language reveals much about the ideological underpinnings that prevent or support change practices. And yet what are the implications of rupturing the codes, of reinscribing the other or what is otherwise as Patti Lather suggests?[22] Kristeva has suggested that language is not the problem but rather what and how we think about language and meaning that may be the greatest inhibiter of change.[23] And Foucault adds that even what and how we think does not account for the more political and economic restraints relative to the production of "truth"/knowledge.[24] So what are the implications of language that suggests rupture when seen in various contexts? How might we understand what traps such a break should/could lead to? For example, rupture implies a bursting of something, a renting or tearing away of some stable element, a complete taking apart. It, indeed, suggests more than interrupting that brings a time-out; it suggests complete undoing. Yet, complete undoing is exactly what Dillard's bird-watcher does. She completely reverses evolution; she completely sees the lizard, even its scales, and still she is capable of seeing the bird.[25] Can rupturing a system from the inside out leave space for possibilities? Perhaps so if we consider Kristeva's thoughts on the break or rupture as "split unification"—both/and.[26] Or Foucault's break as a turning inside out, like a glove.[27] Or will such deconstructive practices simply lead to infinite regression as Gayatri Spivak suggests?[28] I contend that it may be both actions that make possible the space for renewal—interruption in the social order of language or rupture followed by a space to think and act into the future in new ways, critique, on the one hand, and possibility, on the other. A less utopian view, however, is Barbara Johnson's astute commentary, that the most we may hope for is to question the constructs that bind us to the exploitive powerful arrangements we rail against.[29]

What I am, finally, suggesting here, of course, is that neither language (interruption or rupture) depends on dichotomy. For in order to be able to think in terms of multiple possibilities for practice, indeed, for seeing the world, then a complete undoing of some of the language we use may be necessary. A time-out will not work. Time-out leaves room for turning something inside out, but it may not create the time or the space for renewal for further becoming.[30] Thus rupturing some of the language codes seems the place to begin.

Language

A project of possibility may begin by critiquing or saying what's good and what's bad with the old and suggesting possible new ways to proceed. In one sense, critique and possibility would incorporate both Foucault's notion of reassembling and Williams's notion of emerging meanings and practices.[31] But it seems essentially more complex than that. For example, we may need to examine the mirror and claim for ourselves multiple interpretations/new images of teachers and schooling, but, and perhaps even more important, we also need to make problematic the language we use to express how we see teachers and schooling. In other words, we need to look at the tain or underside of the mirror[32]—from the inside where our ideologies often get in the way of making "real" change. Seeing from the inside out, making the familiar strange, undoing false dichotomies like practitioner and scholar, for example, may be one such construct that needs to be examined. When we talk about a practitioner, historically we are talking about a public school teacher. Distinctions tend to lie between the scholar, researcher, and the school practitioner and are often dropped at the threshold of theory and practice. Stephen North, for example, has explored this stratification, and he suggests that practitioners have little of what Pierre Bourdieu calls academic capital.[33] In *Postmodern Education* Aronowitz and Giroux examine the problems of pedagogy without theory and offer this critique: "Privileging practice without due consideration of the complex interactions that mark the totality of theory/practice and language/meaning is not merely reductionistic; it is a form of theoretical tyranny."[34]

It seems here that Aronowitz and Giroux are suggesting a similar notion with respect to rupture. That is, what needs to be questioned and considered is what we call practice and what we call theory and who gets to decide on what is theory and what is practice.[35] As Pierre Bourdieu formulates it that decision occurs in the academy.[36] But that, of course, is what is in need of reformulation. Who decides and thus appropriates language/meaning is as problematic as what is decided upon. Consider, then, Aronowitz and Giroux's notion against Bruffee's notion of language as a social act, particularly with respect to constructing a language that addresses the practitioner who is both scholar and researcher and the scholar and researcher who is also a practitioner.[37] Here Bruffee draws on Bakhtin and Foucault's notion that language is a collective creation.[38] However, Bourdieu reminds us that collective creation has not actually been collective at all; rather, it is the work of academics who have constructed meanings around theory and practice, research and scholarship.[39] In other words, our notions of practitioner do not permit our seeing university teaching as practice; it is not practice because it is professorship—we profess, authorize, appropriate in anything but a collective manner across spheres. The university is one sphere; the public school is another, and we collectively create language, if we collectively create at all, only within our particular spheres of influence.

Bakhtin's sense of language may help tease out these issues. For in describing the social essence and "stratifying forces" of language, Bakhtin reminds us that there are no "neutral words and forms" because language is completely "shot through with intentions . . ." Although the word *practitioner* may mean many different things to many different people, what is held in common is the social intention and implied stratification that such a conception holds. To quote Bakhtin, "As a living, socio-ideological concrete thing, as heteroglot opinion, language, for the individual consciousness, lies on the borderline between oneself and the other."[40] Because language is a collective creation it is always "half someone else's," but it also becomes "one's own" when the language user inscribes meaning and intention. When professors authorize/appropriate language, the particular sphere of influence from which they operate may code language in particularly stratified ways, but there is always the possibility that language will mean something else to someone else depending on "the other's" frame of reference. Therefore what Kristeva calls the ambiguity of language and what Bakhtin calls the multivocalic, heteroglossic nature of language, is the notion I intend when I describe both/and.[41] In the language of inclusion there is multiplicity, and, indeed, there is ambiguity, but there is also the implication that one's language is not totalitarian but partial because it is always both "one's own" and "someone else's." As I see it, then, even when we entertain inclusive constructs—for example, scholar/researcher and practitioner, if we've made our words "our own" in the Bakhtinean sense so that our social forms are "shot through" with our intentions, those forms may nonetheless be potentially problematic as the personal/social intentions of ownership draw us into complicity with and against someone else's meanings and intentions.

The point here is that all our language carries with it the potential to be understood in a variety of possible ways that include ways we do not intend; collectivity seems by its very nature to produce ambiguity and this aspect of language can be perceived both as a constraint and as a possibility. If we accept multiplicity, we may see ambiguity as positive; if, however, we operate within a more positivist framework—that is, if we need certainty or absolute meaning; if we need to see the world in terms of either/or—then such ambiguity becomes a "real" constraint.

Does that mean we should consider collective creations and ambiguity in a negative light? I think not, but what I do think is that such an understanding of language requires more patience with uncertainty, more tolerance for ambiguity, and more acceptance of multiplicity. The very best attributes of language, however, may also suggest its problematic nature—that meaning is both a condition of and conditioned by world view or socio-ideological concerns. Does that mean we should not attempt to move beyond the limitations imposed by some understandings, then, even common understandings? No, it means, I think, we should understand that language itself is problematic, perhaps because it is a collective creation thus ambiguous and also because historically the collective creation that *seems* to count resides within and among hierarchical spheres that depend on our classed, raced, and gendered positions.[42] More than other questions, then, asking what language/meaning counts and who decides may help us understand both why and how we have dichotomized language and thus how we describe what we do.

For example, when we ask teachers to consider themselves teacher-researchers, we are asking them to be the same people we are asking ourselves to be at the university. And when we ask them to be reflective, we are asking the same thing. We are asking them to question, to challenge accepted institutions, to, indeed, be as Giroux suggests "transformative intellectuals."[43] How then can we continue a dichotomy that suggests that teachers are practitioners at the K–12 school level while we are researchers and professors at the university level? This dichotomy will, out of necessity, limit teachers' abilities to see themselves as reflective teachers and intellectuals.

The use of the word reflection and phrases like reflective thinking and practice then may resonate with the often evoked notion of the reflective practitioner. That label, if labels were not so suspect by themselves, would, perhaps, be alright were it to refer to both university/college and K–12 teachers and were reflection taken up as a self-critical, reflexive practice as well as that more exteriorized form of reflection. That, however, is not usually the case. So, lest there be doubts about my intentions here, may I suggest that my reading of reflection/becoming reflective is of a continual process of being and becoming—a process no one can create for us regardless of how we frame practice but one we must create for ourselves through self-critical questioning, self-conscious awareness, and continual (re)evaluation. The perspectives offered by literature and other aesthetic media may, at best, create only the conditions for reflection. Because again, the process of becoming reflective, like the process of appropriating language, is difficult and complex.

Thus, in my attempts to call the language we already have problematic, it is important that we not understand this as an indication to re-create language. It is more an attempt to problematize always—understanding that (re)creation might only be accomplished in narrow spheres of collectivity and as Derrida suggests, even new language may be dichotomized within political systems of power.[44]

This, of course, is not to suggest that collective aspects of language are unimportant; it is merely an attempt to situate this discourse within a wider political context of realities beyond our classrooms and sometimes beyond our capacities to participate. It is an attempt to situate this discussion within matrices of constraint and possibility. The point here as elsewhere is to question the effects of power and to understand the complex set of arguments that all discourses function within.[45]

Perhaps a necessary place to begin further investigation of the power/powerless dichotomy—the dichotomy we continue each time we use either/or language—is back to the previously, but only briefly, dealt with notion of practitioner as seen within the relational contexts of public school teacher to university teacher. For what this dichotomy seems most naturally to suggest is that public school teachers are the practitioners of what we teach them—tell them, *authorize* for them. That is, we, at the university, authorize or author and often hand down in authoritarian ways, the knowledge we believe they should have in order to carry on their work in the classrooms. We talk about constructing knowledge, but more often than not, we pass on information as if it were a "body of knowledge," and frequently it does not matter who of us in the classroom sees it as knowledge and who sees it as information.

For example, I may believe when I give notes at the beginning of class discussion—notes that provide critical constructs that might be useful in helping us to formulate questions that go beneath the surface to explore assumptions within a piece of literature—that my agenda is to enhance discussion. But as this example illustrates, it may not matter what I think I am doing. Say my notes previous to a number of readings are drawn from Rudine Sims's book *Shadow and Substance* and have do to with authentic representations of particular cultural experiences in books—in this instance with authentic representations of African Americans.[46] And say we explore all the ways of recognizing authenticity, but one way I particularly urge—drawn from my own reading of Sims—is from the perspective of the author writing in the culture of his or her birth, the culture he or she would likely be most familiar with. In other words, Sims is talking about black authors writing about black people and what happens when white authors attempt to write authentically about the experiences of black people. Sims merely suggests what a same race author chooses to emphasize may be slightly different than an author who writes out of his or her particular culture. Sims also links these notions to the perpetuation of racial stereotyping in books for children and adolescents.[47]

What happens then when we read *The Education of Little Tree*, supposedly an autobiographical text about Native American life in the Cherokee Tribe?[48] Recently published articles stated that Forrest Carter falsified information with respect to his cultural heritage and that he was a member of the KKK.[49] What happens when these articles become a part of class reading? How shall students read and think with this information? How shall they interpret other potentially racist books against the backdrop of this information? And for the purposes of our course, how shall they view the educational importance of this text—the parts that suggest that both book learning and the kind of hearth and home participatory learning that takes place in the book are valid? And how are students to think with notions of authenticity related to authors when their own experiences are valid measures of authenticity as well? What are the mixed messages in this kind of conversation? What is the young man or young woman whose own growing up experiences resonate with those of Little Tree to think when we have linked in some unbreakable fashion the notion that the authenticity of a book relates to the author not the reader? How in this relational context can the reader see his or her experiences as authentic, important, and worth bringing to bear in our discussions? Even when I believe I am merely giving information that my students, who will become or already are teachers, will reconstrue according to their own particular previous experiences and prior knowledge, often that information is received or assumed to be knowledge, and it is used in the narrowest possible sense. In my example, does my own complicity in what students consider knowledge become more problematic because I have attempted to move between information giving and discussion or does it matter? Is what counts for "knowledge" so reified that position is the only changeable part of the construct?[50] That is, who gave information becomes important under this understanding of knowledge. If information is given by a teacher and if it comes from a book, then somehow it seems automatically construed as knowledge.

To be more specific, what is the difference in my giving a tool to think with and in giving the thought? What if students don't think with an idea; what if they just accept an idea and use it to carry out their own projects? Are we not satisfied as teachers if the latter occurs? Do we not, at times, wish to have students bypass thinking with or through an idea when the result of that thinking might be philosophical rejection of a particular notion we think is important?

Furthermore, we need to examine these assumptions as political arguments related to positioning. In other words, often in attempting to do our jobs, rather than giving ideas to think with (as if those might not be problematic enough), we and our students—teachers-to-be—assume a stance that suggests teachers are not capable of coming up with their own workable plans for teaching or making decisions appropriate to their own classrooms. In other words, sometimes, even if not consciously, we give lesson plans. Then the language our position suggests becomes a matter to be dealt with. As I have just illustrated, the stance we think we are taking may not be the stance our students see. For regardless of whether we see ourselves as a teacher who models good teaching or a teacher who gives lesson plans from a more authoritative, even authoritarian position, we *are* modeling something and it may not be what we expect.

For example, sometimes even along with a teacher preparation stance that is well intended, we give recipes or specific lessons or teaching ideas that we and students, perhaps unintentionally, assume will work. These ideas are rapidly reified and teachers go about using them unquestioningly. This kind of "what to do on Monday approach" makes us at the university truly complicit in teachers' lack of reflective practice. For what we have suggested is a universal classroom with a singular response to the right kind of stimuli. Not to simplify the problem, but again to show its likeness to other phenomena, these specific teaching ideas tend to be used like recipes you follow to bake a cake. The notion suggests if you follow it precisely you will not fail to turn out good students or good cakes. The trouble is, as anyone who has dabbled with either knows, any change in condition, for example the oven temperature is uneven, can cause the "kitchen-tested" recipe to flop.

I recently experienced this phenomenon firsthand and not metaphorically. For example, I attempted to bake my daughter's, birthday cake in my oven that needed repair. The baking coil was making a poor connection, which left the oven temperature uneven. I set the timer; the cake baked for the requisite 35 minutes, and it looked done when I opened the oven door. Because it was a sheet cake for Tiffany's party, it did not have to be turned onto another plate before icing. In my haste I forgot to do the toothpick test as any good baker knows to do. It looked done; seemed ready to ice and decorate, so I did. But alas, when I tried to serve this cake later that day at the party, I discovered the cake had not cooked in the middle. The children laughed at the idea of getting to eat cake dough instead of birthday cake, but I learned a valuable lesson about recipes.

What I learned can be extended here. If kitchen-tested recipes can flop as my cake did with the relatively small number of variables that exist when we bake, how very true it is for students. Students who come in all shapes and sizes, all colors, all socioeconomic and ethnic backgrounds, all abilities, and so forth. How then could we possibly expect recipes to work in classes?

Traditional methods then that encourage a narrow, functionary approach to teaching are deprofessionalizing and limiting. They generally seem to assume teacher's will not think, rather will only act and react. Even if we insert Donald Schon's definition of reflective thinking here, what we are left with is a notion of a teacher thinking on her or his feet.[51] In other words, as I read it, there is still in Schon's definition a lot of certainty about the act of teaching. Rather than drawing out complexities, Schon shows us close-up what teachers look like when they think and act at the same time. Schon's reflective teacher construes and reconstrues the act of teaching, but I am not sure how much uncertainty accompanies the teacher who figures out what to do and does it. Of course, teachers must act, but uncertainty does not mean inaction; it means that when we act as we must when we teach, we are always aware of the possibility that there are other possible ways of acting that might be better. Being uncertain does not have to mean we are paralyzed; rather, it can mean that we are always open to the possibility that some other way of thinking, responding, acting is also plausible and that, indeed, there are structures that may mitigate against desirable human actions.

By politicizing reflective acts—that is, by taking up, puzzling over, and questioning not only institutional hierarchies but all relations of power—reflection can become a site of operationalized resistance and struggle that allows us to both fight our politically regulated educational spaces as we recognize and embody the subjectivities, contradictions, and conflicts of teachers-of-learners and learners-as-teachers. When we position ourselves with and against broader social structures as well as local structures and understand that teacher agency implies a relationship somewhere in between the limitations that such structures erect and the individual capabilities they enable, then we may see reflection as that moment of radical praxis when the interlocking wires of constraint and possibility are loosened and we act, even if tentatively, to meld struggle with potential. Sheila Rowbotham refers to such a moment as a "problematic potentiality" where success is "never guaranteed yet . . . nevertheless possible."[52]

Therefore, I challenge any definition or conception of the word *reflection* that suggests simple solutions to the complex job of teaching. When we frame a reflective teacher simply as one who can think about a potential dilemma and who can construct solutions that allow that teacher to move on, I believe we risk simplifying the act of reflection. I believe we risk reductionist thinking as a problem-solving logic often does, seeing a problem and immediately seeing its solution or a pathway for solving it. It is, of course, not inconceivable that teachers are problem solvers—thinking teachers functioned this way long before we had a phrase like "reflective practitioner." My challenge to Schon and others, however, is that reflection may not depend entirely on thinking or questioning as usual; it may depend on asking harder questions—ones that begin with a self-critical, self-conscious awareness and then extend to wider political contexts that include always questions about knowledge, power, voice, and position.

If it is true that in order for teachers to be other than functionaries in the system they need to see themselves as "transformative intellectuals," in charge of their own destinies and capable of creating change, then we have to create a space for that kind of freedom.[53] Difficult as that may be, the alternative is hopelessness. Part of creating that space, then, is getting rid of the we/they dichotomy that I have used to illustrate the ways in which sometimes our language mediates against our efforts at all levels.

We/they dichotomies, of course, also contain the question of who decides what counts for legitimate knowledge. Indeed, who owns that knowledge is one that teachers know historically and one that has been institutionalized through privilege and tradition. How then can we ask teachers to be reflective until we rupture such language? What will we reflect upon? What will we be free to challenge? What institutional structures will we be justified in questioning?

As a feminist educator concerned with oppressive structures, I am painfully aware of what our language does and what it does not do. For example, I'm aware of how our language often seems to structure-in oppression (i.e., the way in which the names of particular roles have gendered descriptions is perhaps the most easily recognizable instance of structured-in oppression)[54] and of the needs it meets and those it does not begin to meet. Therefore, other ideas expressed in this text through the use of words like *empowerment* and *student-teacher* need some clarification here. Throughout this book I will refer to students who are in teacher preparation programs as student-teachers or teachers-to-be or prospective teachers instead of preservice teachers for several reasons.

First, student-teachers are operating on several very problematic planes. With teachers in the schools having one goal, the administration having another goal (and these not always being in the best interests of teachers or of students), and still the university having another, student-teachers are truly split. Additionally, the hyphenation itself suggests something about how they must feel at this particular moment in their histories. Hyphenated, split, torn between two worlds. We ask them to be students for two years, if not more, during which time we also send them out to the schools to be teachers. We ask them to perform, to model, to have their acts together, to preserve the dignity of their teacher education programs, at the same time that they are trying to survive as strangers in a strange land.[55]

Finally, embedded within the language of preservice teacher is the assumption that students can postpone commitment, that they do not need to be completely responsible while they are still *pre*-teacher. By referring to students who are student-teachers as prospective teachers rather than preservice teachers, I believe we begin at a much earlier date to encourage commitment and to encourage teacher thinking.

Yet, even the words *teacher thinking* are full of problematic assumptions. For example, some teacher thinking is autocratic. Some teacher thinking denies that students should play an active role in their educations. However, the teacher thinking that I would like to suggest by using the hyphenated word student-teacher is very close to the frequently used expression teacher-learner. In other words, I would like students to think of themselves as both learners and teachers, at the same time. I would like for them to understand this construct while they are still in the university and considered by many to be learners only. A continued negotiation of the terms *teacher* and *learner* (re)expressed as student-teacher may also help students who cling to the idea that their classes should have one privileged voice, the university teacher's, rather than multiple voices, theirs and their peers.[56] If students can begin to see themselves as teachers while still in teacher preparation programs, then perhaps some of the regression associated with first-year teacher socialization may be avoided.

I see many prospective teachers who seem to understand the concept of teacher-learner for their future classrooms. Unfortunately, however, what seems like understanding may be lipservice only, for teachers-to-be often believe that they will not learn to teach if their college teachers do not give them some particular lesson plans—what I earlier called recipes. Prospective teachers often seem to want directions not ideas to think with. What is not often considered is that the idea of relying on any teacher-proof materials, either teacher-proof textbooks or kitchen-tested teaching ideas is associated, then, with the lack of decision-making capabilities and autonomy—the idea of autonomy might suggest teachers have agency to work collectively toward common educational goals.

Instead of considering that teachers work within and against both constraint and possibility, we often formulate language that is, again, frequently thought of in terms of an oppositional construct. The language I'm referring to here is "empowerment."

We often see the constrained teacher as the opposite of the empowered teacher—the teacher who has agency, or who is confident and sees possibilities for affecting his or her environment and for making a contribution to society. And though we have sufficient language to define the term, we frequently are unable to describe in concrete ways what it looks like. Further, we tend to think of teachers as either being empowered or not being empowered. However, the notion of empowerment I would like to foster does not depend on an either/or construct. Because teachers tend to function within tensions of *both* structure *and* agency, a notion of empowerment based on a both/and way of seeing the world tends to be more grounded in the political realities of teachers' lives. To recognize limitations as well as possibilities does not take away from the concept, rather it seems to strengthen the argument Maxine Greene makes with respect to teachers having a consciousness of possibility—that is, having the capacity to see obstacles to one's freedom, to name obstacles as problems, and to find a public arena in which to pose alternatives.[57] To extend that concept to include reflective thinking when it includes self-critical questioning or reflexivity provides a view of empowerment that recognizes that we work always with and against constraint and possibility.

Yet as we know it, the word is seldom used inclusively; when I use the word in teacher education courses, student-teachers respond as if it were some sort of amorphous blob. Both the concept and their reactions to it. I use the blob notion in two ways here: one, because it is a slippery term and difficult to describe and two, because students hear it as some "touchy-feely" concept that does not seem grounded in the subjective realities of their lives. It is difficult to explain, but partly because we are asking students to buy into a concept that seems to have no relation to their immediate contexts. In other words, teachers-to-be seem particularly torn between constraint and possibility, feeling largely overwhelmed and powerless both at the public school and university level.

If I try to talk about this concept, even as I have discussed it here, the class lets out a simultaneous yawn. Perhaps, it is that definitions name and categorize, but they do not really create associations or help us make connections. So, I resort to stories—stories of teachers and their students whose behaviors indicate that they operate within a range of possibility that occurs largely out of their willingness to question power and authority. No story makes the point quite like this one of first-graders who show agency within the limitations of their school structure.

A teacher tells of a first-grade class in which the students became frustrated about always being last in the lunch line therefore never finishing their lunch. They asked their teacher if something could be done about this situation. The teacher explained lunchroom procedures but also suggested that students visit the principal's office with their complaint. One child, speaking for the group, volunteered to meet the principal with their problem. She walked into the office sat down and began.

"You see this?" she says, pointing to the spaces where two front teeth should be.

The principal looks at the child with concern and replies, "What?"

Once again the child says, "This!" "You ever tried to eat meat with this?" "Without these."

Immediately, the principal sees her problem and replies

"Oh, you mean without your two front teeth."

Seeing that she had finally gotten through to the principal, the child sighs and continues to explain that she and her classmates need a longer lunch hour in order to finish their lunches. Because the older kids are first in line, the younger ones, many of whom have missing teeth, do not get to finish eating lunch. Believing that this is unfair, she requests that the principal take their situation into consideration. The principal does, indeed, listen to the child and decides to let first-graders go to lunch five minutes earlier so that they will not continue to be last in the lunch line.[58]

Student-teachers have no trouble recognizing that these first-graders have voiced their concerns regardless of their positions. My students also recognize that these children seem confident to use that voice because their teacher had confidence in them. This three-minute story of empowered first-graders illustrates two things. One refers to the notion of not being able to give empowerment; about the most we can do is create a climate in which such tendencies might have the chance to flourish—create a space for such freedom where restrictive systems of thought and behavior can be questioned. In such an environment students may find that they too have a voice and that voice helps them accomplish important real world things.

Another point the story illustrates has to do with teaching without giving recipes. If our teacher preparation courses convey that we do not have confidence in teachers' capabilities to make good decisions (as the giving of recipes may convey), then we may be perpetuating a kind of dependency that thwarts any possibility for teacher growth toward autonomy. Not that independence is the answer to the empowerment question either. Dichotomous language, once again, is the problem. Either we are independent or we are dependent. Marie Nelson suggests that interdependence may be the key in this case (each of us needing the other interdependently), moving us closer to a both/and construct.[59]

In order to illustrate the complexity of this concept, let me explain how I perceive that interdependence, and then I shall problematize it against what my students' perceptions might look like (let me emphasize "might" for I do not intend to speak for students here). For example, I depend on my students for helping me continue to learn, reformulating all the while what that learning is. And they seem to depend on me to raise questions with them they have not considered. Though they count on me to provide a safe place for them to voice their understandings and concerns, on the other hand, they know I will gently nudge or even push, if need be, to help them extend their thinking to new ways of knowing. But remember, this is not wholly innocent. The politics of schooling in and of itself suggests that it is more than a possibility that my students' new ways of knowing will likely be my way—that their stories and their language will become the same as mine. That what I have gently nudged them to do is take on my language or the language of a particular text.

If in this setting, however, students can come to depend on each other, collectively their experiences will be richer. Despite my years of study, what each unique student, with his or her unique background of experience, brings to any classroom is greater than what I alone am capable of giving. When we politicize the classroom, when we question our own and each other's assumptions, when we work back and forth to mediate all meanings against the collective experiences represented in our classes, we may begin to create a climate for reflection. That reflection then may make possible the conditions for empowerment.

Thus, the language of empowerment seems problematic because of its association with power and because teachers assume that the simple definition many give (e.g., "to share power," "to be with power") reflects a simple rather than complex concept even though the idea of sharing power attempts to conceptualize a both/and construct in addressing unequal relations. A laudable goal, nonetheless, one that tends to be constructed naively and may overlook the political implications related to harmful effects of institutional power both within educational hierarchies and in the larger society. Adrienne Rich argues that we cannot rid ourselves of dichotomous relations when we continue to work with language that describes the most powerful dichotomy of all, the power/powerless dichotomy.[60] That language, like the language of preservice teacher, needs to be examined and problematized against the politics of "sharing power" and the politics of schooling hierarchies into which new teachers are socialized.

For example, as a woman writing and as a teacher, I have a particularly important, but not very powerful, role to play in helping students politicize these language constructs. I understand that questions of power and authority underlie nearly all that I produce and that my students produce in ways that are privileged by tradition. I understand that it is difficult to move away from the traditional role of student and to conceive of oneself as a nontraditional teacher. Of all the disabling beliefs students and teachers have, beliefs that are embedded in notions of power and authority may be the most difficult to shake. The hidden agenda that students tend to understand makes it sometimes seem ludicrous to use language like "empowerment." It suggests a power that many of us do not have to share. For women, it may even suggest complicity in the very system from which we are marginalized.

In that traditional system, we and our students are not much different; we are both taught exclusion as we are enculturated into the culture of schools. As we learn who owns the knowledge, we are sure it is not us. Though I attempt to break with authoritarian traditions in class, still students tend to have a difficult time valuing their personally constructed knowledge, and I have a tendency to replace lecture models with other practices that may be just as directive and steeped in domination. (I examine these practices in detail in Chapter 7.) Before questions of empowerment may be advanced, questions about knowledge and who decides what that knowledge will be are basic.

All efforts at school reform then may require close examination of our theories about knowledge. In other words, if knowledge is represented as a set of cultural artifacts, bound by time and tradition, transmitted for the purposes of perpetuating dominant ideologies and social control, then human agency is lost and deterministic as it sounds; we are but automatons in the system. However, if knowledge is socially produced or constructed, then it is capable of being constructed/produced again and again (this version of social construction does not necessarily assume reproduction). When we question the effects of power within the production of knowledge, what we contest is who produces and what is counted as most valid. When we contest a notion of cultural reproduction through particular views of culture and particular forms of knowledge, we, indeed, do contest both knowledge and culture as a fixed entity.

If culture is capable of being remade, if it is, indeed, social practice, then who the actors are is an important question. And if human agency is not lost but is vital to an emerging view of culture then it is also vital to any view of knowledge as a socially constructed product of culture. What has to be questioned in any notion of agency, however, is the structure within which knowledge is produced; put another way, we need to question the effects of power within particular discursive practices that tend to produce "regimes of truth" or the powerful arrangements that mediate what is counted and who decides.[61] Thus an emerging view of knowledge, power, and culture is the cornerstone of any project of critique and possibility.

This critique of some of the language frequently used in naming our reform projects stands to remind us of the contradictory nature of any practice, especially self-consciously critical, reflective practice. Again, I do not disagree that the language we use is the language we have, but I do suggest the need to problematize what such language represents and what it might mean politically for students and for teachers. We and our students operate under a set of assumptions about culture and social practices. Whether our perceived realities match our desired realities may depend on our assumptions about knowledge. Culturally, we and our students are specifically located within social categories that define our positions along gender, class, race, and ethnic lines. Whether we perceive culture as a social construct or as an instrument of the status quo may thus have the greatest impact on how we see ourselves socially. For each of us operates out of a history and a world view and each of us views schooling accordingly, but it may be the extent to which we consider ourselves capable of repositioning, capable of dislocating boundaries, and capable of negotiating meaning in any given situation that may define our roles as teachers and learners.

In this text I support a position of possibilities that I believe grows out of critical inquiry and reflection. Thus I invite readers to think about the particular ways in which our beliefs about teaching, in general, and about teacher education, specifically, can limit our possibilities for practice unless we ask harder questions that may seem to stand logic on its head.

Having defined reflective activity as wondering, doubting, questioning, in ways that support an attitude of what Dewey calls "effective thought,"[62] discussion of two final ideas remains crucial to my thesis. First, dialogue, again which is *both* public *and* private, necessitates valuing multiplicity—multiple voices/perspectives *open* to multiple possibilities. In both critical dialogue and reflection with self and others, a "dialogic" is created that embraces a difference of struggle and conflict. The term *dialogic* as used by Bakhtin seems to more intentionally embrace notions of a both/and construct. On the other hand, language or thought that tends to bipolarize or represent the world in either/or extremes leaves nothing to mediate, no meanings to attribute, and little use in reflective thinking and practice (see also Chapter 1).[63]

And finally, in relating multiplicity to our own pedagogies, it seems important to tease out some of what is problematic and seems polarized about what we call our radical pedagogies. For example, we tend to distinguish between "critical pedagogies" and "feminist pedagogies" on the basis of one tending toward a more masculine use of language, thereby objective and fraught with elitism while the other, if we are feminists, is grounded in the subjective, the particulars of human experience. Of course, that is an oversimplification of those notions and is problematic because it too assumes a masculine/feminine dichotomy.

Chandra Mohanty states in her essay on race and voice that polarities undermine any understanding of historical and relational connectedness. She says that we cannot understand difference until we can share responsibilities for particular histories that have tended to define both white and black peoples and women and men. Moreover, while shared experiences can become a prelude to further understanding, Mohanty makes clear that unless experience is "explicitly understood as historical, contingent, and the result of interpretation, it can coagulate into frozen, binary psychologistic positions."[64]

Some critics argue, on the other hand, that the chief cause for concern is oppression. That is, how can white male critics, who are linked to patriarchal oppression through race and gender, tell women how to fight oppression—particularly if in that telling, they create a totalizing discourse that seems to give them more power and is thus oppressive? Additionally, Jennifer Gore suggests that the word *pedagogy* itself is linked *both* to having a social vision *and* to specific practices.[65] This claim may suggest that critical pedagogies do not deal with specific practices but are still experiencing modernity at the level of grand ideas/social visions. Yet if we are to make progress in our endeavors to dislocate boundaries, push on limitations, and disrupt static practices in order to find a space for alternative discourses that include multiple possibilities—to live without borders,[66] might we not examine the dichotomous language we use to describe what we do and think particularly about what we suggest when we attribute one or the other with the words *critical* or *feminist*? Perhaps we might ask what else is masked in the use of this language. If both deal with issues of power and authority, if both deal with issues of domination/subordination, if both deal with issues of ideology and culture, if both deal with social injustices that are enacted along class, race, ethnic, and gender lines, and if both deal with change practices, why then the need to dichotomize?

Although the way we question knowledge, power, and authority might tend to effect the way we perceive our sense-making processes and in turn our professional discourses, these processes are not inherently, biologically, male or female according to Ruth Hubbard and other feminist scientists.[67] As Hubbard expresses those intersections of social and political, class and gender, she says, "Because the Western world-view values objectivity over subjectivity and men's knowledge over women's, 'feminine' ways to know are by their nature inferior."[68] Yet she makes clear that "these limitations are not inherent in the nature of women and men, any more than in the nature of science. They result from the ways scientific work, facts, and theories are constructed and from the ways we construct sex and gender."[69]

While Ruth Bleier maintains that thought processes are biologically neither male nor female, she adds that if thinking becomes gendered then it is socially gendered. The integration of subjective and objective thought, she says, is a human process not a male and female one.[70] The only way to construct knowledge is to first make sense of the new by seeing how it fits into our lives—making the public personal, the political private. As we further particularize more general or abstract ideas, we connect or weave new knowledge with old. We make local knowledge. We make it through situation, example, story, and once we have made it ours, we can explain it using our language with examples familiar to our experiences.

For instance, I offer this story as an example of how I came to fully understand, to construct knowledge, from the words of Virginia Woolf in *A Room of One's Own*.[71] On a beautiful spring day, I am tucked away in my work room writing this manuscript. I have my door closed as Woolf suggests women who wish to write should do. I even have a lock on the door, but I do not have it bolted. It is Sunday and my children and husband are at home. Tif is playing with her friend Molly and Chris is just back from fishing. And Roger is perched somewhere in the house with a good book.

They do not know how entranced I am with the passage I am working to create. They do not know how important it is to me. They do not know how I struggle to find just the right words. They do, however, know how my shoulders begin to ache after many hours at my computer, and they do know that I would rather be outdoors on this sunny, warm Michigan Sunday. So they bother me ever so often just to keep me from feeling neglected. Now, I do not generally feel neglected when I am working, but they want me to play so they sense I am feeling this way. And they keep on bothering me. It's not the kind of bother like when they really need me for something; rather, they're really beginning to annoy. Every few minutes, I hear, "Are you done yet?" "Is it almost finished?"

I yell back, "No, it is not done, and it won't be done anytime soon." This time, I also lose my patience and say, "Please stop doing this, I'm trying to think. This is not easy, and it is made especially difficult when you keep popping in. Yes, I want to play, and you are not only making it hard for me to resist, you are making it hard for me to think. This is important stuff I'm working on right now, and I have to be able to get it just right. So. . . . "

But before I can finish that sentence, I hear Roger mutter, "Ha!"

That does it for me, I start to cry. Not only will my family not leave me alone to do my work, now Roger, my usually very supportive husband, is not taking seriously the thing I have spent the better part of the year working on. He hugs me and apologizes, and apologizes, and apologizes. He says that he was teasing, and that, of course, he did not mean to hurt my feelings. But, at that moment like no other did I fully realize the meaning of these lines, "Write if you choose; it makes no difference to me. The world said with a guffaw, Write? What's the good of writing?"[72]

Through personal experience, we come to know. Through story we make it known. In narrative we weave the fabric of our lives (and others) connecting information with experience to construct knowledge.[73]

So though political questions of power and knowledge and embedded notions of patriarchy and privilege seem central to any examination of dichotomous language and practice—especially respective to the ways in which we seem to have polarized what we call critical pedagogies and feminist pedagogies, I am struck by yet another dimension of this problem (perhaps, equally as unpopular as raising this issue in the first place). For me, the dilemma in acting on one side or the other of pedagogical stances both of which offer alternatives to tradition and the status quo is more than political; it is also moral and ethical. That is, moral and ethical issues are embedded within the political arrangements that both constrain and make possible conditions for freedom. And because my "real" goal is reform that creates spaces for freedom and because that freedom may not be achieved without rupturing codes that consign difference to the margins, it is important for me to enter this argument. As a woman, as a mother, as a teacher, as a researcher, as a thinker, and as a writer, it is important for me to raise these questions. It is important for the sake of all our children that we find some "possible ways forward," some ways not to give up and "degenerate into cynical apathy."[74]

The process Williams describes in *The Long Revolution* suggests the possibility that "consciousness really [can] change," but he also suggests critique of "not only meanings and values, but [of] their 'real' context."[75] He writes:

> If, for example, we are to be co-operative, responsible, non-violent, where exactly in our actual world, are we expected to live? Is the economy co-operative, is the culture responsible, are the politics non-violent? . . . The only useful social argument is that which follows the meanings and values [questions] through to the point where real contradictions are disturbing . . . [76]

And I would add that we make this argument and launch this protest for the plight of children who live in neighborhoods where violence is the norm and for children who can't play in parks because of drugs and gang violence, for the children who don't seem to learn because no one expects them to, for children whose days are spent on the streets instead of in schools, for children who don't read and whose only form of entertainment is the television, for children who have never had a decent bed to sleep in nor clean clothes to wear, for children who go to bed hungry and come to school hungry.[77] There is pain in the world and as Barbara Eckstein reminds us in *The Language of Fiction in a World of Pain*, "[uncertainty] does not mean no responsibility."[78]

With pain we cannot afford lack of responsibility, lack of action, yet I fear we may not find those ways forward if we take up the battle on different sides. Then, of course, there are two battles to fight, and the one for the children becomes the one less fought. When it comes to children, if issues of hope and possibility are not a part of our varied political projects, then I have to ask whose interests are being served?

Although problematic, these questions may be worth considering: When Jo Anne Pagano asks, "What if our common sense notions of authority, responsibility, and power were different,"[79] I cannot help asking, what then? If we refuse to accept commonsense notions of power, will we cease dichotomizing and pushing both women and children farther to the margins? Will we be capable of providing hope for children who seem to be without hope? Will the price for change seem too high? Will an *un*common understanding of the complexity and problematic nature of a world of whiteness and blackness, femaleness and maleness, and so forth, seem so difficult to entertain that we somehow lapse into the taken-for-grantedness that we've heretofore railed about? And if our overturned commonsense notions of responsibility suggest wider political participation does that mean local discourse is unimportant or less valued? And if we come to see local discourse or particularized local experience as unimportant, then will it seem useless to work at all? Will derailing common sense make theory and practice any less problematic?

Perhaps Gramsci's thoughts on the matter will explain my concerns. For he suggested that though the world deposits many traces—hegemonic ideas and "prejudices from all phases of past history," the seeds of historical change are contained in the individual's capacity for self-critique.[80] In other words, though we contest hegemony, it may be that perhaps all conscious awareness is so infiltrated with commonsense understandings derived both from hegemonic ideas and other sources that it becomes impossible simply to reject ideas wholesale, that are always part of a collective, and start over at any particular point in history. Yet the practice of self-critique or the critical, reflexive examination against one's experiences with and in the world may offer possibility for change. That practice seems to engage the self who critiques against experiences that are both unique and personal and part of a wider collective self and whose ideas foster an ongoing, back and forth struggle, an internalized process of crossexamining previous thoughts and actions against possible future thoughts and actions. The self who critiques against the self may be uncertain, but that uncertainty does not suggest lack of awareness or lack of concern or even lack of ability to act; uncertainty in this instance may reveal instead the organic nature of critical constructive thought that is embedded in controversy, and that shifts and sorts and emerges forever containing seeds of what is past and what is possible.

Therefore, I ask "what then" not to suggest that I disagree with questioning our commonsense notions of power, authority, and so forth, but to suggest that questioning is simply not enough. I am driven by the idea that continual, reflexive examination may somehow result in action, in a stab at the possible, at the what then. Despite our uncertainty, a world in pain cries out for action, even if that action is only that of one person at a time practicing change.

Practice

In *An Apple for My Teacher*, Louis Rubin, Jr. collects the stories of twelve authors telling about teachers who made a difference in their lives.[81] Rubin profiles the "perfect teacher" as someone who loves language, literature, and poetry and sits among students as a co-conspirator shifting authority to them. This teacher treats everyone as equals, supports the underprivileged, listens to opinions with respect, never embarrasses with criticism, and does not accuse or condemn, but merely *corrects*. Not the most romanticized image of a teacher, still not the image of a teacher as a human being who loves, who feels pain, who cares deeply about lots of things, who reacts, who questions, who doubts much including self. It is, indeed, a public image—an image that denies the self. But what of the private image, what of the self turned inside out? What of the teacher who seeks to create a counter image? What of the teacher for whom "thinking-as-usual becomes untenable . . . [who] experience[s] a crisis of consciousness . . . , [for whom] the formerly unquestioned . . . become[s] questionable, the submerged . . . become[s] visible?"[82] What of the reflective teacher who has doubts and who engages in self-critical inquiry in addition to critique of local and wide (social) problems?

Perhaps the schooling narrative in the book *One Child* by Torey Hayden best illustrates the teacher for whom thinking-as-usual is not only untenable, but unconscionable.[83] *One Child* is the story of Sheila, a severely mentally disturbed child with a genius intellect. This true story portrays Torey in the role of teacher for eight autistic children with varying degrees of autism. Through love and pain, questioning and doubting, Torey reaches Sheila's tortured soul and the transformation is overwhelming. In the beginning, Sheila seldom speaks and is destructive and violent. Though she has been tortured both mentally and physically by her family, she has never cried. Finally, Torey reaches her sharp mind and closed heart through patience, tough love, and a refusal to give up even when Sheila's behavior reverts to old habits and the case worker for Sheila finally gets a placement at the state hospital.

Throughout the book, Torey questions her teaching, questions her motives, questions her loyalty, even questions her right to care for this child. What we see most is the kind of self-critical, reflexive questioning necessary for reflective practice.

Yet all our images of teachers as reflective thinkers may be largely unsuitable until as in the case of language, we do more than interrupt to create a temporal space for such a teacher. For teachers cannot practice reflection in a time-out-of-time moment. As students who need many years to get over the years and years of being socialized into an institution that privileges and marginalizes, so too do teachers need many years to get over their institutionalized roles.

We might wish for a bird-watcher who can reverse evolution and see a different society or a different version of schooling, but having a vision is not enough.[84] Most of us have a vision. Being able to puzzle out what keeps us from recognizing that vision, however, is as important as having it. Therefore, a teacher who seeks to understand the ways in which society often depicts the "good teacher" and the roles he or she is asked to play is, perhaps, a teacher questioning tradition and trying to interrupt the system.

Still in such an instance, the image of the "good teacher," can have a strong inculcating effect on teachers-to-be and experienced teachers. For example, Greene portrays the "good teacher," according to school/social expectations, as "infinitely controlled and accommodating, technically efficient, impervious to moods . . . with all . . . loose ends gathered up and all . . . doubts removed."[85] If this image or role model is offset only by other overly romanticized images, it may be little wonder that the culture of teachers and teaching is slow to change. Furthermore, and, perhaps, even more to the detriment of school change as a whole, the teacher Greene describes may be close to the good teacher in Schon's definition of a reflective teacher—no doubts, just thinking while acting[86] or to Gene Maeroff's vision of the empowered teacher as professional.[87] What in our practice binds us to that image of teacher?

If Dillard's bird-watching scenario sets the stage for seeing things in new ways, for seeing alternatives, for seeing possibilities that tend to push back the tedium of everyday living, for allowing the invisible to emerge and the unquestionable to be questioned, then that may be the metaphor we need in order to begin the process of rupturing the codes that impede reflective thinking and practice.[88] Moreover, Greene's description of the traveler who returns home to find everything that was once familiar now strange may, indeed, also provide an image of rupture.[89] Although both metaphors portray a sense of wonder, the person returning home notices things never seen before—"has to think about local rituals and customs to make sense of them once more."[90] Things taken for granted are examined in a new light. The traveler recognizes the arbitrary nature of those rituals, and when arbitrariness is understood, dismissal is possible. What is in need of rupture, then, is *taken for grantedness or given-ness*, what Herbert Marcuse calls the "mystifying power of the given."[91]

This need is especially pronounced for the teacher, that individual in society so defined as to sometimes seem invisible not only to the self but to the served. The loss of self or sense of who we are is what Greene is making problematic in her treatise about the homecomer. She describes for us the "teacher as stranger"—stranger to the self. So many things are overlooked: personal histories; expressions of self in language; goals, dreams, ambitions; and perhaps most importantly, the teacher is perceived as one without a world view or perspective on the world from which he or she operates. In fact, teachers' roles are so firmly defined that teachers themselves frequently do not consider questioning the practices they have been assigned to carry out in their schools.[92] In this instance, how then can teachers expect students to become questioners?

In Greene's analysis of the homecomer, she describes that teacher or reflective thinker as one who takes a "stranger's vantage point on everyday reality . . . to look inquiringly and wonderingly on the world. . . . "[93] As the homecomer who returns home to feel out of sync with community rituals begins to see the arbitrariness of culture, so too the teacher has to question, interpret, reconstruct his or her classroom and curriculum in light of new experiences and make problematic those rituals that bind him or her to exploitation. In other words, reflection thus entails a dialogue (both private and public) in which not only are assumptions questioned and mediated against a backdrop of experience, but meanings are politicized as well. This background of personal experience then is what Dewey sees as the prime source of education.[94] Recognizing what is most valuable from that experience requires another step. It requires reflection on the "active, persistent, and careful consideration of belief," binding ideologies, and experience.[95]

Thus a "fusion of the intellectual and the emotional" is required or there cannot be true reflective practice.[96] This practice involves a "felt-thought" or a passion that comes from what Greene calls a "committed rationality."[97] An excerpt from a student's response journal best describes what may be meant here:

> Passion—it's looking at the world with the fresh wonder of a child. It's caring so much that you want to share it. Not all of the lessons are fun or easy, but they're all real—just like the Velveteen Rabbit. It's loving learning so much that you need to help

[students] understand, help them feel, make the struggle for understanding worth it. It's the pleasure of realizing your own humanity and wanting and helping others to find theirs also. In English class, it's found in the literature and discussions that make you think. It's when you hear the primal scream (so to speak) of Holden Caufield in *The Catcher in the Rye*, when you feel rage in *The Color Purple*, or when you hurt for Esther in *The Bell Jar*. It's the part of teaching that makes you feel alive, and you want your students to [feel it] also. It's the intangible, unexplainable everyman's land between art and life, and the reward of its revelation. I refuse to be a sleeping teacher.[98]

In this instance commitment means not only dedication to a cause, it means caring and connectedness. It means building community. And rational commitment means acting deliberately. As Thoreau went to the woods to learn "to live deliberately," teachers who have a committed rationality experience their daily lives deliberately.[99] They experience what the philosopher Alfred Schutz calls "wide-awakeness" or a "plane of consciousness of highest tension originating in an attitude of full attention to life and its requirements."[100] They are not sleeping teachers, as Jody suggests she refuses to be. That is, reflective teachers make a conscious decision to actively engage in "critical thinking and authentic choosing."[101]

In part, then, rational commitment means authentic choosing—choosing teacher work, choosing debate, choosing community, choosing hopefulness. It means choosing, period! And it is liberating to the extent that deciding to make choices, rather than accepting without question whatever happens to bump against us, gives one a certain freedom. This emancipatory shift is best described by Greene in *Landscapes of Learning*:

> Freedom is the power of vision and the power to choose. It involves the capacity to assess situations in such a way that lacks can be defined, openings identified, and possibilities revealed. It is realized only when action is taken to . . . move through the openings, to try to pursue real possibilities.[102]

Out of this sense of freedom we construct our world; we may be a player rather than one who is played. Our stance as chooser does not mean limits do not exist; according to Dewey, it means we as teachers do not set limits on "opportunities for continuing growth in new directions."[103] Nor do we lead "lives of quiet desperation" as Thoreau said.[104] Rational commitment means having a sense of the possible. And it is encouraged, indeed, nurtured by self-conscious inquiry. It means we are "continuously engaged in interpreting a reality forever new."[105] But it may not occur, and it cannot last in our present system.

Too much about a teacher's work day mediates against this. Not only short-term interruption, but also rupture is needed, and with that rupture continued self-critique. Feelings of victimization and powerlessness can stem both from loss of identity and from choices not made, but to say this is all that causes such feelings is a simplistic and micro-level response to a macro-level problem. As the bird-watcher sees the bird from a different vantage point and the homecomer, who is now an outsider, sees differently what was once taken for granted, so too reflective teachers may see that they need to be intrinsically involved in the deconstruction of "illusions that bind . . . exploitation."[106] But to dismantle illusions implies choice. And making choice a possibility necessitates that we make it problematic discovering all the risks associated with making choices. Often for teachers these risks seem limitless and at odds with what we sense is "real."[107]

Here feelings seem consistent with what Williams calls a "structure of feeling" or a "process, often indeed not yet recognised as social but taken to be private, idiosyncratic, and even isolating."[108] Williams further elaborates a structure of feeling as social experiences in "solution." By stating solution in this way, he is neither referring to it as "mere flux" nor is he suggesting that it is already a social formation or a solution as we have come to think of the word. Although in some instances, as Williams describes, art that represents opposition to existing formations can be said to define a structure of feeling, not all art can be seen in this way. What Williams most seeks to represent here, as I see it, is the connection between, in this instance the obstacles humans (teachers) face, and what is a social manifestation with a structured hypothesis or worldview. These structures, then, are the ones I suggest here are in need of rupture—those dominant and residual meanings and practices. Marilyn Frye defines such structures in her "birdcage analogy" as a "network of systematically related barriers."[109]

Williams agrees on the complexity of rupturing systems that are as Frye suggests, systematically related:

The actual alternative to the received and produced fixed forms is not silence: not the absence, the unconscious, which bourgeois culture has mythicized. It is a kind of feeling and thinking which is indeed social and material, but each in an embryonic phase before it can become fully articulate and defined exchange. Its relations with the already articulate and defined are then exceptionally complex.[110]

In this statement of resistance to dominate forms, Williams reminds us that we cannot create spaces for freedom, for transformation of existing social orders if we remain silent and fixed in our gaze. Though taking up a position of articulation and action is complex, it is a part of the "journey of hope" that oppositional cultures must enjoin. In *The Year 2000* he writes:

... the relations between small-group initiatives and potentials and a dominant system are at the very centre of the problem. It is there we have learned how new work can be incorporated, specialised, labelled: pushed into corners of society where the very fact that it becomes known brings with it its own displacements.[111]

Thus whether we take up, debate, and meet power head on is not only a personal issue but also a collective struggle. In any event, not doing so allows those already fixed obstacles, that would keep us from dislocating boundaries within our classrooms and within our own lives, to remain formidable, systematically related barriers.

Research

Within the question, what counts as legitimate research, is also the question, what counts as legitimate knowledge. Here, I do not wish to spend time examining issues related to how traditional research in education limits and denies access to the teaching community and to how it reinforces patriarchal relations.[112] I do want to suggest, however, that an interruption in this tradition and an eventual rupturing of the power relations that are evident in this "quest for professionalism" might lead the way to our listening *for* the story as Eudora Welty says of the storyteller who does more than listen *to* the story.[113]

What I am suggesting here is that a respect for the story as a form of learning is as Robert Coles writes in *The Call of Stories*, "everyone's rock-bottom capacity."[114] He continues, "Their story, yours, mine—it's what we all carry with us on this trip we take, and we owe it to each other to respect our stories and learn from them."[115] What we, of course, do with those stories shows much about our respect for them, and thus is the aspect of this form of research that must be politicized. For example, in Daphne Patai's article on the ethical dilemmas of personal narrative research, she writes:

> As I sit down to write about Teresa other problems emerge. Did she imagine that I would describe her street and the poverty of her house? . . . her weaknesses more than her strengths? . . . How would she have felt about it had she known? And do these things matter?[116]

Patai's article does not pretend solutions; rather, it raises questions with respect to narrative research. She reminds us that we not only have agendas, but we also have obligations and that responsibility and intentionality operate at different levels, sometimes connecting, sometimes conflicting.[117]

When we include stories gathered from research settings or classroom settings in our texts, as I do here, we have an obligation to preserve the dignity of that storyteller. And Coles reminds us that as people bring their stories to us, they can only hope we understand them; when we interpret a story, we are interpreting a life.[118]

Coles, a scholar and practicing psychiatrist, speaks directly of a political dilemma among educational researchers that reflects how deeply rooted in a positivist tradition we still are. That dilemma is, of course, our continued debate over analyzing the story or letting the storyteller speak for himself or herself, and why? For example, a recent conversation with another researcher revealed this in response to why he analyzed the stories from his interview research. He replied simply, his publisher insisted on categorizing profiles from that research.[119] However, those categories will, in one way or another, provide labels for the profiles he constructed from his interview data. And those profiles belong to people. People whose words, whose lives will end up either being labeled by readers or in categories in the researcher's book—where, indeed, a person's *life* is made a text.[120]

Creating new spaces for learning from research means broadened agendas that allow for more anecdotal evidence and less justifying of the form. Yet we need always to be mindful of the power issues on which these new research relationships center.[121]

Remembering then Patai's questions and the title of her article, "Who Should Eat the Last Piece of Cake?,"[122] I cannot help asking, who is being served by our research, and who is being marginalized? And where do we draw the lines? About this, each of us will have to decide.

In the meantime, however, such stories provide a rich way of telling us many things, particularly about schools and teaching that we have not been able to learn under traditional methods of research. For example, little in the way of research into teachers' beliefs or about reflective inquiry has been discovered in more standard ways. No, we cannot measure reflectivity in the traditional sense—it is a way of thinking. Researchers who need "defensible benchmarks by which reflectivity can be assessed"[123] will likely find them only in the actions of a reflective teacher and in their stories. However, the lack of such research has limited meaningful attempts to organize, plan, and assess school reform movements.

STORIES OF SCHOOLING AND THE DEVELOPING TEACHER

Many of the ideas prospective teachers have about their roles as teachers and about schooling, in general, are developed long before they enter teacher education programs. To examine new approaches to curriculum and not take into account students' "personal knowledge"[124] has traditionally been a blindspot in teacher reform movements (problematic as the notion of a blindspot may be, particularly when conceived as a lack or a gap to be filled). Therefore, in looking at ways in which teachers' personal knowledge is shaped, I shall consider the impact of stories of schooling in literature and the arts.

Because teachers' beliefs are often based on experiences prior to teaching, dispositions, feelings, guiding images, and principles may have a cumulative effect on students' developing teacher selves.[125] William Pinar refers to this phenomenon as the architecture of self or how we integrate beliefs and values from past experience.[126] This suggests that teachers, especially prospective teachers, might benefit from the opportunity to examine the ways in which they have come to define their role as teachers—what it means to teach. Educative activities that lead students to reflect on their past experiences in order to discover what is most valuable and what will best serve them as teachers may provide significant learning.

In *Landscapes of Learning*, Maxine Greene argues that an engagement with literature and the arts connects us with the past as it reminds us of the ways in which we bring meaning into being.[127] And Margaret Buchman writes that "contemplative" response to literature may effect teacher thinking more than any other single teaching enterprise.[128] In addition to contemplation, I would add that critical/reflective assessment of both literature and other aesthetic media such as films, television, and songs, which may have already provided a significant though perhaps unrecognized education, may also be integral to the development of a teacher self.

Therefore, as we seek to create some spaces for freedom and renewal in teacher education, I suggest we consider a curriculum that pairs stories of schooling with readings that display a variety of critical social theories of education. Dramatizations of schooling situate for students issues of class, race, and gender and make more accessible theories of resistance, hidden curriculum, politics of student voice and position, power and its distribution, relationships between school and society, and the social construction of knowledge.

Through inquiry and reflection in an extensive study of stories of schooling read in parity with professional texts, teachers may be helped to question, if not dismantle, many preconceived assumptions about teaching as they develop a greater capacity for understanding the meanings students make about schooling. This is important for several reasons. First, understanding how all students make sense of curriculum (and in particular, how students learn to read and write) renders a teacher far more capable of making important decisions about pedagogy and content. On the other hand, until teachers know what they believe about teaching and learning, reflect on that, and see themselves in relation to other students, teachers, and administrators, a clear articulation of their own rationale for curriculum and classroom dynamics may be difficult to achieve if not impossible. Moreover, without some understanding of how school as a social institution tends to structure inequality, teachers may not see the complex ways in which inequitable situations tend to mediate against students' learning. Narrative practice that includes readings in literature and other media; for example, films, television, songs, and so on may help teachers-to-be develop what Maxine Greene calls a "committed rationality" that may, indeed, lead teachers to make connections between school and the wider society.[129]

I take Greene's use of the word *rationality* here to mean deliberate, fully awake to life and all its possibilities and thus I connect that sense of wide-awakeness to critical inquiry and reflection and to how narrative both frames and is framed by such practices. What I want to make clear, however, is that I use the word *narrative* more broadly than is suggested simply through an engagement with literature and other artistic media. That is, as a way of thinking/reading the world, literary narratives are but, perhaps, one place to begin inquiry that may lead to the kind of reflective activity that necessitates our grappling with to make sense of the cultural and political milieu in which teachers and students do more than simply exist and act out diverse but well-defined roles within schools and outside in wider social contexts.

Examples of those roles can be seen throughout the pages of literary history when schooling emerges as an important theme and when it may be no accident that culture/society is shown as shaping the destinies of school children. That shaping is shown repeatedly in texts chosen for this book and in the opening lines of the classic, *Madame Bovary*, when we meet Charles Bovary, a new "boy dressed in ordinary clothes" who on entering his new school is so intimidated by classmates and their daily rituals that he is incapable of joining them, is rendered speechless, and is laughed at pathetically.[130] As Freire describes "the culture of silence" in the Third World, we see that programmed conformity is no less at work in this nineteenth century novel.[131] The descriptions of Charles and the recitations that were a part of every class are not much different from our introduction to Welton Academy and to Neal in the contemporary movie, *Dead Poets' Society*.[132] Like Charles Bovary, Neal comes from a lower socioeconomic class than other boys we meet at Welton. Both stories are tragic, both reveal something of the bondage and human sacrifice from which culture is made, and both show us something about how schools tend to reproduce society along class lines[133]—where "crossing boundaries," to use Mike Rose's words, is extremely difficult if not impossible.[134] In the movie and the book, prospective teachers can challenge the romanticized image of teachers while they question the privileging of elitist forms of knowledge.

Placing ourselves today in relation to this kind of historical look at schooling, at literacy, and at culture creates what Mikhail Bakhtin calls a "dialogic" relation.[135] When a novel or a film text creates a story capable of showing the multivocal nature of the past, rich with voices from the people, then and only then in Bakhtin's words is it worthy of being canonized. And as inquiry into the dialogic relation among language, school, and society becomes a struggle for meaning, narrative practice and reflective practice may emerge synergistically as a moment of connection that marks not merely a language event articulated as story but an event through which meanings are made and acknowledged. When and if these meanings become a part of a wider critique, such moments may be said to reflect the wide-awakeness Greene refers to as committed rationality.[136] But the sense of narrative in this text is always more than representation. In other words, it is as a means of finding and forming language to articulate meanings that narrative practice unfolds to make possible wide-awakeness and critical inquiry/reflection.

Thus, within this space in which renewal may occur, I argue for reading different kinds of texts in parity for purposes of drawing on multiple voices but also for two other reasons that seem obvious. First, students often have difficulty reading critically some literature and viewing popular movies (*Dead Poets' Society, Lean on Me, Teachers, Educating Rita,* etc.) and television programs (e.g., *Head of the Class, Parker Lewis Can't Lose,* etc.), but critical professional readings can provide a lens for such a reading.[137] And second, critical readings (e.g., *Pedagogy of the Oppressed, Literacy: Reading the Word and the World,* etc.) may be difficult to unpack without situating them in some greater approximation to reality.[138] In other words, making the leap from abstraction to situation can be difficult without a bridge. But stories or narrative can provide such a link and may be the key to making meaning.

REFLECTIVE PRACTICE AS CONTRADICTORY PRACTICE

Therefore, as I write this story about the possibilities inherent within the framework of the narrative—specifically schooling narratives—and the powers of the fictive world to connect us, to move us, to allow us to see through the eyes of characters we can know or become, I invite you to join me in this conversation. I invite you to participate in the possibility that our conversation may suggest to you ways of thinking about teaching and learning that seem contrary to all you have considered heretofore as appropriate content, especially in teacher education. I invite you to consider the ways you view texts and how you read them and what you consider textual material. I invite you to consider your stories and their values, your beliefs about teaching and how they guide your work. I invite you to consider how much your public self is a reflection of your private self and how those worlds collide in classrooms. And most of all, I invite you consider the reform question. I invite you to consider the politics of reform as well as the possibilities. I invite you to consider with me who reform is for, who stands to gain the most and who does not, and what reform would look like if its success were measured in terms of reflective, critical thinkers/empowered students and teachers. Therefore, in Chapter 3 I look more closely at reform that is related to conceptions of liberal education and how teacher preparation becomes a part of that discussion and debate.

CHAPTER 3

Education as a Liberal Art

"Liberal education has been conceived as pertaining to the development of the mind. . . . [However,] those concerned with the preparation of teachers—including those now engaged in its reform—emphasize the sort of skill development employment-related competencies, and technical rationality that are the very antipathy of the guiding principles of liberal education."
(from Landon E. Beyer, *Knowing & Acting: Inquiry, Ideology & Educational Studies*)[1]

The dilemma addressed in this epigraph speaks to the issues many of us are dealing with at this particular moment in our histories as educators. That is, what is liberal education when it comes to the preparation of teachers? Is it, as some proposals suggest, more work in the disciplines—work that occurs in the beginning and is later taken up in discussions that surround the teaching of that subject matter? And is that project political; does it see teacher preparation as a "counterpublic sphere" that is part of a "wider social movement," or is it based in an attempt to refine teaching methodologies?[2] Does not the separation of applied studies and subject matter actually reinforce the bifurcation that exists between theory and practice?[3] And central to these questions is the question that Beyer and others raise with respect to "knowing and acting."

As Beyer's work challenges the "epistemological and political bases of the distinction between liberal and applied studies"—between "knowing and acting,"[4] I continue that argument with questions related to how we define liberal studies. For example, do we mean traditional liberal studies in which a body of cultural knowledge is handed down as proposed in the writings of E. D. Hirsch, Jr. and mastered for employment-related purposes,[5] or do we conceive of a liberal education as a liberating education—one that encompasses the desire to have teachers-to-be see themselves as culture makers (i.e., subjects of their own histories), reflecting on and questioning the dominant images of teachers and schooling within a wider political discourse? This latter notion of liberal education is not based in traditional cultural studies where culture is seen as fully formed. It is a view of culture and practice or activity as Raymond Williams expresses it—a view that is not deterministic but emergent[6] though not completely free of traditional meanings and practices either.

Not unaware of the social and political constraints society places on teachers but fully aware is the position to which Alfred Schutz refers when he suggests the need for "wide-awakeness"—what he describes as being deliberate or fully awake to life and all its possibilities.[7] Thus a liberatory education, perhaps, might work in the contradictory space between constraint and freedom to help teachers-to-be shift from seeing themselves as merely pawns in the system—or as Christopher Lasch suggests "minimal selves"—to a subject position, albeit a position still in need of problematizing.[8] Therefore, to the degree that all of us operate within formations of constraint and possibility, a revision of liberal education would include then the opportunity to question and, indeed, act on our socially constructed positions as a part of a wider struggle. That is, our programs might deal with "general, human issues, and ideas" through inquiry into a topic, subject, piece of literature, and so forth; they might be more concerned with raising the intellect than with "concerns of future employees."[9] Our programs might offer the possibilities Joseph Campbell raises in *The Power of Myth*—what he calls engagement with a subject.[10] They might look less like "job training" where the focus is generally "how to" and more like forums of debate where the focus is "why." This, of course, is not to suggest exclusion of the "how" of teaching, but inclusion of "how" with "why"—a both/and construct where theory is as inseparable from practice as content is from form.

An example of the way literature and media arts are used in parity with critical readings seems appropriate here. Related to this discussion of cultural studies and to the inclusive practice of "how" teaching and learning occurs with "why" some content is privileged and some is marginalized and "why" some students seem to have a voice while others are silenced is a particular instance of a pairing of aesthetic media with critical readings to illustrate the alternative practices on which this text is based.

TEACHING THROUGH LITERATURE AND THE ARTS

Often in both literature and other media texts we see *one* vision of schooling, and it is powerful. That vision is largely negative, authoritarian, skill driven, and uncaring. Even when we have a character like Mr. Keating, the featured teacher in *Dead Poets' Society* who exemplifies other qualities (for example, he is caring and his teaching is not skill driven), supporting characters in this instance, other teachers, and the administration as well as parents provide negative imagery.[11]

The movie opens with a graduation that shows all the pomp and circumstance that is a part of the tradition at Welton Academy, a school of white middle- to upper-class male students. Neal emerges as one of the central characters in the story. Coming from a lower socioeconomic background than other young men, Neal's dominating father forces Neal to drop all extracurricular activities and concentrate only on his studies, as he sees Welton as Neal's opportunity for success, which is measured in terms of a rise in cultural status. Not long after the opening of the school year, Neal and friends discover an old yearbook that shows Mr. Keating, their English teacher, involved in a club known as "The Dead Poets' Society." Though the content of Keating's class is highly traditional, his methods are a combination of ritualized memorization and high anxiety chanting. Eccentrically, he marches students through the courtyard of Welton chanting literature and verse as students follow with excitement. He encourages a carpediem notion among students as he draws out independent thinking that challenges authority. When Neal and friends organize their own "Dead Poets' Society," Neal takes Keating's suggestion to "live for the moment" seriously. Neal goes against his father to pursue his love for acting by taking a part in a Shakespearean performance. The story ends tragically when Neal is found out, and he and his father come to blows. In his father's study, Neal finds a gun in the desk drawer and uses it to exercise what might be considered his one last option in freedom—in independent thinking. Keating is, of course, forced to leave Welton, and the story ends with friends of Keating's and Neal's questioning both the system that would hold Keating responsible and the society that would call Neal's hand.

The response to this movie is mixed. Though Keating is a character who addresses some important educational concerns (i.e., thinking for oneself, risk-taking, and the pursuit of excellence), his role, however, is portrayed as extreme and romantic. In one article we examine, Mark Collins says, "The teacher wins over the class/audience by the sheer force of humor, visible energy, confidence, and a passion for words."[12] And what may be more problematic here than the stereotyping to which Collins refers is who Keating addresses through his character.

Though Keating stands on his desk to remind himself that he "must constantly look at things in a different way," he looks at a privileged class. Within the context of *Dead Poets' Society*, the audience does not see a view of teachers consonant with a multicultural world. Though some of his methods may be nontraditional, Keating reflects the cultural elitism that is an approach to canonical literature in keeping with E. D. Hirsch, Jr.'s vision of cultural literacy.[13] Although Keating's presentation may not be at fault, media images link the opening of one's mind directly with the opening of it to a particular view of culture, and in the context of Welton Academy, link the knowledge of cultural forms through the classics to status in a privileged class. With Keating's ability to work students into a frenzy, he could have had revolutionaries had they been fighting for a cause. Instead, they were becoming "members of the club," perpetuating dominant class interests. And Keating's punishment after Neal's suicide serves only to reinforce society's notions that schools must be strict, rule-enforcing agencies where its members, from teachers to pupils, must be controlled.

Students found the stereotyping problematic, yet in order to encourage discussion to go beneath the surface, a more critical pairing became necessary. For this we examined a piece by Stanley Aronowitz and Henry Giroux entitled "Schooling, Culture, and Literacy in the Age of Broken Dreams."[14] The reading situated the problems students already saw in the film with respect to relations of power between Keating and the headmaster of Welton and between Keating and parents—especially Neal's parents. Students were also moved to consider Keating's interactions with students and how the particular content of his classes and the entertaining form of his teaching somehow enacted another kind of power. In other words, the reading pointed out the various ways in which teaching is often related to classroom management and discipline and learning to mastery of discrete skills and select information. In terms of larger structures, however, the reading helped students consider how those hierarchical arrangements between parents, administrators, teachers, and students became a particular form of social authority and control. Moreover, the article helped move students to consider the structures operating in the film as part of a larger interrelated network of structures that extend to the wider society. From the obvious power relations to the not so obvious (to students) understanding of how that power resulted in a particular view of knowledge and history as "merely an artifact, a warehouse of goods, posited either as a canon of knowledge or a canon of information that has simply to be transmitted as a means of promoting social order and control,"[15] the article paired with the film moved students to a deeper critique of schooling/teaching.

In particular, the combined film/article study helped students raise questions about what they assume knowledge is. In other words, the study created an opening for us to begin to consider what counts as knowledge and who decides what counts and what the differences between information and knowledge might be. Recognizing already the favorite notion that *knowledge is power,* students seemed pushed to consider if knowledge is power then whose knowledge are we talking about—do they as students have and make knowledge that holds any power? or does someone else have and make the knowledge that counts? In order to decide if what they had heretofore taken as knowledge was, indeed, the kind of knowledge that gave them some power (whether or not that power was desirable), students began to consider when in the past knowing a particular thing had actually resulted in any "real" power. In examining who seemed to have power and what "real" power might be, students began to question the nature of privilege and who and what is marginalized at Welton Academy. What groups are represented? What languages are valued? What literatures and authors are valued? How is teaching and learning enacted and valued? And when connections to everyday lived experiences are made, what are the outcomes of those connections and who is responsible?

These and other questions created space for me and my students (teachers-to-be) to examine the problematic relationship between knowledge and truth as we began to unravel the particular forms of cultural authority embedded within the "body of knowledge" Hirsch and Bloom referred to as what every American should know.[16] Regardless of what students seemed to understand about power and control issues as they related to knowledge, our conversations after viewing *Dead Poets' Society* and reading the Aronowitz and Giroux article created an opening for further exploration of such issues and the possibility of extending these issues to other school and nonschool contexts.[17] Additionally, in order to make problematic other sites of contestation in the film, I juxtaposed Giroux's article on "Critical Literacy and Student Experience."[18] This text posed questions related to the notion of self-determined thinking as seen in the film. Students raised questions about the idea of self-determined thinking as they worked to understand the implications of such thinking on Neal's suicide. For example, they wondered if Keating's "live for the moment" theme and thinking for oneself was always the same? They questioned whether living for the moment and self-determined thinking could be construed as individual acts. And if so, were people capable of living that kind of autonomous life? Or does thinking for oneself involve a more critical act—an act that forces us to examine issues relationally? Is thinking for oneself in the film related to a notion of individual freedom, when individuals do not consider how they are connected to others in social communities? And what about the idea of community in this film?

These and other questions are raised within the corpus of critical texts and media selections used in classes to challenge students to look not only at the form and the content of the teaching in texts we read/view, but also to examine critical/theoretical implications of that form and that content in light of practices that we are each a part of. Because popular film depicts a range of power relations, cultural conflicts, and personal as well as collective struggles, in addition to a variety of raced, classed, and gendered roles, and because students are bombarded daily with various forms of popular media that need to be questioned, bringing contemporary movies into the classroom along with other critical materials can create a site of interrogation and contestation that not only serves to remove some of the Hollywood glitz associated with media productions but that also creates fertile ground for the further development of critical literacy.

When students raise questions about the hierarchical nature of the various relations within, for example, *Dead Poets' Society* and the relationship between power and what is viewed as appropriate content and teaching,[19] they are also led to question the various social forms of production and reproduction in their own classrooms both at the university and in their field placements.

This kind of critical thinking may lead students to challenge assumptions embedded within notions of a monolithic "cultural literacy" that depends on cultural uniformity, and it may extend their understandings of what it means to be a literate person in society. If we can help teachers-to-be and experienced teachers pose harder questions about the nature of cultural literacy and critical literacy and popular culture and the reified versions of culture to which Bloom and Hirsch refer,[20] teachers and students alike may begin to surface other views of culture, literacy, teaching, and learning. Other possibilities may include an understanding that power, conflict, and struggle are a part of any culture; that literacy education should not marginalize the voices, languages, and cultures of subordinate groups; and that teaching and learning is more than implementation and mastery.

From our discussions on power and knowledge surrounding the theme of self-determined thinking in the film and from Giroux's article in *Language Arts*,[21] Jenny wrote this in her double-entry notebook. Notes from the reading are in the right column and Jenny's reflections are on the left:

Self-determined thinkers? I am reminded of my readings in curriculum 450. I wonder if indeed we have developing "self-determined" thinkers in mind at all when "those who count" yell for more standardized curriculum. Sometimes, I think the ideal student, according to those who advocate more generalized curriculum must resemble those old glass milk bottles I remember in my dad's bottling plant. They marched along on a ball bearing conveyor. They marched in [empty] rows, in neat rows got filled by the world of

Giroux's article provided crucial insight into the learning process by showing how Graves links the nature of learning itself with the dreams, experiences, histories, and language that students bring to school.

mechanization, plunked with
a paper cap and were packed
in nice neat rows, 25 to a
case. They all looked alike,
sterile, sealed. Are we as
teachers becoming the filling
machines? God, I hope not.

Two other books, and a music video are useful for the pairings previously discussed: Bel Kaufman's *Up the Down Staircase*[22] and Muriel Spark's *The Prime of Miss Jean Brodie*,[23] and Pink Floyd's *The Wall*.[24] The books focus on a "body of cultural knowledge" and *The Wall* deals with mechanization aspects of power as students are depicted moving on a conveyor belt. These materials help bridge into another discussion surrounding power and knowledge (and with gender inequities that are also a focus in the books). Challenging dominant methods helps create discussion that spans the raced, classed, and gendered categories both within schools and outward to society.

In other words, linking content and pedagogy that recognizes particular cultural lenses necessitates that teaching raise questions about how it is we come to our particular subject positions and how we understand our subject histories. This makes knowledge and power problematic especially as it relates to how the particulars of teaching take up the multiplicity of narratives that make both history and society—as in Neal's special circumstances revealed through his character or the narrative that's a part of Jenny's response to the reading. Indeed, as Freire and Giroux suggest in a foreword entitled "Pedagogy, Popular Culture, and Public Life," programs need to include in these discussions of knowledge and power how "knowledge and power come together in *various* educational spheres to both enable and silence the voices of different students."[25] Accordingly, then, emphases on community and collaboration need to get at understanding pluralistic difference because focusing on "harmony" tends to co-opt or norm difference. For as Mohanty states, "This results in depoliticization and dehistoricization of the idea of culture and makes possible the implicit management of race [and I would add gender and class] in the name of cooperation and harmony."[26] Yet even as I consider these alternatives spaces in which culture is taken up, I find my discussion problematic. For implicit within this discourse is the notion of "the better way" that if not questioned continually runs the risk of co-opting my own arguments in this book, as a whole, and in this chapter on liberal education, in particular—especially those arguments that suggest we embrace the contradictions and tensions that lie between constraint and possibility and that in this space we may discover how to back our way of totalitarian structures.

My work here then combines the vision of critical educators who propose cultural studies (see, for example, Giroux, Shumway, Smith, and Sosnoski[27]) with Maxine Greene[28] and others who propose that teacher education include literature and the arts as a vehicle for reflection. Further, I draw on the work of Raymond Williams, who suggests that all of culture can be viewed through television and films; he says, we can see "intense particular worlds . . . under stress, in conflict, in personal isolation, in dream or in nightmare."[29]

In addition, I borrow from a new movement in literature, "New Historicism," which argues for the pairing of unlike texts in order to make more obvious the historical moment from which canonical texts as well as popular texts emerge, including films and television. New historical perspectives seek to discover elements in history that explain literature and the complicated relationship between the two. Although, I pair unlike texts, I diverge from this perspective by using literature and the arts to illuminate historically grounded critical educational theories.

Drawing on Foucault, "new historicist," Stephen Greenblatt sees the ambiguity of language as "the supreme instance of a collective creation."[30] So too, we discover, is history, as he explores complex relations between contradictory texts. For example, in *Shakespearean Negotiations*, Greenblatt relies on Pierre Bourdieu[31] for insights into historical relations between economic interests and cultural or aesthetic interests. Greenblatt terms this enterprise a *poetics of culture*; that is, a "study of the collective making of distinct cultural practices and inquiry into the relations among these practices."[32] I too argue for the pairing of a variety of disparate texts. I too want to know how culture shapes our beliefs. I too want to guard against further reinforcing culture as a fixed and maintainable instrument of the status quo. And like Greenblatt, Mohanty, and others,[33] I too see culture as related to a wider historic struggle. In the next section, I examine the usefulness of various approaches to the study of culture through literature and the arts.

Relational Contexts

Reading the tensions in literature is important, but the relational contexts of film, television, music, and advertising texts (in short, the popular media arts) seems an equally important place to begin a project that seeks to question schooling practices.[34] From a semiological perspective, then, seeing and hearing may be said to be acts of reading. Scholes assumption that "all the world's a text" suggests the importance of drawing on relational contexts for studying our practice.[35] Furthermore, Scholes suggests that nothing exists beyond our capacity to read it through signs. Therefore, we are reminded that even our gendered, raced, and classed selves are constructed from signs we have read. This is especially important to remember when we question our own belief systems and those of beginning teachers. Therefore, as we examine texts in relational contexts and as we interrogate relations of power including the power of textual authority, we are encouraged to see that no text represents truth but presents fertile ground for raising questions and testing our assumptions about life and history. For as Williams and Eagleton suggest, the particular viewpoint most often presented in texts is one that reinforces a dominant world view.[36] Thus, film and television texts, like other texts, need to be read with resistance—a position of critical reading in which the reader reads the text against her or his experiences, questioning assumptions that tend to suggest how the world works.[37] According to Judith Fetterly, Todd Gitlin, and Evan Watkins, literature, films, and television are so political that deliberate confrontive encounters, as I am suggesting in this text, may actually encourage us, both teachers and students, to pose cultural and ideological "problem-themes" out of our own experiences.[38]

For example, consider the notion of choice or choosing a "committed rationality," as described in Chapter 2 and how it is related to women and particularly to women who decide to teach. Although I will withhold discussion of the images of "women's work" until the next chapter, I do want at this time to illustrate what I mean here by resistant reading against the problematic nature of choice for women. I justify readings like these in educational courses because of what Greene refers to "as the problematic application of gendered categories, at odds with our sense of what is real."[39] and also because of writings by Jo Anne Pagano and Madeleine Grumet that describe women's roles within a patriarchal education system.[40]

When we begin discussions on gender construction, a few critical essays are particularly useful because they ask us to examine early influences and to focus on issues of social order (see, for example, R. G. Kelly, "Mother Was a Lady," L. J. Weitzman, "Sex-role Socialization in Picture Books for Preschool Children," M. R. Lieberman, "Some Day My Prince Will Come").[41] As we read these essays, many students confess to having never considered that their notions of femininity were social constructions that perpetuated a given social order—predominantly constructed by white, middle-class males. Following critical readings with Kate Chopin's *The Awakening*, students begin to feel a particular kinship to Edna Pontellier who describes a reality not unlike the interpreted reality of many women for whom nearly all life experiences have in some way revolved around the *desire to please* in a male-dominated world.[42] In one particular scene in the book, Edna describes her habit of being as she submits to her husband's wishes with no thought for her desires. She describes her life as if it were a hypnotic state in which thinking, feeling, and acting are so taken-for-granted that it becomes a kind of "treadmill."[43]

Male and female students who are teachers-to-be agree that there is much taken-for-grantedness about their current roles as students preparing for a career in teaching. But female students, in particular, claim to share feelings with Edna, even with respect to the degree of choice they felt they had in deciding on teaching as a profession and in coming to a particular university. Many students note this sense of a treadmill-like existence, but it is women, in particular, who agree that much of their lives have been spent learning how to please.

Such behavior becomes particularly problematic then when it translates into teaching behavior because what knowing how to please may suggest is that we don't question; we act—we please regardless of what pleases us. And because women have historically represented the largest percentage of teachers in public schools, questioning traditional schooling structures that revolve around patriarchal teaching practices that interfere with one's ability to have agency makes the desire to please all the more problematic. With respect, for example, to where this text is situated—that is, within both literature on teacher empowerment and on school reform vis-à-vis this particular series—not questioning

a gender specific attitude of pleasing (though male students conform, their conformity does not seem to be located in a desire to
please) then becomes not just problematic but also frightfully suspect. For teachers are not empowered as Goodman suggests under
traditional schooling structures,[44] and if we are to examine what
lies beneath the surface of much that prohibits agency (as Grumet
has begun in *Bitter Milk*),[45] we simply must include gender construction as an important subject for study in teacher education
programs.

Though frequently a subject of study in some programs more
than others, the situation women teachers encounter requires that
attention to gender issues is more than recognized in class, but
that it is also questioned. What needs to be questioned, in particular, is how the school functions within what Helene Cixous
describes as the "discourse of man."[46]

That discourse often results in what Toni Morrison's (*Beloved*)
Sethe calls "helpless, apologetic resignation" because her world
tells her she has no choice.[47] Both Chopin's Edna and Sethe seem
to feel victimized and powerless to change their plights. They
remind us of what Alfred Schutz calls our "ready-made" world
handed down.[48] In both novels the lack of being fully awake
is problematized but what is not made problematic are the
constraints to "wide-awakeness." On the one hand, readers may
believe both Edna and Sethe are somehow complicit in their own
situations; however, what readers do not so easily read with
resistance are the taken-for-granted constraints that are, indeed,
problematic. Partly, I sense that this lack of recognition is
because we seem more likely to see constraint as a given. It is
easier, in fact, to project possible ways out of a problem than it is
to dig beneath the surface to examine the nature of our problems. For projection is just that—projection. But earnest digging
means we actually do want to find a way out, and we are willing
to work. All of which is, of course, messy and layered with complexity.

Had Sethe and Edna been able to understand as we might
come to understand that one *can* choose, that reality *is* constructed and if it is constructed then it may be altered, that life is
not merely filled with inevitability, and that we all live within
matrices of constraint and possibility, then, perhaps, they might
have been able to resist some of the roles they were forced to play.
Here when I use the word *force*, I do not refer to physical coer-

cion, but to the Gramscian notion of hegemonic direction—the more subtle kind of moral and intellectual persuasion.[49] This kind of force is often harder to resist because, as with many of my students, it lies somewhere just beneath conscious recognition but drives us nonetheless. In pondering the need for a future with possibility—a future that does not simply accept taken-for-grantedness, Paul D eloquently says to Sethe, "you your best thing" as Morrison leaves us to puzzle over the structure/agency continuum that raises questions with respect to whether through human agency we can re-create, reconstruct, remake our social realities.[50]

Like Edna and Sethe's lives, teachers' lives are socially constructed in the perpetual legitimation of social order. If as Taxel states, "both the formal and informal knowledge presented in schools contribute to the formation of . . . subjectivities: values, ideals, world view, belief systems, etc,"[51] then I cannot help asking how teachers' subjectivities and dispositions are created. Is our sense of who we are and of our roles a given? Are we under what Marcuse suggests is "the mystifying power of the given"?[52] If so, then, as Carol Gould reminds, we need to do everything possible to demystify the "illusions that bind us to exploitation."[53] Perhaps as choice is problematized, we may, like Edna, hear the voice of Mademoiselle Reisz echoing in the distance, "The artist [/teacher] must possess the courageous soul that dares and defies."[54]

If teacher preparation wants to be recognized as liberal education, then some work will be given to the political project of helping teachers understand their gendered constructions. Perhaps this help will come through confrontive encounters with literature and other relational texts. And, perhaps, when we have the soul Mademoiselle Reisz's echo describes, then discussion of empowerment will make more sense.

According to Bill Nichols, however, we are not in the habit of confronting literature or film texts against existing social conditions.[55] In particular, we are not in the habit of connecting those social conditions relationally to conditions within education—especially when those conditions have to do with power/powerlessness. For that reason, and with respect to images of teachers and schooling, we tend not to notice the ambiguity of images. Yet to show how a change in context can alter the meaning one ascribes to a particular object, Nichols arranges (on a single page) photos of the same object used in scenes from several movies. In each of the different film clips, the object of focus, a gun, is the same, yet the background or the facial expression of the person holding the gun, or even the lighting affects the meanings we ascribe to particular scenes and to the object itself.[56] This illustrates the necessity to examine each text and each image individually against the existing context in order not to attach fixed meanings. If the object or subject were to have been teachers, children, or schools, it would be especially necessary to examine each image presented against existing social conditions. So that images do not come to represent something permanent or have fixed meaning, we need to read images semiotically instead of symbolically.[57] In other words, as Nichols explicitly states, we need to examine "the image's referent at that single instant in time of its capture."[58]

Criteria for selecting all literature, films, television programs, and songs used in this text are two: First, those selected dramatize schooling situations, and second, no selection represents an ideal; rather, each offers a range of contextualized schooling environments with a range of teaching and learning styles. What is common is that all provide rich areas for critique and all are capable both of moving us to visions of alternative possibilities for schooling arrangements and practices and of helping us to make those visions problematic. The necessity to remain open, to let the story work toward raising critical questions is extremely important. As literature calls forth a reader to reflection, critically viewing/reading other aesthetic texts may also provoke response and reflection. What is not clear, of course, is how and to what extent aesthetic texts approximate reality in the minds of readers and how images from such texts tend to become a part of our framework for understanding the world.

Approximating Reality

Movies, like books and television, seem to create a fiction world in which students can become the characters, try on roles they have not experienced in life.[59] However, here I want to focus on films and television because of what Gilles Deleuze calls a privileged instant.[60] In a media text, we tend to experience that lived-through moment to which Rosenblatt refers with greater intensity due to the time frame of most movies or television programs.[61] The camera directs our attention to key elements within the narrative, certain movements receive more attention than others, and the plot is easily resolved within the required time limitations.

Consequently, we need to ask how movies and television affect us in ways that books may not. Virginia Woolf addresses this question briefly. The visual narrative holds a "surprising power," writes Woolf in "The Movies and Reality." Woolf says that if thoughts and emotions are connected to visual perceptions, then the more realistic the cinematography, the greater power of suggestion it has.[62]

Georg Lukacs describes this process as "social realism" in art—or reality capable of being objectified, reality that transcends the here and now, and reality that demands belief—what Woolf calls *exactitude*, or the process of creating images that appear real.[63] This exactitude, to which both Woolf and Lukacs refer, seems problematic in that what it suggests is symbolic representation fixed in certainty rather than multiple interpretations—making it, of course, all the more necessary to read visual texts as critically as we do written texts. Furthermore, when we consider the potential power that such certainty claims for itself, it is little wonder that media productions (which tend to depict negative images of teachers and schooling) tend to play the role Watkins suggests popular media plays in an overall process of enculturation.[64] In his book *Work Time*, Watkins says that despite the role teachers of literature may think they play in presenting a particular tradition and culture, the popular media may have an even greater impact on students.

And further drawing on Lukacs, Todd Gitlin says, ". . . symbolic expression[s] through which creators articulate meanings . . . [whether] 'magical' or 'religious' . . . [are] more than imitations or training exercises."[65] Social identities and political statements are made manifest in song and story, in films and television.[66] Additionally, in "Television Programming and Household Flow," Evan Watkins writes of the particular "intersections of economic, technological, and ideological factors involved in . . . commercial television broadcasting in the U.S.,"[67] and as stated earlier, of its ability to inculcate. Thus, as if Woolf had prophesied the impact of the visual image,[68] we are literally, at this moment in history, bombarded with images of schooling in movies and in television. This popular culture representation of the teaching profession, though usually negative, seems to powerfully affect our definitions of schooling. Guiding images from films and television tend to do more than produce visual emotions, they tend to influence our world views and ideological perspectives as much as representations do from books. Both the form and the content of such narratives need to be examined and questioned then if we are to understand more about how developing teachers see their roles.

Tensions between Form and Content

Current reading/literary theorists are debating the role of form and content in the act of reading and interpretation. Some theorists argue that the difficulty in reading particular texts lies in the form or structure of the text more than with its content. Explication of information versus telling a story is often given as the difference. But teasing out those tensions is a difficult and sometimes circular process.

Let me pose a reading/writing problem here and some questions to think with. For example, when we write with intent to build a world through what might represent a literary narrative, our work is descriptive; therefore, character building and development, scenery, and so forth are extremely important. However, we need to ask whose world we are building. Sometimes we build our world the way we perceive that it is, or sometimes we build it the way we would like it to be, or sometimes we build it the way we perceive readers will expect it to be, or if we want to publish our narrative in the wider context, we may build it the way we perceive a publisher with a political economic interest expects it to be. Although political reality may suggest the latter, I will pose here some other possibilities to suggest the multifaceted nature of hypothesizing relations that make up what seems to be an interrelated set of arguments that exist in both local and wider political structures. The key to avoiding reductive thinking here seems to lie with the idea of both/and—with shuttling back and forth between personal and public spaces.

Before going further it may be important to ask, on what do readers base their interpretations of a world? Are readers' interpretations based on their experiences as they actually are? Or are they based on perceptions borrowed from others about how or what experiences are or might be valid? In other words, do we examine our perceptions against a background of one, ourselves, or against a background of social community? Do those impressions ever come from texts—either books or media texts, and if they do, to what extent do those texts affect our subjective interpretations? How do we mediate those impressions? And if we examine impressions of our experiences against a take that resembles society as we know it—as it has been shown to us by those in power—who directs that experience? The point is that all of our impressions about the world and the way people function within it are subjective. And our subjectivities seem to be based on some set of values. How closely those match the values of dominant culture probably depends on our positioning within that culture or on our capacity to resist hegemonic enculturation. The latter may or may not be wholly possible. Again, we are limited, in some respects, to what we can know because of our cultural lens.

Likewise, how values appear in fiction may or may not be related to the author's subject position. In fact, it may lie more with a political economy of publishing than with other factors—with who gets represented in positive ways and who gets represented in negative ways, with who is seen as dominant and in power and who is seen as powerless, and finally, how much money the publisher stands to make becomes part of the decision with respect to represented values.[69] In other words, whether an author chooses to write in or out of her or his cultural experience may have to do with the market for particular books—that is, the author may be responding to a perceived need to represent class, race, or gender in a particular way, a way that perpetuates the dominant culture. Indeed, with respect to the political economy question, whether or not an author breaks into fiction at all may relate, more directly than we suspect, to how well a particular vision of society is represented in her or his text.

Therefore, neither the author's textual representations nor the reader's response to those textual representations are the only factors at work when we talk about enculturation through textual materials. Likewise, then, our understandings of texts and the negotiations readers make with respect to tensions perceived over form and content is equally complex.

Another point relates to the form and content of texts. I am referring here to what researchers James L. Collins and Michael Williamson have defined as "semantic abbreviation."[70] They use this terminology to refer to a phenomenon in children's writing that suggests what is written on the page may be an abbreviated version of what is in the head. Collins and Williamson suggest that the abbreviation may occur because children are egocentric and have not learned that other people have different representations from their past experiences, and that what they as a writer may know, a reader may not necessarily know. Collins and Williamson use this as an argument for peer group instruction as a means of decentering—to get what's in the head out through questions posed by peers in a conferencelike arrangement.

Although it may be accurate to suggest egocentrism as one of the causes of children semantically abbreviating their texts, adults who write may abbreviate also. It is highly improbable that any writer will know, with any degree of certainty, what is in the reader's head—therefore, what needs to be elaborated and what can be abbreviated.

As I suggested in Chapter 2, even the idea that we think we can know anything for certain is problematic. Certainty may mean, for example, not reading the signs; certainty seems, at least, to remove part of the complexity if not to remove it completely in our minds. Certainty seems to reduce to simplicity that which may not be simple at all. Egocentrism or not, then, it is unlikely that either adults or children can easily know what is in the mind of a reader. We can no more step into a reader's experience and know what she or he knows than we can trust that what readers and writers share in conferences is anything more than what they want us to know.

Therefore, what children experience because they may not recognize other points of view, adults may experience for similar reasons. For it may be true that adults should be less egocentric, yet it remains to be seen whether we are. What's more, when we write, we write what we think we know against whatever culturally embedded framework we have, and sometimes we forget that readers do not necessarily have the same information nor would they necessarily understand what information they do have in the same way that we might understand it.

Semantic abbreviation, maybe. Because our experiences vary, so should our meanings. Here, however, may lie one of the greatest contradictions—a part of what also makes our language problematic. In other words, if our meanings do not vary because of the nature of the cultural embeddedness of our language, then it may be in part because the form and the content of artistic texts both written and visual help to perpetuate a single vision—a singleness of mind giving the impression of harmony. However, even an impression may be problematic if it suggests cultural norming.

Even when we blend personal impressions/stories into our work in order to try to make our meanings known, still we are limited by what we can know and cannot, by what our language can do and what it cannot, and sometimes, as in this text, we use language that we assume is shared by an audience we have in mind. Though we resist cultural norming, we may actually prefer to think of our experiences as shared, as common, as harmonious. Though we may have a reader in mind, still we cannot assume what that reader knows or how theory and practice are connected and understood in that readers frame of reference. As I said in Chapter 2, language may be problematic, but it is the language we have.

If we wrote professional materials like we might write fiction, language would be no less a problem. Though fiction, on the one hand, makes use of a language that is much less professionally coded. On the other hand, when it attempts to use a common language as it may be more likely to do, it begs the question of whose common language. It may do a better job of attaching words to recognizable phenomena, but then we have to ask the question, whose recognizable phenomena? Because fiction is a representation of some world, questions of whose world and whose representations have to be addressed.

Here I have examined the difficulty of producing (in the act of writing and reconstructing in the act of reading) a common language in literary narrative and professional writing with content that does not reproduce harmful social images (including stereotypical understandings of power, knowledge, authorship, and so forth) but that incorporates cultural positioning and ideologies and understands "difference as historical and relational."[71] Such language seems as problematic in narrative as it is in professional writing. Although Frederic Jameson posits that narrative is a socially symbolic act [read sociopolitically symbolic];[72] I assume that all acts of composing meaning/interpreting in reading and writing—narrative or otherwise—are socially symbolic because such acts use language that is collective albeit not necessarily mutual to understand personal and social experiences. With Bakhtin, however, I understand that intentions create stratifying forces that would suggest to some that particular acts may seem more sociopolitically symbolic than others;[73] however, I perceive that the both/and hetero-ideologic nature of language itself makes it social and therefore symbolic.

Because language seems to be culturally instantiated, how we use language in the act of creating meaning seems, out of necessity, to be socially symbolic. Even if not consciously, language users may not escape extending social constructs when words and meanings are socially embedded—"populated and overpopulated" to use Bakhtin's words.[74] For example, that writing is capable of perpetuating racism, sexism, classism, heterosexism, ablebodiedness, and so forth, seems to make it as symbolic as if it resists dominant ideologies and symbolically (re)writes textual authority. To dominant groups the former may even make such writing a socially significant act; to marginal groups the latter. Problematic here is whether or not social symbolism depends on social significance—that is, does narrative need to be socially significant in order to be symbolic?

I would suggest that even psycholinguistic (meanings in the mind of the language user) and sociolinguistic perspectives (meanings derived from social context) do not have to be mutually exclusive constructs. If we consider Bakhtin's notion of collaboratively constructing a language to talk about multiple discourses,[75] then it seems that this construct may apply to both/and formulations as easily as it might apply to either/or. And if we consider writing an act of construing meaning by the language user/interpreter, who lives not in isolation but in particular communities at particular moments in history and who constructs meaning out of social experiences that are mediated against his or her own background of experience in community with others,[76] then, perhaps the idea of writing as a socially symbolic act functioning within the political unconsciousness, as Jameson suggests, may not seem unreasonable.

Though Jameson uses this construct to talk about interpreting texts from a Marxist framework,[77] I am borrowing his words to talk about language from a both/and perspective and that, in many respects, creates a contradictory argument. However, again, my point is to show how contradictory tensions are between form and content, between theory and practice, between professional and personal, and between intellectual and political. When we talk about complexities of language, we necessarily talk about contradiction, and we talk about limitations and possibilities.

In part, then, tensions between form and content may arise because of the problematics of language. Perhaps it is easier to represent those problems in professional texts; practically any work of theory will do as an adequate example. However, it is not as easy to recognize what is problematic in fiction because fiction tends to arouse passions and evoke emotions, and sometimes those passions and emotions cause us to overlook potentially harmful images. Yet narrative does seem capable of decreasing the separation of words we read and worlds we live in as Shor and Freire suggest.[78] Barbara Hardy's work on storytelling/narrative relates to this. She says that the meaning-making potential of narrative occurs because stories are a "primary act of mind transferred to art from life."[79] It may be then in the space where art and life seem to merge that the "ethno-poetics" of what Gloria Anzaldua calls "invoked art" occur.[80] Anzaldua's ethnopoetic narrative blends the functional with the artistic, the sacred with the aesthetic, and the purposes of art with everyday life, as both the story she spins and the kind of narrative she writes about draws us into a world. From inside this story world we may begin to see our past connected to our present and each to a future that is not yet arranged, therefore, capable of being altered. For as Barbara Eckstein suggests in *The Language of Fiction in a World of Pain*, fictive language is uncertain language;[81] therefore, both the language and the worlds we see ourselves in can become sites of multiple interpretation.

So while, on the one hand, the argument over form may be a moot point; on the other, it seems relevant if it encourages us to examine textual form and thereby to examine textual authority. In raising questions we might ask how the form of the writing works with and against any reading of the content? or, how particular forms privilege particular texts and particular meanings? In any case, finding a way to use both/and—that is both professional texts that name problems and literary texts and other aesthetic media that illumine those issues and invite vicarious participation—may provide a rich supply of resources for teaching and learning—not, however, the *only* resource. Though I would argue that what readers bring to texts is by far more complex than anything that might be reductively determined, still I would argue that the way a reader reads against a text—especially if an author represents the world in terms of binary oppositions—is an important part of that reader's meaning making process.

EDUCATIONAL TEXTS AND MEANING MAKING

Meaning making suggests a particular take on questions of what counts for knowledge and who decides what counts. Though binary opposites like good/bad, weak/strong, and so forth are frequently seen in literary and media texts, educational texts offer up a similar kind of bipolarization that needs to be interpreted against a social and political framework—one that leads to questions of power and knowledge. In this instance, I am including a variety of textual materials under the idea of educational texts in much the same way that Michael Apple does in *Teachers and Texts*.[82] I am particularly referring here to the texts practicing teachers and prospective teachers make out of their own experiences. Teachers/readers seem to understand textual representations or images of their texts through extensions of their own memory. The text a teacher understands then may have much to do with experiences either as a student or currently as a teacher—or, in the case of prospective teachers, from limited field experience. How teacher texts are read against literary texts is not clearly understood, yet there does seem to be some connection.

Despite attempts to diffuse bipolar images of teachers that suggest simplistic personae, we still do seem to have within our own teacher texts as well as from the plethora of literary and media schooling narratives, interpretations of teachers as good or bad. A traditional portrait of the good teacher is one in which the teacher is in *control*. (See, for example, how teachers are contrasted in *Dead Poets' Society*.[83]) Both form and content of teaching tend to revolve around the issue of control. From previous experience both personal and vicarious, it is not hard to imagine how teachers-to-be have limited their roles as teachers.

For example, teachers-to-be who participated in one phase of this study by allowing our taped in-class discussions to be reported here, showed in a variety of ways that both schooling experiences and images of teachers had an impact on their thinking. One way, in particular, was the almost unanimous documentation by the thirty-one prospective teachers who participated that they believed social and cultural change, especially school change, was completely beyond their capabilities. When I asked if this sense of powerlessness had to do with their being new teachers, many replied that most teachers they had known had relatively little power outside their own classrooms. As the many teachers they both read about and had seen in movies or on television revealed, participants in this study also believed themselves ultimately powerless within the structure of schools.

Lasch's notion of schools educating for "minimal selves"[84] does not seem unreasonable, then, given the realization that students, who have attended private or public schools through high school and then through four or five years of college, could see themselves as so powerless. What they had observed and experienced apparently had taught them much about teachers. For example, prospective teachers in this study saw only the need to inculcate and to do so in an authoritarian manner; that is, the word *control* came up as least ten times more often in any discussion, even discussions of content, than did content words having to do with language and literature. This supports Linda McNeil's study of four high schools in which teachers' attempts to maintain their own authority generated "defensive teaching" strategies in which content was either mystified or lost altogether through oversimplified facts processed as worksheets, list-filled lectures, and short answer tests. McNeil's work shows that when "control and credentialling become the rationale for the educational experience, substance is lost."[85] If teachers entering the profession are disenfranchised "minimal selves" who view culture as fixed and defined rather than emergent and who assume it is their task to transform official "school knowledge" into small bits of knowledge that can be transmitted, how then will they serve *all* students—minority and otherwise—or see their work as a part of a larger struggle for social change?

As the educational texts from this class tend to suggest, either we are good teachers or we are bad teachers, and control is seen as a positive attribute of a good teacher. After all, who wants to align themselves with teachers who have noisy classes? Noise in the classroom is traditionally seen as negative—if not by viewers, then at least by depicted administrators like the controlling principal in the popular sitcom "Parker Lewis Can't Lose."[86] A noisy classroom presents a situation in which it is assumed that the teacher has no control.

Instead of portraits that depict active learning through student participation, shared responsibilities in the classroom, and so forth, images of schooling—both in teachers' own texts and through popular culture representations—have traditionally shown "good students" silently taking notes or raising their hands to speak. A "good classroom" then is assumed to have conforming (if not completely passive) students and a teacher who is always in charge. In the traditional view of schooling, cooperative students do not necessarily signal progressive classrooms because students are not generally cooperating with each other; rather, they are obeying the teacher. See also, for example, the social studies teacher in *Ferris Beuller's Day Off* who asks questions but allows no response time before answering the questions himself.[87] Instead, he simply says, "Anybody? Anybody?" Typically, only in portraits that present negative images do we see students interacting with other students or teachers interacting with students. For example, the overly romanticized versions of teachers like Mr. Keating in *Dead Poets' Society* or Alex Jarrell in *Teachers* are presented as heroes in the classroom, taking personal interests in kids' problems and being a friend to everyone, but the films also show us that the administration sees these actions in a negative light.[88]

Traditional images do not represent the complexities of teaching, and contemporary images do much to distort teachers' lives. Creating a new stereotype, however, can only reinforce the dichotomous either/or and severely limit our abilities to see the complexities of teachers' lives and their work.

The importance, then, of examining teacher images from both literature and popular culture representations of schooling as well as from the teacher texts both experienced and prospective teachers offer through their own stories of schooling may lie in creating the space to question images that attempt to narrowly characterize/define teachers and schooling. Work that occurs in this space is an act in resisting a single perspective, infusing our own cultural understandings and experiences into all our texts. In this instance, readers produce a "heteroglossic" text.[89] That is, though some texts may present history through one voice or one perspective, representing the dominant world view in any single text, as we read, challenge, and rewrite that text, we make it multivocal— changing its one privileged voice/perspective to multiple voices/perspectives. In other words, then, in a space created for questioning all educational texts, our own reading/rewriting, which becomes the curriculum of the moment, gives rise to multiple possibilities for "seizing . . . a range of meanings by persons open to the world."[90]

Representative, Productive, and Generative Texts

Studying the culture of schooling through a medium or text that Scholes describes as representational (i.e., dramatizes or represents a particular image)[91] but that is also productive (i.e., capable of being shaped through active responding) can act as an invitation to dialogue. According to Scholes, because of the representational manner of all texts, text structures demand interpretation—a kind of seeing in which the interpretant constructs a visual text. However, if all texts have the potential to represent a dominant image as Williams and Eagleton have suggested,[92] which for teachers may be a negative image, the role of the reader then becomes increasingly important as it is the reader who is capable of resisting a single perspective, who refuses to close off possibilities, who produces multiple interpretations. Thus, I would argue again that reader stance (regardless of text structure) may be the key ingredient in meaning making, and especially when those meanings are mediated through dialogue or what Shor and Freire call transformative communication,[93] texts tend to take on a multivocal character.

Raymond Williams treats this interactionist theory of communication thoroughly in *Television and the Working Class*.[94] He describes an active viewer who mediates responses through involvement with a variety of other viewers (e.g., neighbors, work associates, etc.) within a given social context. Williams contrasts the interactive model with a linear model that assumes a one-way relationship with an undifferentiated audience. This one-way relationship may approximate what I have previously referred to as a reader/viewer whose stance is not resistant/critical and for whom conversation and critique about particular images is either not an option or not valued. It appears to be much easier to accept that a particular image represents *the way things are* when we do not interact with others, exchanging ideas that might inform our meaning making.

Additionally when, for example, prospective teachers originally viewed *Dead Poets' Society*,[95] before they began a deeper critical analysis assisted by critical professional readings, their response to the movie did not offer much of a reshaping. Rather, they commented on the stereotypes of English teachers without going deeper and challenging the forms of knowledge and the power structures at work within the movie.

Williams's interactionist theory may be applied here to the kinds of transformative communication to which Shor and Freire refer when in the course of classroom dialogue students are challenged to question the images and representations in particular aesthetic texts.[96] Philip Wexler's commentary on the interactive nature of texts may also be applied here. Indebted to literary the-

ory for much of his rendering of the "new sociology of education," Wexler suggests that texts are "structures which *produce*
textual effect," that is, this can range from an actual text to the
interaction between text and reader or even the *thinking* that produces response to the collective recording of historical social life
and class struggle.[97]

Umberto Eco and Wolfgang Iser further elaborate on the
importance of viewing texts as productive structures through
which readers make meaning.[98] Openness, incompleteness, and
contradiction, features of books, films, and television call for constructive, interpretive activity—for further remaking. Roland
Barthes labels this kind of text a "writerly text" because through
it readers are capable of remaking their social, political, and historical realities.[99] Construction of new images or a "reconceptualization" of teachers and schooling, to use Pinar's and Grumet's
term,[100] might well be fostered through a political teaching project that works to create spaces for interactive text making.

Texts that are representational and productive, however, are
also generative. Stanley Straw defines a generative text as one that
has the potential to generate particular ways of thinking and knowing.[101] That is, generative texts often evoke stories. His use of the
word story here is close to Rosenblatt's notion of a kind of reading
response that creates a poem or a mind text filtered through the
reader's particular experience.[102] Though Straw deals almost exclu-
sively with a text in which an evocative form (e.g., narrative)
evokes a poem or story, he like Rosenblatt realizes that the story
comes from the reader who draws on a particular worldview or
lens. And like Rosenblatt, Straw's interpretation of a generative text
also suggests something to do with purpose. That is, readings are
framed as point-driven (what Rosenblatt calls "efferent" reading or
reading for information), inquiry-driven (for which Rosenblatt
does not seem to have an equivalent), and reflection-driven readings (what Rosenblatt calls aesthetic reading).[103] Further, "poems"
or stories told or evoked, according to Rosenblatt or Straw, may or
may not be a retelling (via one's own experience) to create a new
version of the narrative; rather, stories may be a new text, created
wholly anew, and related only by association to the work. A memory associated with a particular story but that deviates from the
original text in all other ways may be an example of such an evoca-
tion. I will elaborate on this further in the next section.

Evoking Meaning

Meaning making is the way we make sense of all texts. Yet some texts may help readers to more easily reach what Lukacs refers to as experiences of the "here and now," or what Rosenblatt calls a lived-through or "virtual" experience.[104] Finding those texts and creating a receptive space is my hope when I juxtapose literature or other aesthetic media with professional readings to deal with issues of critical teaching. Though professional readings may invite readers into a discussion of issues of power and its distribution or raise questions about culture and ideology, still these readings do not often provide adequate grounding of teaching situations. For example, on the topic of women teaching in a patriarchal system, selections from Grumet's *Bitter Milk* or Apple's essay "Gendered Teaching, Gendered Labor" raise issues of power within schooling hierarchies that establish the historical positioning of women's roles in education.[105] Yet the old television program *Our Miss Brooks*, and the movie/book *Up the Down Staircase*, as well as the book *The Prime of Miss Jean Brodie* provide fully contextualized literary examples of what Grumet and Apple call "women's work."[106] The professional selections name the problem, the latter narratives illumine it.

Professional readings alone seem to be inadequate, at least in my classes, for providing prospective teachers with a necessary framework for understanding the meanings their students may make about themselves and school. Although critical texts provide useful, maybe even necessary, stimulus for questioning the assumptions in aesthetic texts, they tend to fall short of providing enough context for teachers-to-be who may have little to no background in schools outside their own experiences as students. Their lack of "teacherly" backgrounds may make many important concepts difficult to understand. However, despite the difficulty of concepts like the *culture of silence*[107] or *tracking as a device for reproducing class, gender, and racial inequality*,[108] both may be, nonetheless, as important for beginning teachers as they are for experienced teachers.

This story may sound familiar. As a first-, second-, third-, and even fourth-year teacher, I made many mistakes. I put students through drills that silenced them. I didn't have to separate the brighter students from those who we were told would "slip through the cracks anyway"; my school already had ability grouping in place. These groupings were all too easy to recognize. It largely meant that black students were separated from white and poorly dressed students from those who looked like they'd just stepped off the cover of *Vogue*. But even with my own working-class background, I participated in this structured inequality. I helped push students further into the margins. I bought into the notion that we couldn't reach all of the students, that we were there to teach our subject matter (eleventh- and twelfth-grade English). If students didn't "get it" and we had presented it, at least, we had done our jobs. Students suffered as a result. In one term alone, I failed over half the students in one English class. The saddest part of this story is that I was proud of my toughness. I did not until much later see that it was I who had failed. Yes, I had failed my students, but not by giving them F's. I had failed to be their teacher. I had failed to care. I had failed to see what I was really teaching them—what meanings they made—and how that affected their schooling experience. I had failed to see what they were internalizing about themselves; I had failed to hear what their silence spoke. I had failed to see the tracks or classist structures I was reproducing in my own classroom. My good students who came from well-to-do families were headed for college and respectable, if not lucrative, careers. My other students were headed for assembly lines, gas stations, or the streets—for drug trade or whatever other nonchoices the hopelessness they received from teachers like me suggested.

When I returned to graduate school and began to read theories of learning, social criticism, literary criticism, and so forth, I said, "Ah-ha!" A lightbulb went off in my head and things I had puzzled over began to make sense. Why, I asked, was I to wait until now to learn things that would have been so important to know then? Why was I sent into the schools well-equipped with subject matter knowledge but with no way to understand why what I was doing could be so harmful? I never even thought about what sense my students were making of the whole experience. Why, indeed, is a good question.

My teacher preparation—not unlike what is proposed for teacher preparation today—drew heavily on subject-matter knowledge but was not located in the wider discourse of social reform. Though a liberal education in the sense of learning a discipline, it was not liberating in any sense that might allow me to see myself connected to a wider struggle. Teacher preparation had not prepared me to see my students' lives as a part of a larger political reality. But, perhaps it is problematic to suggest programs are at fault here. Perhaps it was my own naivete that kept me from recognizing students' realities. Whatever the reason, not recognizing the importance of understanding the meanings students make of schooling suggests the experience of schooling is for teachers. Clearly, my students were not having a meaningful learning experience in my classes. Though I suspect they were learning that the hidden agenda in my class was that I was in charge, that learning to me meant conforming, accepting the materials I presented without question, or adhering to my rules and the like. Learning became confused with discipline, and as McNeil suggests, content was used to control.[109] And why, indeed?

Obviously, there are lots of answers to this question. Although some of those answers may have to do with being an inexperienced teacher, unpracticed at technique and so forth, I suspect a potential answer that I and possibly other practicing teachers would not want to admit is lack of an ability to understand what students needed—because admission of not knowing means uncertainty, and we were taught to be certain. Yet, certainty in this instance, as in most, leaves no room to doubt who is right and who is wrong. Obviously, in my opinion, students were wrong; I was right. Our positivist paradigm teaches us that it's either one way or the other, but never both at the same time. If there are other interpretations different from my own then I have to be either right or wrong. Insecurity often forces a judgment call. And I was insecure as many prospective and practicing teachers are. The one other interpretation over which I do remember some conjecture was apathy, but I didn't understand or perhaps I didn't even try to understand what their apathy suggested. Inability to understand or desire to know what meanings students were making, inability to see the mixed messages I was giving, inability to politicize my classroom, meant school, for my students, had no value, no meaningful place in their lives.

"But why?" I asked. And, yes, my graduate professors had a good answer to this question. Their answer was, of course, that it did no good to teach theories that would have helped me understand my students better prior to having any students.

"Prospective teachers do not have the necessary framework/experiences on which to hang theory—nothing on which to understand what experienced teachers understand so easily," was their collective reply. It made sense. I was absolved.

Yet, in the midst of years of school reform and curricular change, we are still sending teachers into the schools ill-prepared to understand or even question what sense students are making of their schooling experiences. Although students are much better prepared than I was then to attend to processes of learning (i.e., we've given them the tools to teach reading and writing, even mathematics, as a process), still much of this teaching and learning is quickly curricularized and becomes routine, even thoughtless. Even the kind of reflection Schon suggests, thinking while doing, or what he calls "reflection-in-action"[110] continues to escape many new teachers.

And if part of the problem is not providing social theories to prospective teachers at the undergraduate level, it is just that—*part* of a complexity of interrelated arguments that needs to be addressed at all levels of teacher preparation and simply providing theories will not be enough. Although readings on a "culture of silence" from Paulo Freire's *Education for Critical Consciousness*[111] or on the institutionalized structures of tracking from Giroux and McLaren's essay titled "Reproducing Reproduction: The Politics of Tracking" may be important,[112] they are exceedingly difficult for undergraduate students in teacher education to unpack without more help than sometimes even the best teacher can provide. Perhaps it is, as my graduate teachers suggested, prospective teachers' lack of experience, or, perhaps, it is the coded language that results in abstraction rather than situation. Despite the reasons, many teachers-to-be cannot make the necessary leap to understand what those texts offer.

But narrative seems to help; it provides a bridge; it creates a world that students can enter. And once students have begun to make those connections, critical readings can provide another kind of bridge. One that helps them ask harder questions, reading more critically for a wider range of meanings. In other words, the particular readings on tracking and silence seemed to add a range of meanings to *A Hero Ain't Nothing but a Sandwich*, the story of Benjie, a thirteen-year-old drug addict, for whom school seems to have no meaning or purpose.[113] Critical texts read in concert with aesthetic texts then may enrich the perspectives students need for critically reading against and reshaping their educational texts and terrains. As students are invited to experience the world of teaching and schools vicariously through aesthetic texts (in addition to whatever field experiences may be available), they may be better able to connect unfamiliar concepts either with what is remembered or with what is made apparent through narrative. For as Jerome Bruner reminds us in *Actual Minds, Possible Worlds*, narrative is, indeed, a vehicle for connecting and making sense of new information, new experiences, and unfamiliar concepts.[114] However Hardy lends this caution, "Narrative is not to be regarded as an aesthetic invention used by artists to control, manipulate, [or merely] order experience"[115]—that is, the potential of narrative lies in its ability to particularize experience and to enlarge as well as to personalize issues.

It is the generative nature of narrative that gives it potential to generate particular ways of thinking, knowing, even criticizing— to have a memory and to extend or formulate application of that memory to particular experiences. For example, Annie Dillard writes of this memory of early reading experiences in her autobiography, *An American Childhood*.[116] She says that reading was a subversive act. She looked for things in books that matched her feelings, what she calls her "interior life." She says that in the world of thought and imagination she carried "secrets" with her— "a secret joy . . . and hope." The possible worlds to which Bruner alludes. In Dillard's memory, reading was an act of resistance. The joys and hopes, the secrets, did not necessarily match her lived-experiences; rather, reading experiences allowed her to participate in a world less limited by the social constraints her femaleness carried.[117]

What generated Dillard's particular memory as an adult is not known to the reader of her autobiographical narrative. What is interesting, however, is that Dillard fades into this memory in the midst of describing a particular occurrence in school. Dillard remembers air-raid drills and teachers marching students into the school basement, where gym teachers lined students against walls and lockers and showed them how to cover their heads in case of an attack. In this memory she is particularly aware of the European women who teach French, history, and German in her school. They each have their respective stories to tell about their flights from Hitler. Then Dillard flashes to her home with its basement and canned goods stored there for just such an emergency. And she remembers the story of Anne Frank and her family. Suddenly, and without warning, Dillard remembers the world of books and how she had lived for those experiences.[118] In other words, what seems interesting is the progression of Dillard's memory back to the moment it connects with story where she is as Victor Nell suggests *Lost in a Book*.[119]

That generative texts often generate stories is no surprise. That those stories are sometimes the stories of how reader's connect with texts is not surprising. But what is little understood is how or why stories work on the variety of levels in which they do seem to operate. For example, two modes of thought seem to characterize the process of storying out meaning: critical/analytical thought and imaginative thought. Both seem important for construing meaning. Both seem important for locating ourselves in relation to the particular identities we have forged over time—in response to teachers we've had in school, in response to particular structures within schooling hierarchies we have experienced firsthand, and, perhaps, in response to images we have internalized from books, films, and television. Perhaps, it is when we recognize that the way we use language, the way we relate to other people, and the way we see ourselves in the world is no accident, but is, instead, socially constructed, that we are capable of imagining other worlds—possibilities for ourselves and for our practices. Examining our socially constructed identities may then lead us to question who we identify with and what or whom we resist. These seem to be especially important points of inquiry for prospective and practicing teachers and may be possible through extended conversation over a text like *Lean on Me*.[120]

For example, after viewing this movie and thinking about students' voicing their pleasure or displeasure with the totalitarian rule of Joe Clark, I began to think of my junior high school principal. Though Mr. Browning did not have to police students in the ways that Joe Clark did, he was, nonetheless, easily as authoritarian in his delivery of discipline and punishment. While students debated whether or not Clark would have been capable of changing existing social conditions at the school under a more democratic rule, I faded in and out of my junior high experiences. I remembered having to stand in the hall during fifth-hour social studies class when I verbally objected to a male classmate who sat behind me and picked on me daily. I was singled out as the distraction; he offered no explanation. I was sent into the hall without a pass, and who should happen along but Mr. Browning. Striking fear in the hearts of junior-high schoolers and me at this moment, in particular, Mr. Browning said, "Come with me to the office, young lady." He called my mother, and I was sent home for the remainder of the day. Extreme punishment for the particular offense or not, Mr. Browning ran that school with an iron fist, and he had *no* discipline problems.

His wife was an English teacher; mine, in fact, and one of the best teachers in junior high. But it wasn't his wife who influenced me to want to teach English. With my own students' conversations in the background, still hotly debating the movie and the practicalities of democracy at Eastside High, I am drifting ahead to my eleventh-grade English teacher, Mrs. Blay. She was the first English teacher I strongly identified with. I liked her for several reasons; one of which was that I knew her personally before being assigned to her eleventh-grade English class. Because my mother sewed for her daughters, I had known Mrs. Blay for a long time. Strangely enough, I felt privileged in her class. She knew me and had been to my house. To me she was more than a teacher; Mrs. Blay was a real person.

She lectured on self-reliance and civil disobedience. Though I find this a strange irony today, then it was eloquent. She made me love Emerson and Thoreau. They were her favorites. They became my favorites, too. I never questioned her mode of presentation. I do, however, remember thinking it odd that such a traditional teacher loved such revolutionary literature, and I think today that Mrs. Blay was aware of those conflicting interests and of her position or what she believed to be her role as English teacher. That her nature was often abrupt may have been both a symptom and an outcome of disruptive theories in conflict with her practice. Nonetheless, she was the person who triggered my desire to be an English teacher though it was not until much later that I actually saw that as a possibility.

I also identified strongly with another American literature teacher many years later. A New Englander, Dr. Bigelow was an American literature professor at my undergraduate institution. I took every course he offered. In between lectures, he read to us. Though he lectured, Dr. Bigelow also seemed in contradiction to the traditional English professor, particularly when it came to legitimized forms of writing.

For example, in the first course I took from him (literature of the twenties), I produced a term paper that I perceived would suit his requirements. I became really involved in my project. It was on the Sacco-Vanzetti case—the struggle of two young men being tried for anarchy. I read about the trial in newspapers from the late twenties stored in the microfilm collection. I read with excitement in one account that Edna St. Vincent Milay spent the night in jail on the eve of their execution to protest the court's decision.

Yet when I wrote the paper, I used only what the critics said about this issue. Though I had seldom felt this passionately about any issue, I kept my opinions to myself the way I had been taught. I used the same strategies I had always used to produce good papers, and I expected this paper to be no exception. I was sure it was an A paper. It received a C- and a note to see Dr. Bigelow in his office. I visited his office with skepticism and a renewed sense of fear and more than mild irritation. My perception of my position shifted once more as I humbled myself before this teacher whom I had admired and respected. His comments, however, were not what I expected. He was kind and judicious. He asked me what I thought about the case, and I spewed forth with the same degree of passion that I felt while reading about the case. What came next was a total surprise. Dr. Bigelow said I should write the paper over and say what I had just told him, infusing all of the personal connections I made with the research I had done and using critics' responses only when they supported the points I wanted to make. Reflection, passion, and criticism all in one piece of writing. That stuck with me; his suggestions gave me permission to voice my concerns. Dr. Bigelow, like Mrs. Blay, had an extraordinary influence on me.

Though two teachers stood out in my mind, they did not necessarily drive my early teaching. Much about those first years is so complex that even now I cannot completely understand what motivated me (if I had two or three memorable teachers, I had many more that remained in my subconscious whose patterns I am sure I must have adopted). What creates those early predispositions, we may never know. Memories of childhood play experiences tell me that I often recalled the most authoritarian teachers I had—even from first grade. The choices we make, then, (or those we do not think we've made) do often range a wide span of events and are not always what we perceive to be our most favorable experiences.

Although early teaching often seems marked by certainty, the appearance of certainty may signal instead a good deal of insecurity. I suspect that was the case in my first years of teaching. Those years left me feeling more confused than successful and very concerned about what it meant to be a teacher. I turned a lot of that early experience back inside me internalizing what I didn't understand as personal failure. When I left my first teaching appointment to return to graduate school for something else, I didn't even know what to look for. But that doubt forged the way for me to begin to understand the contradictions in both my preparation and in my practice. What I had learned from Mrs. Blay and Dr. Bigelow I began to read against the contradictions I felt about those early teaching experiences where failing students with no regard for what they were or were not learning marked both failure and transformation. Remembering, reflecting, and eventually coming to know what I valued in practice also eventually led to knowing what I resisted. And *finally*, it led to the belief that there is no finally—no completed structure at the end that allows us to say this is how good teaching looks and this is how learning looks or how bad teaching and no learning looks. That is, teaching may be/tends to be for me, at least, a continuous practice of learning, questioning, doubting, and reflecting. None of this happens in a linear fashion but occurs in contradictory ways—sometimes all at once, sometimes recursively.

So, what does this all mean? As with other texts, there are many readings, and I do not claim to know them all. But I do sense that texts capable of generating particular memories are worth examination because such texts may have the potential to raise those memories to a level of critical consciousness. That is, they may encourage active theorizing of the whys that underpin nearly all experience.

Suzanne Langer suggests that analytical thinking may be a matter of seeing relationships.[121] In this particular case, I saw a relationship between Mr. Browning and Joe Clark which in turn led to other thought patterns that helped me to better understand my socially constructed identity. Again, until we begin to understand why we see the world in the particular ways that we see it, we cannot begin to think how we might change either our position in the world or our practice. This fits with Ann Berthoff's notion that seeing relationships is also a matter of seeing what she calls oppositions, juxtapositions, and coordinates in order to examine diversity.[122] Until we think of ourselves and our world as socially constructed, we may have difficulty understanding human potential. And teachers as much as other groups of people need to see themselves as having agency to change that which is inequitable.

Thus, when analysis of our own experience engages the imagination, we may become more capable of writing a new script, of creating a new image, of reconceptualizing what it is we are about. Connections that are linked to personal experiences and sometimes to other texts seem to more naturally tend to engage both the imagination and our capacity for critical reasoning. For example, in a discussion of the movie, *Stand and Deliver*,[123] this response, to Andy Garcia's saying that lowering standards for minority students is as discriminatory as making it harder, seems to strike a balance between critical/analytical and imaginative thinking, illustrating the generative nature of this text:

> I don't know why no one challenged him on the issue of standards. He [meaning Garcia, the representative from the testing service] did not realize that just the standard itself represented discrimination. Who established the standard? What criteria did they use? Struggling with poverty was the major focus of this movie: the homes—overcrowded, poorly furnished—families—both parents working, students working in the family business or at home so parents could work. Also, during the movie presentation, someone referred to the officials investigating the test results as the "salt and pepper team." Even though one was light and one was dark, this may have been an accurate label, due to the fact that they were African and Hispanic. The term salt and pepper was a popular way to refer to the police squad teams following the Detroit riots in 1967. In order to quell the well-founded charges of police brutality, the officials decided to create mixed teams of black and white officers. The term drifted north a bit in the late 60s and 70s. Then it was attached to the campus parties in which all the black dudes brought white dates. In neither case was salt and pepper a term of endearment. African Americans resented the harsh treatment still afforded them, now by some racially mixed police teams. In the spirit of black pride many African Americans particularly African American women resented interracial dating. [from transcript of class]

The nature of this response focuses on aspects of standards and who decides what standards are important. Note also after a few sentences, the student clicked into telling a story (i.e., "The term salt and pepper was a popular way . . . "). The next response follows immediately:

Just to add to that, there was, I think, only one scene at the beginning of the movie showing resistance. I don't think that's quite realistic for any classroom regardless of social-economic background. The teacher just walked in and after one day, coming in wearing a chef's hat, suddenly boom the kids are tuning in. [also verbatim transcript]

This movie is discussed in connection with several professional readings, some more critical than others. For example, with Mike Rose's text, *Lives on the Boundary*,[124] I read to the class selected passages from *Theory and Resistance in Education.*[125] *Lives on the Boundary* describes Rose's successes and failures teaching minority students, many of whose schooling experiences mirrored his own. Viewing/reading this popular film text along side the autobiographical text of Rose's own growing-up-poor story, with schooling experiences—his own and other students'— that describe what it is like to be dispossessed or disenfranchised, may have contributed to the discussion's focus. That is, class discussion focused on what the students in this story seem to have been understanding about their teacher, Mr. Escalante, about credentialing, and about the testing service. The film combined with Rose's book and with selected passages from *Theory and Resistance* seemed to evoked responses that bordered on being both critical and imaginative. Students seemed to be connecting the past and thinking about the future.

In other words, my own student teachers' attention seemed directed more toward the meanings students in the movie were making of their experience than with the technical aspects of what teachers taught and tests tested. The first response, in particular, lets us see a teacher-to-be questioning who sets standards and how those standards compare to economic structures. In the second response, though we hear the word resistance, what seems most important is the students' willingness to consider whether or not Heime Escalante's classroom is authentically described.

The particular use of an expression like *resistance* does not necessarily indicate a more critical response but may simply be the student's impressions about how to articulate this situation in ways that sound professional and well theorized. Students hear this word a lot in education courses; they may or may not understand its political implications. Regardless, the content of each segment seems to suggest a particular understanding of resistance and how students relate it to the "real" world of schools—real, according to some of my students, means public school—and to their own lives.

These response segments are added to illuminate the generative nature of narrative especially as it is combined with professional readings; that is, the two segments seem to illustrate the capacity of narrative to evoke emotional response that is connected to personal experience as the lens provided by the professional reading helps students begin to structure that response into a critique. Discussion that takes the form of stories (as in the first segment) may provide students with the opportunity to rehearse or try out what they're thinking through narration—a format that seems natural when we share experiences. Or as Shor and Freire suggest, it may be an opportunity for students to discover what they know.[126]

Learning opportunities that infuse the imagination with whatever we happen to be teaching may suggest to students that we consider both their social and their intellectual worlds as integral to our educational agendas. Narrative, then, may help connect us and what we try to know to other people, places, and things. Gordon Wells suggests that language is the tool of story making;[127] I suggest that story making may be the tool of culture making. And the culture of teaching and schooling may be created by the stories shared within.

Questions about teachers' beliefs and how teachers see the practice of schooling may be integral to curriculum reform in teacher education if we are to move that project into a political arena. As students are called on to explore their own personal histories, their social, political, economic, and cultural realities through a curriculum of multiple voices, their predispositions tend to become more apparent. Recognizing what one believes is important, how those beliefs impinge on future practices is another matter and may depend on how we approach teacher education.

Cultural studies that emphasize a variety of professional and aesthetic texts, including films and television, may arouse tensions to a point where students willingly question the nature of specific schooling practices—practices that tend to marginalize and dehumanize and reduce teaching and learning to a practice of mastery and implementation. With professional readings that form a social critique of meanings and practices, literary and media stories may provide another lens for seeing issues of power, ideology, and culture. Examining stories in concert with professional readings then may allow for more than a literary or pop cultural experience. Stories may, indeed, illumine our past, help us rediscover our raced, classed, and gendered selves, help us unlearn images that tend to perpetuate negative practices, and may lead the way for making culture. Additionally, narrative may have the potential to elicit our own stories of schooling that may, indeed, provoke reflection that becomes both self-critical and extends to the wider society. In this instance, both reflection and self-critique may come close to what Janet Miller refers to as "generative criticism."[128]

Miller describes tensions or "points of dissonance" that "propel us toward forms of interaction and dialogue that can enable each of us to enter into multiple and shifting relations and identifications without relinquishing our own desires."[129] This seems especially important when thinking about teachers' images of themselves—shifting positions and identities without giving up desires. It seems especially important also as we talk about practice—practice in which we participate "within particular socially and historically situated conversations about teaching, research, and curriculum."[130] In Chapter 4 I examine schooling narratives that offer an opportunity for generative criticism. These narratives frame particular raced, classed, and gendered images of teachers as they function within "multiple and shifting relations and identifications."[131]

CHAPTER 4

Teaching and Teachers in Stories of Schooling

Exposing myths may be the most important work of this chapter. Like many of my students who grow up learning American culture via the technology of television, over the years I have had to do a good deal of unlearning. In other words, I grew up with "Our Miss Brooks," the wacky caricature of a teacher, and with the Beaver's very motherly schoolteacher on "Leave it to Beaver," and I fantasized about being a schoolteacher.[1] Actually, I did more than fantasize; I played school nearly every afternoon. What kind of teacher was I? Well, I made my one student (my friend, Mildred) sit for as long as she would tolerate me and do what teachers today call seatwork. Perched on the top doorstep in front of my house, I shrieked with teacherly control and insisted on silence except when spoken to. Before we could scarcely read and write, I had Mildred filling out what we now call dittos. I was not unlike the character named "Ditto" in the movie *Teachers*, whose students came into the classroom, picked up the ditto for the day, and worked quietly for the remainder of the hour.[2] So my student worked in silence except when I asked her to recite her ABCs or to read a passage aloud from a book. And my first-grade teacher reinforced this behavior. Then I would call on Mildred to read a difficult passage and she would trip over her words, and I would mimic my teacher's behavior by pretending to hit Mildred across the knuckles with a ruler. That action usually stopped our play. But play like movies, books, and television can teach us many things. It can, as Dorothy Heathcote says of drama, teach us "how it feels to be in someone else's shoes . . . to *pre*-live situations of importance . . . without having the actual experience."[3]

Later, much later, I began to study the implications of that play experience. What I question from that memory-bank experience now are the effects of power acted out by the controlling playschool teacher whose one and only playschool student resisted. I think about my positioning in relation to Mildred's— how I had to be on the top step literally towering above her, how I demanded silence, and how I pretended to rap her knuckles for not being a "proper" student, and how, to some degree, that role allowed me to enact a kind of resistance. That is, I think about the implications of playing teacher instead of playing house, and why I played teacher instead of nurse and how, perhaps, each of those play choices in some way related to powerful roles of men—my working-class father who had little power outside his home but commanded an enormous amount of power over my mother and me and my sisters, the principals who abrasively dealt with teachers who could not control their classes (which seemed to mean keep them silent) but who seemed to leave those controlling teachers alone who posed no particular problems for them, and male physicians (I saw mostly on television) who both flirted with nurses and gave orders to them.

When I examine the implications of that memory-bank experience, my choice also seems to inextricably link resistance to power—by choosing the role of teacher, an accepted role for women, I could resist male control by taking on the male role I had seen modeled both in principal as well as teacher roles. That is, in my playschool role, in order to resist the domination of a powerful (male) principal, I enacted the kind of power over my charge that would result in having the principal leave me alone. The trouble with that picture and what needs to be problematized again and again, is that we do not actually ever resist power by conforming or by taking on what appears to be a powerful role over those subordinate to us, we simply perpetuate power and powerlessness. To resist being constantly overpowered I became overpowering in a different arena. (I had seen this played out before in my own father's subordinate-in-the-workplace/dominant-at-home role.) To understand power and control, I became as controlling as the controller with those I perceived less powerful than me. But I, nonetheless, conformed. And in my playschool role, neither consciously nor subconsciously did I question the wide-ranging effects of that behavior.

But I question it now and that questioning seems to lead to unlearning. What happens, however, if my students do not question; will they be able to unlearn the harmful effects of power?

Will they be able to understand that there are other possible ways to resist oppression than becoming an oppressor through conformity to a particular code of behavior? Will prospective teachers understand that closing the door and doing one's work, even, perhaps, subversively, without attempting to understand the hierarchical structures of schools against a wider context is also, in a sense, conformity?

Without exposing some of our most popular myths, how will our prospective teachers be prepared to do more than play school? The myths of our childhood are powerful, and they seem to indelibly imprint a world view that becomes accepted knowledge—"social blueprints" as Linda Christensen calls them "that inhibit [our] ability to question . . . when we are older."[4] From the childhood favorite *Cinderella* we learn that women are helpless and in need of rescue by prince charming;[5] likewise, perhaps our first learning about teacher behavior comes also from childhood favorites in which schooling is dramatized. That teaching behavior then is often reinforced by our teachers in school and a perpetual cycle is begun. Thus much of our work in teacher education becomes a matter of helping student-teachers unlearn harmful images of teachers and schooling by offering opportunities to critique inequitable structures. For if our students do not challenge words and images as presented in books and popular aesthetic materials, then as Paulo Freire says, they just "walk on the words."[6] Of that other education, that "hidden curriculum," in texts and aesthetic media, Ariel Dorfman has this to say in *The Empire's Old Clothes: What The Lone Ranger, Babar, and Other Innocent Heroes do to our Minds*:

> Industrially produced fiction has become one of the primary shapers of our emotions and our intellect in the 20th Century. Although these stories are supposed to merely entertain us, they constantly give us a secret education. We are not only taught certain styles of violence, the latest fashions, and sex roles by TV, movies, magazines, and comic strips, we are also taught how to succeed, how to love, how to buy, how to conquer, how to forget the past and suppress the future. We are taught more than anything else, how not to rebel.[7]

In the next section I examine schooling narratives that portray the controlling teacher. We may posit many explanations for that behavior, as I have suggested earlier with respect to my playschool role. However, of greater import perhaps is how we might encourage students to make those roles problematic.

IMAGES OF CONTROLLING TEACHERS

"School is discipline, control, and fear."
(from "Parker Lewis Can't Lose")[8]

As I walked through the halls of a high school in North Georgia, the principal said to me, "Listen to how quiet it is."

I'm thinking, "Yeah, it's deadly quiet here. Is there any life in this school?"

But before I had an opportunity to respond, he said, "The teachers all have their classrooms under control."

Of the dominant images of teachers, controlling stands out. In almost every form of media, we see the stern, severe looks that have tended to characterize teachers over the decades. Student-teachers are told to "develop a stare," "not to smile until Christmas," or "never to let the class get the upper hand." Control equals classroom management. Being in control shows who's in charge.

"The Legend of Sleepy Hollow" is the story of Ichabod Crane, a schoolmaster, and a portrait of control.[9] Despite the much loved fantasy of the headless horseman, what is of interest here is the dramatization of the traditional student-teacher relationship based in domination and control. A favorite of many students, reading this story against a teacher education curriculum that infuses social theories with curricular issues and reads both against a background of language arts methodology, the story becomes a frightening indictment of how easily we accept dominant/subordinate relationships—in fact, how we assume such relationships as a given. In other words, Ichabod's students love him even though the only sound in this otherwise quiet setting of his classroom is the sound of his "menacing voice" accompanied by a birch cane to keep them on task with their memory work. One student in my class tells this story after we read "The Legend of Sleepy Hollow" and discussed aspects of Ichabod's disciplinary regime:

> My granddad who used to teach back in the 1920s or so had his rod. It was a ruler, he did the old knuckle-cracking things. But

he doesn't believe in that sort of thing nowadays. He thinks people are on the right track today to get away from that sort of thing.

Another student-teacher remembers this about a previous schooling experience and compares memory work then to now:

> I had a teacher in fourth grade who was an older lady probably near retirement at the time, and she had some very old-fashioned ways of thinking about schooling. She had long vocabulary lists that we had to memorize. Not much different from today. Now the lists are SAT lists but kids still have to memorize them. Things haven't changed much in that regard.

Then as now students seemed to accept whatever is handed down as the way it's suppose to be. If students who are our teachers of tomorrow continue to accept without question things like lists of decontexualized vocabulary, teaching for the test, and so forth, then how can we progress into the twenty-first century with teaching/learning that is meaningful for all students? How can we teach for tomorrow with outdated strategies? How can we teach narrowly when technology is changing so rapidly that we cannot possibly keep up with it. Eliot Wigginton has a saying, that goes something like this, if what we are teaching today will not be useful twenty-five years from now, then we'd better rethink what we're teaching (closely paraphrased).[10]

Ichabod's students never seemed to question his intentions but, indeed, seemed thankful for their taskmaster (I am not equating Ichabod's students with my own; rather, I am merely suggesting that in the traditional role teachers lead, students follow, and they follow unquestionably whether teachers provide a meaningful learning experience or not). In fact, Ichabod's students never even questioned his authority to completely control their actions and interactions. They and their parents seemed to trust him completely. He would go home with many of them and actually rotated living with them. He had an attitude of superiority and people did not resent that either. He was a "jack-of-all-trades" (which, of course, is problematic as an image of teachers for reasons that have nothing to do with control).

And yet Ichabod commands the respect that many teachers say they wish they had from their students today—an issue we need to make problematic with our students. My own students often raise these questions, "How will students respect me if I am not absolutely in control? How will they believe what I say unless I prove I am an authority? How can I make them do what I want them to do?" When we discuss their questions against a view of discipline that grows out of a sense of worth and dignity, students seem to see the ludicrous nature of respect through force.

The discipline to be courteous to both teachers and peers does not depend on control. It seems to be inextricably linked with value—not material value in the economic sense but the value of human life. In other words, the value of each person's right to speak and be heard, seems to be at the center of the kind of respect and courteous behavior that allows both teachers and students voices to be heard in democratic classrooms and in democratic societies.

Pat Conroy's *The Water is Wide* is the story of Tom Wingo's teaching experiences on an island off the South Carolina coast.[11] Wingo's goal is not just to help his students become literate, but to give them choices if they ever want to leave the island. He calls his method of teaching before students know how to read and write, the pep-rally method. Wingo teaches the children geography by pointing to a map and showing where something comes from. The next day he asks, "where did we say coffee comes from?" for example. Students learned about their world orally.

Though Wingo's teaching seems laudable on the surface, what I want to focus on in this section is the other teacher, Mrs. Brown. Mrs. Brown controlled through harsh disciplinary measures, evoking fear with a strap to reinforce the importance of memorization. She wanted so much to be respected by the school board that she told the board her students were learning to read and write by going through the book.

In addition to paddling the children when they could not say their lessons, Mrs. Brown attempted to turn the school board against Tom Wingo for his unorthodox methods of teaching (the school board did not know of hers). Though both kids and parents loved Wingo and his methods, Mrs. Brown succeeded in having him fired.

Although the unfortunate aspects of Wingo's dismissal can be discussed, what is perhaps worse than his dismissal is what teachers-to-be understand about it. First, it may suggest that if you try innovative methods, you may lose your job. And second, the fact that the school board listened to an abusive teacher who taught by fear and violence may suggest something worse yet. That is, control whether through content or punishment is what society adheres to. The school board's decision reflects the view of the wider society, and, in fact, seems to act in its stead as if it were commissioned to preserve the status quo no matter the cost.

The Class of Miss MacMichael is a film about a violent and abusive controlling headmaster.[12] At Selkirk, an alternative school, all teachers, but especially Miss MacMichael, stand in stark contrast to the headmaster, Mr. Sutton, who is controlling and both physically (punches kids in stomach) and mentally abusive (has students digging clay for craft class which school doesn't have). He is unaffectionately called the "hedgehog" (for his porcupine-like spines). Sutton is constantly worried about appearances and wants to keep a student named Gaylord, who has been labeled educably mentally retarded, at Selkirk so he (Sutton) can take credit for "daily miracles *he* performs."

Because competence is a big issue in this movie and because control is often confused with competence here and in schools, teachers-to-be may benefit from examining what Linda McNeil refers to as "contradictions of control."[13] Since the idea of control is so exaggerated in the film, contradictions are easy to spot. Mr. Sutton's behavior tends to make all teachers seem admirable by contrast; therefore, students need to closely examine the attitudes, practices, and expectations of the teachers in this movie as well. In the following passage, McNeil discusses the defensive teaching styles and classroom control found in the four high schools she studied. This passage seems useful for framing discussion of many of the literary selections here, especially the movie *The Class of Miss MacMichael*:

Ideals implied open-ended, long-term learning, begun by broad-ranging, depth-seeking inquiry and discussion. Yet the content presented was often limited to brief, "right" answers, easily transmitted, easily answered, easily graded. The divergence implied by teachers' vision of "real learning" was contradicted by the uniformity of student behavior and lesson content typical of most class sessions. The teachers at the very first school (Forest Hills High School) demonstrated this contradiction between teaching goals and teaching style. They justified their over-simplified lessons as their way of accommodating to a school where their only power came from the classroom. What the students saw as teacher strictness was for the teachers a complicated accommodation to changing power relations in the school, relations which over time had diminished teachers' voice in program and school policy. This accommodation has direct effects on classroom instruction.

Our image of the one-room schoolteacher, or the master of a Latin-grammar school, is of a teacher wielding the hickory stick to make students learn. Student discipline—sitting on hard benches, standing to recite, maintaining absolute silence unless spoken to—was instrumental to mastering the content. This study of four high schools reveals that today meany teachers reverse those ends and means. They maintain discipline by the very ways they present course content. They choose to simplify content and reduce demands on students in return for classroom order and minimal student compliance on assignments. Feeling less authority than their Latin-grammar school counterpart, they teach "defensively," choosing methods of presentation and evaluation that they hope will make their workload more efficient and create as little student resistance as possible.[14]

McNeil states that the purpose of her study was to "trace school knowledge to its sources in the institutional setting."[15] Therefore, she raises these questions that I also like to raise with my students as we think about the glaring contradictions between Mr. Sutton and the other teachers at Selkirk:

What kinds of knowledge do schools make accessible? How is school knowledge a product of the ways of knowing students encounter in school? At the institutional level, How is the treatment of school knowledge a factor of the way the school works, the way it is organized?[16]

Another schooling situation in which corporal punishment is used to control showed up in an episode of "Little House on the Prairie."[17] In this episode we meet Laura Engles's teacher, Mrs. Olson, who believes Laura is a troublemaker. No matter what Laura does, she cannot change this image of herself in the eyes of Mrs. Olson. First, Mrs. Olson rapped Laura across the knuckles, then she "whipped" her, and then she sent Laura home. Another student, Elmer, who witnesses Laura's mistreatment, tries to bully the teacher. Elmer dares Mrs. Olson to hurt him with her ruler. Mrs. Olson raps Elmer across the knuckles to teach him a lesson, and he responds by not moving a muscle. He just stares.

I mention this episode here (a student brought it up in class) to make a point about social practices and a kind of selectivity that seems to operate in popular media. That is, the clip raises an issue that Kathleen Weiler raises again and again in *Women Teaching for Change* (and Henry Giroux and Paulo Freire discuss in the introduction to the book). The question raised is, "How does the interruption of resistance work within social practices that seem to be about reproducing other social practices?" Giroux and Freire say that Weiler sees resistance and reproduction as "mutually informing relations of contradiction that produce forms of social and moral governance."[18] In this instance, the social practice being reproduced through television is control through fear and physical violence. Elmer's resistance to that form of control seems, on the surface, to add a dimension of judicious social action or a least a moment in which the audience can say, "Thank goodness somebody did something to defend poor Laura."

Though my student discussed only Elmer's portrayal as bully because he resisted Mrs. Olson's control, what also needs to be made problematic is whether or not such an action would have been allowed into the script if the character under attack had not been Laura (or another female). And our reaction or how a producer perceives an audience might react also needs to be questioned. Although my students point is very important, issues of the negative portrayal of women (in any role) in the media is also problematic.

Nonetheless, in a Rousseauean sense, the instance of resistance here may be like the serpent in the garden. It seems to legitimate a new form of knowledge that is produced by actors exercising a degree of human agency within a determined structure. Of course, whether resistance would have served the same function had it been pro-active rather than re-active needs to be discussed. Or whether resistance would have even made its way into the script had it been a female defending Laura needs also to be discussed. Yet the momentary interruption of Elmer's spontaneous act created a space or an opening through which a different cultural pattern could be imagined. A nontraditional teacher education curriculum could also create such a space in which different cultural patterns might be imagined. I do not mean to suggest here that acts of questioning authority are simple; rather, Elmer's spontaneous act like the complex business of questioning or contradicting textual authority—or in this sense an official curriculum—is a political act that has a variety of consequences.

The Chocolate War by Robert Cormier also depicts images of controlling teachers.[19] However, control in this story is not limited to teachers. Students also are controlling and manipulative.

The relational context in which acts of power and control are played out produced what might seem like a domino effect.

Most of the action in the story takes place in a Catholic school or on the playing field. Jerry Renault refuses to be bullied into selling chocolates for Trinity's annual fund raiser. He meets Archie Costello, the school's gang leader on a psychological battleground.

This book seems to speak to the control people and institutions have over one another especially when, at times, control is subtle and people are unaware. My students found the book frightening. They were psychologically terrorized by teachers, especially Brother Leon who seemed the most sinister of them all (and the teacher many of my students connected with their own parochial schooling). Angry about the slow sale of chocolates, Leon plotted revenge. And as if Leon's psychological games were not enough, the book addresses another whole level of control parochial schools play. In other words, besides teachers being the one's to judge, students in the book acted as if they felt God were judging them, too.

Control, then, in *The Chocolate War* may be due to the maintenance of a particular world view. According to Gramsci, that control is subtle and persuasive, quiet and seductive; it appeals to our moral and intellectual side, and causes us to give in to power without our even recognizing it.[20] And Leon and the church here seem to represent the physical embodiment of what Gramsci calls hegemonic direction.

In Charles Dickens's *Nicholas Nickleby* we get a historical perspective of schooling prior to standardized education but no less a portrait of control.[21] On the contrary, what may have seemed quiet and seductive in one setting, seems masterfully orchestrated in the other. Here, we have the opportunity to carefully examine what Williams refers to as "rules" that are formally articulated for the purposes of domination and "hegemony," that is a practice—a cultural process—loosely resembling ideology but distinctly different at the level of consciousness—of what people do versus what they think they do.[22]

Dickens shows us three distinctly different ways/tracks in which people can be educated: (1) apprenticeship, (2) tutoring, and (3) the private schools. Under the apprenticeship system, if I wanted to be a blacksmith (and I were male), I would work and train with a blacksmith until the blacksmith to whom I was apprenticed said I knew enough to call myself a blacksmith. Nicholas's sister, Kate, for example, was apprenticed to a seamstress. Families who could afford to do so hired a tutor for their child. Under the pseudonym of Mr. Johnson, Nicholas, is hired to be a French tutor because he has had some teaching experience.

Through the narration of the story, Dickens ridicules the low qualifications needed to become a tutor. He makes fun of a public who would believe that if one sounded reasonably intelligent, one could teach children to speak French or anything else. The only qualification for becoming a teacher was simply to be educated, and it was assumed that you would be capable of educating others.

Teachers were hired in the private schools too with little or no education; certification was not necessary. Children (mostly boys) were sent to private schools to be "raised up proper." Often the schoolmaster was more interested in money than in educating children. As a measure of control, the schoolmaster gave each child a dose of medicine in the morning before classes began. Once students had their medicine, they would be less likely to complain about their lessons.

Several aspects of the control theme can be made problematic through this window on history. First, sending children away to learn to be "proper" suggests a form of social control often seen through particular curricula. For example, one method of control that ensures that students do not know the difference between a fact and a belief (which, in this instance can be particular moral beliefs) is to present content as discrete skills or in ways that do not allow for questions that might help students differentiate. Understanding one's worldview as if it were a fact gives tremendous power to the owner of the worldview whether that owner be a representative of the dominant culture whose job it is to perpetuate the status quo or not. Here control by inclusion/exclusion of curricular content illuminates the relation between a particular kind of knowledge and codes of power and control. Conformity is the key. Power (and subsequently knowledge), or the desire for it, is at the roots of domination and control, no matter how it is carried out.[23]

Second, though, of course not all control equals corporal punishment; giving medicine to control children comes close. How many times in contemporary society have we heard of giving drugs to students with special needs, perhaps, to help them remain calm enough to learn (children who have been labeled hyperactive, for example) but also as a way to keep them under control? In fact, the description of corporal punishment and resistance to it in the "Little House on the Prairie" television episode described previously understates the degree to which other forms of control operate in schools.

Social control is most frequently accomplished by teaching a particular view of the world, one that preserves the status quo through a selective or preshaped tradition.[24] By selecting a particular version of history or privileging a particular kind of knowledge, the dominant culture ensures the regulation of human relations through structures of inequality.

The Blackboard Jungle by Evan Hunter illustrates this issue.[25] A line from the movie *Lean on Me*,[26] "treat 'em like animals; they'll behave like animals," seems to speak especially to the degradation of human relations in Hunter's book.

The Blackboard Jungle centers around a teacher's first year of teaching in a vocational high school in New York City, North Manual Trades High School (even the name of the school suggests something of the social expectations for the students who go there). Hunter captures the frustrations felt by many teachers who fight against poverty, violence, and what is commonly referred to as student apathy. Teachers call this school the "garbage can" of the educational system and say their job is to keep the lid from overflowing into the streets.

Rick Dadier is the central character in the book and the new teacher. His philosophy is that if you keep them busy, you keep them quiet, then you control them. Because his philosophy is shared by other teachers and administrators in the school, the climate of the school is negative. Students are bored.

However, on one occasion, while reading a story, Dadier breaks through to his students. They begin to listen, to discuss, and Dadier begins to listen to them. Unfortunately, at the same time Dadier breaks through to his students, he has a personal crisis and is away from his classroom for several weeks. When he returns, everything has regressed to the way it was before—chaotic classrooms with students showing little interest in curriculum, and try as he might, Dadier is not able to pull things back together. He missed what he considered his teachable moment, and the book ends with Dadier trying to recapture that moment. Here students might ask what they perceive as a teachable moment. They might puzzle over the particular curriculum attempted in a school whose very name (North Manual Trades) indicates something of the social expectation for students attending.

A character sketch in insecurity, Rick Dadier is afraid of his students. Fear seems to motivate his desire to control. In a setting where rape and other social problems abound (Dadier breaks up a rape and later is severely beaten), having students sit in their seats and be quiet seems to be the only solution Dadier can come up with. As my students begin to problematize Dadier's way of handling the situation, one student comments not on the dilemma at hand but on the value of using literature to help expose student-teachers to such dilemmas. She says, "It's not just theory in this book. *The Blackboard Jungle* shows so vividly the consequences of those kinds of judgments. It's something you don't get from just reading a textbook. You can just blow that off. But this really shows you what can happen."

Additionally, an essay by Alan Peshkin entitled "Whom Shall the Schools Serve?" provides an important look at the politics of control and power as played out in the roles, experiences, and expectations of administrators, teachers, parents, and students.[27] Peshkin politicizes the circumstances through which Mansfield High School, a small school in a rural midwestern community, attempts to "maintain Mansfield's sense of community" while the community's interest is "in maintaining Mansfield High School."[28] Against this professional reading and any number of other aesthetic texts like *The Blackboard Jungle*, I raise Gramsci's and Williams's notion of "hegemony" to re-emphasize that whole communities (not just those in power) help to perpetuate the status quo through hegemonic direction or the subtle moral and intellectual persuasion to conform to what appears to be the way *things are supposed to be*. Hunter's book and Peshkin's essay remind us, however, that *things* don't just happen; people make them happen. Yet often in this society, it seems to be much easier to accept what is than to try to do something to change it. Acceptance and not challenge seems particularly easier when whole groups of people become so overwhelmed by external circumstances that they tend to minimize their capabilities to effect change. And, yet, that too may be part of the process about which both Gramsci and Williams write. For example, Gramsci in *Selections from the Prison Notebooks* and Williams in *Marxism and Literature* discuss hegemony not as a set of "rules" but as a whole "process."[29] In fact,

Williams states that hegemonic relations of domination and subordination are in effect:

> a saturation of the whole process of living . . . the whole substance of lived identities and relationships, to such a depth that the pressures and limits of what can ultimately be seen as a specific economic, political, and cultural system seem to most of us the pressures and limits of simple experience and common sense. . . . Society is never only the "dead husk" which limits social and individual fulfillment. . . . [Rather, it is] a constitutive process with very powerful pressures which are expressed in political, economic, and cultural formations . . . and are internalized and become individual wills.[30]

Against Williams's explanation of hegemony as a process, I contrast Joseph Heller's *Catch-22,* where unwritten rules function to order the social practices that keep the "machinery" in place.[31]

It may be then the interrelatedness or embeddedness of these social structures that helps to create what appears on some level to be a kind of conspiracy but according to Gramsci is more the effects of "the entire social complex they express."[32] In other words, inequality may continue because schools (especially vocational schools) tend to "perpetuate traditional social differences" while "within these differences, [they] tend to encourage internal diversification [and] give the impression of being democratic. . . . "[33] By making problematic the frequently accepted notion that culture is fixed (i.e., by taking up Williams's[34] and Gramsci's work that re-evaluates determinism and suggests that history is a fluid process), both inexperienced and experienced teachers may be encouraged to think of their roles within this process. Both may be encouraged to consider this point: As members of a society we can either settle for or we can contest the status quo, remembering here what Williams suggested. That is, that the creation of a counterhegemonic culture would/could come from the margins of society.[35]

In *Lean on Me*,[36] many of the teachers have similar feelings about students as those expressed by teachers in *The Blackboard Jungle.* To the newly acquired principal, Joe Clark, however, being tough seems the only means of handling a volatile situation in which, perhaps, loss of value, identity, and human worth and not simply ignorance or a desire to create havoc and destruction seem responsible for the chaos that disrupts all learning. However, this is not unproblematic. As a part of a cultural image, the "big screen" gets us inside a "school out of control" being run by "savages." The message seems to be one of "I told you so. If you don't keep the reigns tight, this is what happens." It's a particularly timely message too because it appears at a time in which the back-to-basics conservative restoration *appears* to be losing to educators who talk about wanting to educate all students in the service of democracy and freedom (appears here is the key word because I do not see any *real* evidence that back-to-basics campaigners have let up at all). The chaos in this movie seems to suggest the impossibility of democratic schooling among other things.

For example, *Lean on Me* might also suggest a kind of cultural revolution in which those who have become nameless and faceless decide to fight back at institutions that they believe are responsible. Things may not be as willy nilly as they seem within the context of the movie, and this needs to be examined. Teachers and teachers-to-be might examine the relationship between society and what is considered for the purposes of this movie "undesirable tension created by undesirable groups." They might also consider the source of the rage and violence that plagues Eastside High and other inner-city schools.

Regardless of how we critique the film, schooling cannot occur under the situation we come to know in the movie, something must be done and Joe Clark is sent to do it. The following is a conversation between students that occurred after viewing the film in class:

CHRIS. Wouldn't you be more fearful to be a student in that school? I actually had no problems with what he [Clark] did or how he treated anybody. Before you can have these nice democratic classrooms, you [the teacher] have the responsibility to see that there are no murders in your school.

CATHERINE. Yeah, but he violated the students' right of due process; I mean he just asked for names; rumors could get you thrown out.

JOE. You're missing the point. They should have been processed individually, then expelled, if that was the case.

CHRIS. They should have been processed through the courts, and put in jail.

CATHERINE. You're supposed to have due process in the school, too.

CHRIS. See now we're talking from green and white middle-class values.

JOE.   Exactly.

CHRIS.   They live by whole different laws.

CATHERINE.   What do you mean they live by whole different laws?

CHRIS.   They do, people in inner-city schools.

JOE.   They are going to die when they are nineteen or twenty because that is the life span of people pushing dope, trying to make a living by selling drugs.

CATHERINE.   For the dopers, too! You have to show everybody that they have the right to due process, everybody whether they're Mexican, black, white, in every level of the system. Maybe Thomas wasn't really dealing drugs; maybe it was just rumored; his rights to due process were violated.

The ways each generation and each individual understands culture seems to be important to study. By examining and deconstructing the classist and racist statements of some of my students, that process can begin. But we need also to examine in close detail the cultural understandings of those students whose lives are represented in the movies. How they view control, for example, may seem obvious but how and where that view is perpetuated is important too and can provide important information for teachers. How teachers and the administration view schooling may be important to examine as well.

The irony here is, of course, that schooling cannot occur under situations of complete docility either, any more than it can under utter chaos as is depicted in the movie. *Lean on Me* is an extreme portrait, but so is the picture of schooling in which students are automatons and teachers are functionaries in an autocratic/technocratic portrait of schooling.

John Williams's novel offers such a contrast.[37] *Stoner* is set in the midwest and is the story of a young man who attends college to study agriculture and falls in love with literature. After deciding to teach, he remains at the university through graduate school and is offered a faculty position after graduation. This schooling narrative is particularly rich with images of *student-teacher relationships, empassioned teaching*, and *resistance to authority*. However, here I deal with the portrait of Archer Sloane, Stoner's English professor, and briefly with Stoner's reaction to Sloane's authoritarianism.

Stoner's first encounter with English literature is in Sloane's class. The experience both troubles and disquiets him. Archer Sloane is in his early fifties. He seems to hate teaching. Not only does he seem to hate teaching, but Sloane also seems to hold a particular disdain for students. Despite his contempt for teaching, Sloane never misses an opportunity to let students know that he could forget more than they would ever know. His superior attitude both in presenting course material—making no effort to close the wide gulf he perceives between him and his students—and in his ability to be detached and distant results in students both disliking him and being afraid of him.

Stoner's reaction to Sloane's insistent "What does it mean?" was fear. Stoner, frozen in his seat, cannot answer, and Sloane makes it clear that he has the "privileged" right answer. Within this context students seem to more easily see the stereotypical banking teacher who is the only authority in the class, the one with all the right answers, whose primary job it is to deposit knowledge and often through intimidation.

When we read *Stoner* for the particular roles of English teachers portrayed in this book, we also examined passages from Paulo Freire's *Education for Critical Consciousness*. The particular passages are those dealing with what Freire calls teaching for a "culture of silence."[38] In a situation where students are subjected to language as well as values that make them feel as if they know nothing, are virtually illiterate, little critical thinking may occur; instead, silence may abound and a "culture of silence" may be created (we learn through Stoner's eyes how Sloane silenced students). Again, *Stoner,* paired with passages on a "culture of silence," may evoke even greater reflection because of the shared experience with the literary world and the critical nature of the professional passage.

Despite the fear Sloane produced within Stoner during his early experiences with literature, there was a special moment when Stoner realized that he loved literature and wanted to teach it. Though the book goes on to show Stoner teaching in the same department as Sloane, having broken through the silence, it never really shows him as a member of the academic club, so to speak. Effects of Sloane's power and control over Stoner early in the book are never completely overcome even though Sloane reaches out to Stoner to become a teacher and seems to support fully Stoner's decision.

Both *The Chocolate War* and *Stoner* deal with psychological control by producing guilt, fear, and anxiety. Moreover, the particularly authoritarian style of Sloane's teaching seems to make participation in one's own learning experiences futile. Both books show a devaluation of any knowledge other than official school knowledge established by a particular tradition and institutionalized over time. In the one instance, religion organizes and establishes the particular status quo at Trinity. In the other, the literary canon with its particular body of knowledge and its particular privileged cultural representations establishes that tradition.

An editorial by William Raspberry relates here.[39] In a contemporary materialist society, school and business partnerships have begun to establish a tradition. In each instance, what is the same is the degree to which each dominant group expects its cultural representations to be reproduced. Any challenge to the status quo is both threatening and enlightening—threatening because contestation of any political or cultural form does not serve dominant interests and enlightening because the very act of contestation itself interrupts and thus reminds us that humans are agents of change and that boundaries are not immutable.

The editorial advocates business coming into schools and taking charge because schools are not adequately preparing people for business. Such partnerships, however, tend to undermine what John Dewey referred to as the democratic function of education[40] and may suggest a rhetoric of failure. Arthur Bestor suggests that no matter what jobs people have, they need to be capable of understanding the complexities of life, of making intelligent decisions, and of exercising human agency within structures of constraint.[41] A technocratic view of education such as Raspberry's editorial suggest may not provide students with a means of coping or excelling in a rapidly changing society. But it will ensure that there are workers.

And tracking or the packaging of information differently for some students also ensures that social class structures remain in tact because even under a school/business partnership some students will be prepared for higher education that leads to professional careers in medicine, law, and so forth and others will not.[42] The forms of control dramatized in the schooling narratives seem to be symptoms of a far greater manifestation of control present in this society. Such visions present a limited view, perhaps a selective view, of control. Yet all forms of control need to be questioned, and we need to understand how images of controlling teachers affect developing teachers. What are the meanings prospective teachers make of such images from literature and popular media as well as from their own experiences as students in schools? How do these images, feelings, and dispositions toward or against control get taken up in learning to be a teacher? How do teachers-to-be relate both curricular control and control as discipline, management, or punishment to the structures of inequity that exist in the wider society? How do they understand the relation of curricular control to management, and so forth? How do they understand the language of "control," "*man*agement," "school*master*," and so forth?[43]

As previously mentioned, the tape-recorded data from an English methods course in which teachers-to-be read and discussed schooling narratives as part of the curriculum showed that the word *control* came up at least ten times more often than other words even in discussions of content. Student-teachers' responses to issues of control by corporal punishment suggested that they no longer believed paddling was done in the schools. Their ideas of control were "to be in charge," "to keep kids in line," "to mold minds like a sculptor molds clay." (This latter quote from a student followed the reading of *Spinster* by Sylvia Ashton-Warner.[44] Though we problematized the idea of molding students, nonetheless, my own students, teachers-to-be, seemed to think this a worthwhile goal.) Student-teachers had few responses that indicated that they thought of themselves as being controlled by others in the system, and those responses were confined to remarks about having limited choices over the content of curricula. When teachers-to-be were specifically asked to remember their own schooling experiences, however, they quickly noted, in general, that they did not remember their teachers having much power except when it came to giving grades or exerting control over their classes. In fact, one teacher-to-be stated in an autobiographical profile of schooling experiences that she had always been independent and a leader; therefore, she wanted to be a teacher so she could "control" a group of people. The idea then of power and control—powerless teachers applying control in their classrooms—became a chief topic of inquiry.

The richness of narrative study provided many opportunities for critical dialogue on issues of power and control, the legitimation of some forms of knowledge over others, and finally, probably most important of all the question of value—that is, "What is valued? Why is it valued? and Who gets to decide?"[45] Topics like tracking surfaced often and were the immediate ways in which students recognized structures of power and inequality and issues of school knowledge. See Chapter 6, for example, for student-teachers' stories of tracking and their particular view of content required for students in lower tracks.

The negative images of teachers in this section address the problem of naming what is socially appropriated—that is, teachers being defined rather than defining themselves. Aside from being useful in terms of helping teachers to think about the social constructs of power and authority, this material may be (has been for me) pivotal in framing discussions of the social impact of power on the lives of teachers. Finding ways to show that teachers' problems are systemic and part of a larger set of social relations may help students deconstruct negative perceptions and create a climate for coming to understand the difficulties teachers face.[46] Because a high percentage of teachers in public schools are women, this issue becomes particularly sensitive and bears close examination.

Apart from selected passages from the aforementioned studies, the professional text I most commonly pair with literary selections that deal with issues of power and control is Kathleen Weiler's *Women Teaching for Change*.[47] Weiler shows not only the effects of domination, but she also shows the ways in which power is contested through a feminist pedagogy. The teacher voices in this book both catalog and authenticate their struggles. Weiler's critical ethnography situates the "subtle ways in which language is used to regulate, silence, and structure expression and expressivity,"[48] and her succinct explanation of critical educational theories makes this a valuable text.

The schooling narratives and the professional readings may help experienced teachers recognize the "powerful structures of curricular, and parental control in high school classrooms. . . . [where they are] seen as functionaries in a technocratic vision of schooling in which they have to meet prescribed goals, and [where] women teachers are all too often seen as a traditional nurturing presence under the 'expert guidance' of male administrators and academics."[49] Teachers-to-be may be encouraged to explore these critical issues against their own experiences as students, student-teachers, and vicariously through literature and the popular media.

By way of further articulating this problem, Madeleine Grumet makes problematic the issue of women teaching in a patriarchal system. She writes, "The ideal teacher is one who would control the children and be controlled by her superiors."[50]

Thus marks the legacy that has come to be known as "women's work"—women, suitable for controlling only small people, such as in the home, and for being controlled by those more powerful—and work that affords women an opportunity to move outside their "place" in the home but to attend in much the same fashion to the caretaking of children and young people.

"WOMEN'S WORK"

Sitting on the green two-cushion sofa bed that had been in my family for a number of years, my mother and I discussed my future. Not that I necessarily had ever considered before much recently that I should have a future apart from marrying the boy I had dated through most of my high school years, on this particular day in my life as a high school student—career day—I was filled both with questions and despair. Though I had every intention of marrying, I also wanted "to be something" I remember saying. As my mother talked on of the joys of motherhood and family, which in my memory I knew to have been somewhat less than joyful on many occasions, mother told me for the ten thousandth time that my children and a full-time job keeping house and paying bills would bring me all the fulfillment I could ever desire. The thought of keeping house as a full-time job sent me reeling into fantasy land where I imagined lots of other options, but when the reeling stopped I was right back to what appeared to me to be my one option at the time—secretarial work. Not exactly what I had in mind when I said I wanted "to be something." Not that being a secretary wasn't something, what I meant was that I wanted to be something that would define me and my particular predilections. But being defined differently was not perceived necessarily as a good thing. While I fantasized aloud some of the things I thought interesting, mother would remind me that none of the aforementioned career choices would leave time for a family. And family was a priority, even to me.

Finally, I hit on teaching. "Oh, what a wonderful choice!" my mother exclaimed. "What a wonderful profession for women. A woman can teach and have her family, provided that she waits until her children are school age to teach. Why, you would get out of school (as if teachers were still students) at the same times and have summers off together. Teaching is like the ministry; it's a calling!" And, I had obviously just been called, I thought.

I remember that conversation like it was yesterday. I remembered it particularly my first year of graduate school when on a departmental retreat, during a discussion of teacher education major recruits, one of the professors in my department stated that she thought most teachers just fell into their professions. I was taken aback. I denied that I thought that was true. I tried to remember why I went into teaching, hoping that my memory would reveal something noble—like I went into teaching because I wanted to help children learn. Instead, I recalled only the conversation on the green couch after school on the day that I decided then and there to make a career choice.

Unfortunately, I hear that story again and again in my students. Many women enter the profession for what appears to be similar reasons to my own. I use to think those reasons had to do with my working-class background and with my mother's lifelong belief in teaching as suitable women's work and a calling from on high. I now recognize those beliefs as part of a broadly based sociology of teaching/schooling that goes much deeper and extends much wider than those surface level reasons both my mother gave and my students give for women becoming teachers.

In *Exiles and Communities*, Jo Anne Pagano speaks to that notion and to her response to it:

> I am a teacher, and I am a woman. I am a woman who teaches. I am a female teacher. I don't mean that I am a teacher because I am a woman. In my case I am a teacher despite my being a woman. . . . Until I actually began teaching, I disdained the profession because of its press as nice work for a woman, and probably because of its association with women's work.[51]

Pagano's introduction is important because it situates every story in this section with a woman's attempt to locate a project that is truly her own. Having learned what is appropriate and scholarly from our male instructors' positions of privilege, women have set about either to reenact or teach that tradition or carve out a space for our "otherness."[52] Regardless of the position taken up, each seems somehow a response to the effects of power.

Women teaching, then, are both the physical and spiritual embodiment of otherness as they attempt to forge a space for their lives. They find that space in connections both to their work and to each other—in what Belenky, Clinchy, Goldberger, and Tarule (1986) call caring and connectedness or a kind of empathic knowing.[53] Or through what Noddings calls an ethic of caring.[54] As Pagano says, "In telling stories we enact connection."[55] Our stories connect us to each other and to the world. And our stories reveal much about our position in the world and about our relationship to knowledge. Our stories tell much about what counts for legitimate knowledge and who decides what counts.

In this story, however, I want to make problematic a particular take on caring so that we can examine the various ways such a notion may be taken up respective to women's roles as teachers— so we can examine how, in fact, various ways of viewing women as caring and nurturing teachers may serve to further marginalize and even deprofessionalize and may be seen as perpetuating relations of domination/subordination. As with the previous section of this chapter, the stories and problems raised here are raised in response to issues of control.

Spinster by Sylvia Ashton-Warner is the story of Anna, a "middle-aged, unmarried" woman and an excellent school teacher.[56] *Spinster* is discussed here to examine ways students might use the literary text to examine women's roles critically. It provides opportunities to critique a range of problems associated with the effects of power; for example, how women (and women teachers especially) see themselves and how they are seen by others and how relations of difference affect teacherwork. (I am not advocating that we need to stop caring about one another or that we need to stop searching for ways to care more and be more connected.)

In *Spinster*, basically a fictionalized account of Ashton-Warner's own experiences teaching Maori children in New Zealand for seventeen years, we have a unique portrait of the teacher as artist striving at her craft. Miss Vorontosov, or as the children lovingly call her Miss Vontop, is reflective as she picks up a child and sits in a low chair beginning to read. She is vexed over an argument with Mr. Abercrombie about her reading program— the children read words about Maori children first then they move on to what she calls imported books. She says reading Maori words—stories that describe Maori experiences—first is the only way the children will learn to bridge the gap between the *pa* and the European schools. In between reading to the child in her lap, she talks to herself. As she bemoans her situation she describes her motherly role with the children and compares pleading for the children's right to read their own books as a mother would "for the life of her firstborn."[57]

An issue that deals directly with power and domination and relates to the reproduction of mothering metaphor is the passage that portrays Anna, the spinster teacher, as the life-giving mother of the Little Ones over whom she has charge. Though her thoughts are of "true motherhood," she represses feelings for *men* in her life by saying that teaching (using "paints, clay, sand") is the only way she can give birth.[58] Here, it seems important to move from Ashton-Warner's birthing metaphor to several interrelated aspects of what has been commonly referred to as cultural reproduction (i.e., from schools reproducing social stratification to the view that nurturing/mothering teachers reproduce binary relationships of domination/subordination).

The reproduction of mothering metaphor can be examined in selected passages from Grumet's *Bitter Milk* and a slightly different perspective can be read in Weiler's *Women Teaching for Change*. Neither positions are wholly contradictory; rather, they show a range of aspects that may have been consciously and unconsciously present in a woman's choice to become a teacher. Weiler's understanding suggests many things form particular gender subjectivities as she sees a dialectical relationship between women's constraints and their choices. Grumet suggests that patriarchal power and the desire to reproduce mothering have created the caring and nurturing roles of teachers. For example, Grumet posits:

> Cut off from their mothers by the harsh masculine authority of church and fathers, theorists like Mann sought the reclamation of mother love by promoting women as teachers of the young. Overwhelmed by the presence of their mothers, women entered teaching in order to gain access to the power and prerogatives of their fathers.[59]

Weiler's view, on the other hand, is not presented by theories but by women teachers whom Weiler interviews in her research. One teacher says, "I think that probably falling into a teaching position was just an extension of everything that women are supposed to be, which is nurturing and all the rest of it and that probably had something to do with my choice of going into teaching."[60] Another woman responds to the interview by saying that she wanted to go into social work but her father refused to pay for graduate school. He would only pay for four years so she went to the school of education instead.[61]

Though in the second response an enactment of patriarchal power seems somewhat obvious, it may be even more important to make the first response problematic in terms of how women's understandings about themselves and how they are "supposed to be" have evolved and how they seem to be perpetuated. In other words, the father's refusal to pay for an education that would allow his daughter to be a social worker may have been purely economic or there could have been the underlying power motive, even if operating only at the subconscious level. Yet what may be even more firmly entrenched, a great deal more elusive, and perhaps more harmful are the effects of power that create social understandings that are not questioned as in the first response. What seems especially important in that response is that women all too often understand themselves through social patterns handed down from male hegemony (e.g., fathers telling daughter's how they are "supposed to be," mothers accepting the "word of the father" and perpetuating that notion with daughters, or even, in some instances, male psychologists diagnosing women's problems sometimes by telling us what we already know: that the world expects one thing and when we try to be otherwise we just create emotional problems for ourselves—they might as well be saying if we'd just admit inferiority and go on being submissive everything would be fine).

Weiler makes another point that relates and is perhaps important to entertain here—a point that particularly seems to ring true in my experience, a point I've made elsewhere about the interrelated nature of what may be a network of barriers that women have to overcome. Weiler says that in nearly every case, women made decisions based on what they saw as a weakness in their academic background or because they were unwilling to fight against what they perceived created their weaknesses.[62] Marilyn Frye's birdcage analogy comes to mind again as I consider my own experiences and how I have accounted for the choices I've made (what I have often referred to as nonchoices)—each wire of the cage interlocked so as to create a more formidable boundary.[63]

Previously and throughout this book, I announce various weaknesses that I say prevented me from various aspects of participation: for example, because of my working-class background, which the counselor knew about, and a tracking system in my school I was counseled to take courses on a more general track (one that left me underprepared for college because as the counselor stated, "My parents couldn't afford college, anyway."), but I blame my youthfulness for not fighting against this particular episode in my life; having worked to overcome this hurdle attending college first, I made it to the university, and I chose English education because I loved literature and wanted to be a teacher; later, other areas interested me, but I crossed them off without consideration because of a weakness in mathematics and science[64] (it's true I was weak in math and science, but it's also true that I didn't perceive fields like geology, for example, something that might take me to exotic places to study volcanoes or rock formations, one of my options); and later after I became a teacher, I blamed my being a poor teacher on a lack of theory in my undergraduate preparation and an insufficient number of positive role models.

The point here is that I always blamed the structures that were in place. Now I wonder if those structures actually prevented anything or did their existence simply give me the impression that there was nothing I could do about them. Did I try hard enough to overcome particular weaknesses? Or were the boundaries I perceived so formidable that I believed them impossible to dislocate? Although I saw myself as very determined, I wonder now to what extent is determination enough, at what level is human agency capable of overriding powerful arrangements? And are the arrangements as powerful as our perceptions of them are? Or in my case was it more convenient to blame existing arrangements than to contest? What price do we pay for blaming, what price for contesting? I don't know the answers here, but what I do perceive is that it was not one or two structures—classism and sexism, but an interrelated network of structures that created barriers. And perhaps some barriers were created out of my own perceptions—barriers that may have prevented my contesting social forces that acted against me.

What I am suggesting here is that I have often found it fairly easy to say, "I was young and didn't know better," when perhaps the truth may have been that I wasn't paying enough attention, I wasn't wide enough awake—living deliberately. At what age do children begin to pay that kind of attention to their surroundings? Though I did not have the language to articulate what I observed in the way that I articulate it here, to say that I was completely unaware would be false also. Do children have capacities to detect their own oppression? Maturation may be a factor, but if it is then perhaps we need to educate even the youngest children in ways that teach them to be more astute and open to the vast array of possibilities that surround them now and for the future in both local and wider contexts. Curricular materials for women's studies have been available for several years for children as young as fifth grade.[65]

In general women's roles are perceived somewhat differently today, but politicization of those roles, particularly in education, reveals there is still much work to be done. Interrogating the effects of power on teachers' lives, especially women teachers' lives, ought to be perhaps a foundational goal in teacher preparation. Grumet's historic commentary explains my concern:

> [M]ale educators invited women into the schools expecting to reclaim their mothers, . . . Accordingly, female teachers complied. . . . Rather than emulate the continuous and extended relation of a mother and her maturing child, they acquiesced to the graded schools—to working with one age group for one year at a time. Rather than demand the extended relation that would bind them over time to individual children, they agreed to large group instruction where the power of the peer collective was at least as powerful as the mother/child bond. Deprived of the classical education that most males who organized the schools enjoyed, normalities accepted the curriculum as bestowed, and deviations from it remained in the privacy of the classroom and were not presented to principals or communities of visitors.[66]

While Dan Lortie's study of school teachers suggests that most teachers are comfortable contesting curriculum with their doors closed, arguing that most rewards of teachers come from their pupils rather than from any formal evaluations by supervisors,[67] there may be other issues embedded within closed door contestation. If teachers, and women teachers specifically, accept the curriculum as bestowed, especially when dealing with male administrators, such acceptance may do more than keep an undesirable curriculum in place, it may perpetuate polarization between administrator/teacher, dominant/subordinate hierarchical relations, and male/female positioning.

Researchers and theorists alike have suggested that because such behaviors do tend to perpetuate the power/powerless

dichotomy, in this way women and other minorities may be complicit or compliant in their own oppression. Though a slightly different take on compliance, Kenneth Zeichner, for example, posits
the notion of a kind of strategic compliance respective to evaluation—compliance that is both self-fulfilling and self-serving.[68]
Although Zeichner's formulation may make compliance seem less
despicable and more grounded in the daily realities of teachers'
situations, it may be, nonetheless, important to question even this
as perhaps too simplistic a response to oppression.

How and why particular persons (female or male) engage in
practices that interrupt mainstream power, that contests uncon-
tested terrains, is anyone's guess. Of all the complex relations
described in the readings thus far, one example of a teacher, a
woman teacher, contesting male privilege and power has yet to be
discussed. That example comes from *Spinster*. In an especially
spirited scene, Anna refuses to concede to Mr. Abercrombie's
requirement that she keep a workbook (interpreted in this context
as planbook) because Anna says she doesn't know how to say
what she's going to do until the moment arises. Her explanation
within the text does not suggest an unprepared teacher but a
teacher who recognizes the importance of teachable moments and
flexibility, of a teacher who recognizes that the concerns children
bring into her classroom are the curricula of the moment and
need not be disregarded. Though we may see Anna's refusal as an
act of social and political resistance, she questions Mr. Abercrombie's authority to make her keep a workbook and she does so out
of what she believes to be sound educational principles, her resistance is taken up by Mr. Abercrombie as an act of insubordination. Indeed, traditionally any noncompliant act by a woman or a
child is seen as an act of insubordination.[69]

That acts by women and children may be compared at all is
part of the problematics associated with relations of difference in
particular spheres of influence. Consequently, role-embedded
relations like the aforementioned are a part of what is at stake
and what needs to be critiqued when we consider the particular
role of male privilege in educating women to be teachers.[70]

As Weiler's interview data makes explicit, many impressions
and understandings help to create women's (and teachers') subjectivities and are responsible for their either seeing the world in
terms of multiple possibilities or seeing it as a given.[71] Though I
will readily admit that our socially constructed understandings do

seem to have been produced and reproduced in male-dominated spheres of influence, any thoroughgoing examination of what Belenky et al. has coined "women's ways of knowing"[72] suggests complexities that are not reducible to a single force but to multiple and interrelated forces that contribute to a network of assumptions on which our world views are based.

Finally, Weiler warns against reifying any metaphor (e.g., woman as nurturer) that suggests roles and behaviors of women as innate—a given. She leads us to question what has been defined as typically characteristic of women, suggesting that we need to examine all the ways in which gender is socially constructed while we learn to value the multiple ways women experience the world. (I do not read Weiler as completely denying patriarchally encoded notions of motherhood; I read her as positing a range of possible responses that do not depend on causality or reduction of phenomena to specifically located social or cultural origins but that leave open the possibility of multiple explanations.) Multiplicity seems central in Weiler's conceptual framework as she resists all notions that have the potential to limit our definitions of ourselves and of other women.[73]

Women like men need to name themselves. It is one thing to be sensitive expressing feeling and emotion; it is quite clearly another to have that capability be considered a handicap. When women are not valued as scholars because they are seen as caregivers, it raises particular problems that have to be addressed if we consider teachers the indispensable ingredient in school reform—reform that is bottom up rather than top down.

The teacher's contract of 1923, as offered in Michael Apple's essay entitled "Gendered Teaching, Gendered Labor," situates the notion of women's work historically and implies much about the kind of top-down management that accompanies top-down reform. As such, it complements many of the literary selections in this section. The contract includes rules that state that women who hold positions as housekeepers and caregivers are not allowed to get married or have a relationship outside of marriage; they are not allowed to be away from their homes in the evening or leave town without permission, drink or smoke, color their hair, use makeup, or wear dresses more than two inches about the ankle.[74] Several stories, in particular, illuminate the problems raised by this contract, showing the effects of the contract on the lives of teachers.

Sherwood Anderson's portrait of a teacher in the *Winesburg, Ohio* collection of stories characterizes Kate Swift as a teacher affected by the teaching contract.[75] For example, she is like Anna, a spinster, living her life through her students and through books, travel, and so forth, but she never has time for herself.[76]

Jessica is another portrait of a teacher playing the mother role, landlord role, and so forth—in general, a caretaking/giving role. Jessica is the central character in the novel *One Year In Autumn* by Kathleen Kranida.[77] Jessica is cast as a good teacher who cares about her students. This books represents the caretaking role taken to the extreme because as much as Jessica cares about her students, she seems to need them to care about her also. Though Jessica seems to see nothing wrong with inviting a couple of students who talk of leaving home to stay with her, readers might deconstruct this notion in light of what may be seen as a co-dependent relationship and especially what such action may involve related to how its viewed by parents, other teachers, other students, and, of course, administrators.

Though the book is filled with excellent teaching ideas (scenes where reading groups are responding to literature—Jessica even explains the reader response theory she espouses), readers need to examine this book carefully as a part of a selective tradition that tends to perpetuate the role of teachers as more caregiver than professional. She explores the content of English curriculum through dialogue with her students, yet the book tips too much in the direction of portraying women's work as mothering (or showing teaching as a fine replacement for the unmarried woman who wants children). Kranida even makes a point of letting readers know that Jessica is forty-two.

Though Jessica appears to have students' best interests at heart when she lets a couple of them move in with her, she neither stands up for them or for herself but submits quickly and without resistance when her principal and superintendent object. When called on this issue, Jessica makes the students move without hesitation. Teachers-to-be might benefit from raising questions related to other options for the students and for Jessica; they might also ask if Jessica made the best choice when she invited them into her home and whether she really had a choice with respect to asking the students to leave. Although students need to know they can count on their teachers, the kind of mothering Kranida portrays may take issues of caring to extremes.

Students also need to question the continual reference to women teachers as spinsters, as subservient, and most importantly as caregivers. Perhaps, they might then be led to extend their questions politically to ask who stands to gain the most when negative roles are portrayed and legitimized in books? Teachers and students together need to explore their own subject histories to see how much affect these images have had on the development of their own inner-subjectivities.

The *Children's Hour*, a play by Lillian Hellman, portrays women not just as teachers but as caregivers in a boarding school for females.[78] Through an unfortunate turn of events, the teachers' lives are exploited and they are unfairly accused of being lesbians because a young girl overhears strange noises and reports to her grandmother that it sounded like they were doing "abnormal" things. The teachers are fired without any opportunity to tell their story.

In another story specifically about lesbian relationships, *Annie on My Mind* by Nancy Garden, there are two older teachers who are self-proclaimed lesbians.[79] The story is sensitively told focusing on the emotions of relationships and specifically on the difficulties other people have with lesbian relationships—the teachers and two students about whom the story is told. When the young students are discovered, the teachers share with them stories of their hardships over the course of a relationship that had lasted nearly fifty years.

The thing students might want to question about both the play and the book is the nature in which society chose to deal with the teachers' sexuality or supposed sexuality as in the play. Teachers-to-be might do well to address issues of women's work embedded in these portrayals as well. In other words, we may question whether the issue of sexuality here is related more to beliefs in a particular moral code that is attached to codes of sexuality, or whether issues of control and subsequent resistance is perceived in the taking up of nondominant forms of sexuality. Students need not assume either/or positions here, for it may be likely that both are operating on some level. The point is teaching seen here as a "women's work" issue is strongly connected to the social, political, and cultural traditions of which schooling practices are a part.

RACIST AND CLASSIST PORTRAITS OF TEACHERS

Racist and classist portraits of teachers frequently intersect with sexist images or those described in the previous section on women's work. The book *Roll of Thunder, Hear My Cry* by Mildred Taylor is one particular example.[80] By contrast, the image here is not one of subservience but of a strong female teacher who has to deal with the racism and classism in her community.

Set during the depression of the thirties, nine-year old Cassie Logan's story is one of physical survival and survival of the human spirit as her family, the only land-owning black family in the area, fight to hold onto their land. Raised by a nurturing family who are determined not to lose their independence because they are black, Cassie is strong and unaware that any white person could consider her inferior. However, in a dramatization of resistance to the "selective tradition" of history texts, Cassie learns a bitter lesson when her mother is visited by three members of the school board and fired for teaching what is not in the book.

In this scene Harlan Granger, Kaleb Wallace, and another board member come to visit Mama's classroom while she is discussing slavery. She expounds on the "cruelty of it" and on the "rich economic cycle" generated for the factories in the North and in Europe because of slavery. She tells of how the country profited from free labor and the inhumane treatment of people enslaved. Before she finishes, Mr. Granger picks up a book and examines the "pasted-over" front cover. Not seeing in the book what Mama is teaching, he argues that Mama is suppose to teach only the curriculum as it is set forth in the books approved by the Board of Education. He tells Mama that she has no right teaching children those things about slavery that are not in their social studies books. When he asks why she would do such a thing, her only reply is that she cannot teach what isn't true.[81]

Raymond Williams's concept of the selective tradition applies here as it does to previously discussed texts (e.g., *One Year in Autumn*).[82] This notion refers to a discriminating version of history, culture, and knowledge presented in schools. Additionally, and especially important here, is again a discussion of Gramsci's notion of hegemony, the subtle direction by moral and intellectual persuasion intended to make people subservient to power without their knowing it. It is important to note here, however, that Gramsci's notion of hegemony seems a great deal more complex than teachers transmitting dominant or selective forms of knowledge.[83] Particularly problematic here and in other recent discussions is the idea that this direction seems most powerful when it is women, minorities, or children who are being directed. *Roll of Thunder* offers a positive view of a woman, an African American woman, engaged in resistance to hegemonic forces—both to the members of the school board and to the tradition selectively being perpetuated in the social studies text. Mama's resistance is overtly political as it is directed toward putting an end to domination by Mr. Granger and his cohorts, but Mama Logan also has a personal stake in putting an end to Granger's oppression. As is often the case with women, the private is political because of the multiple ways in which our lives have been regulated in this male dominated society. In Mama's case, this regulation extends from gender to race and to particular values. As a teacher of black children she finds there is even more at stake than the way in which she is personally treated. How and what children come to understand about themselves and their subject histories is at stake.

Unfortunately, for Mama as for many who are resistant, putting an end to domination in this particular context results in Mama's dismissal. Again, what needs to be made problematic here is how this particular text intersects along race, class, and gender lines and how resistance to domination is especially played out in the life of this courageous woman.

In "Gendered Teaching, Gendered Labor," Apple describes women's ongoing efforts to control their own teaching and curriculum as they battle the social and sexual divisions of labor. He writes:

> [Women have] fought "silently" everyday on their jobs to expand or retain control of their own teaching and curriculum. . . . Overt and covert efforts from the past are of much more than historical interest. . . . [For] the past is still ahead of us.[84]

Indeed, as Apple suggests, Mrs. Logan and the female characters of the previous section are among many women, fictional and otherwise, whose teaching and lives reflect the constant struggle for freedom from social and political constraints.

It is hardly arguable as to whether the story of Mama Logan's trouble stems from racism, classism, or from the lack of power and control women have known in their work outside the home.[85] The intersections within that novel help it speak to each of those issues in varying degrees. I have simply chosen to highlight her personal struggles as they helped create the space for social resistance against the cause of inaccurately representing a "body of knowledge" about the role of African Americans throughout history.

Additionally and perhaps a more poignant racist account of schooling can be seen in the made-for-television special, *Separate but Equal*.[86] The General Motors Mark of Excellence Program, *Separate but Equal*, details the struggles of Thurgood Marshall, then lead attorney for the NAACP who later became Supreme Court Justice, in his fight with the state of South Carolina over the legalized segregation of schools. Attempts by white attorneys to continue segregation became a federal concern. As black children were pushed farther to the margins, dispossessed by a separate and unequal education, self-concepts suffered irreparable damage. And the white children of Clarendon as elsewhere learned moral confusion as those who taught them about democracy also taught them to segregate and discriminate.

A passage from the Feinberg and Soltis text entitled "Equal but Separate" is reminiscent of the television movie that catalogs events in Clarendon County. The *School and Society* text reads as follows:

> Deerpark School of Sylvan is part of the new Madison County Consolidated School District, a planned realignment of educational facilities and government. The new system combines, under a central county administration, the old schools of Jefferson City, which have been dominated by minorities and the urban poor in recent years, with the modern schools of the richer suburbs. This plan was developed as a result of pressure from Jefferson City residents and federal attorneys in order to guarantee educational parity and an acceptable racial balance in the area schools.[87]

Though the Jefferson City account deals with struggles of working class white people as well as people of color, both the professional text and the movie text show how the predesegregration situation perpetuates interests of the dominant class.

In a classist portrait of schooling, we see a teacher's response to his subordinate position in an image of the resistant teacher. James Hilton describes the life of a schoolmaster in *Good-bye, Mr. Chips*.[88] Hilton shows us how he perceives a committed teacher reacts when his values come face to face with a strong power differential, a headmaster who represents highly respected members of an elitist English society. Chips is being asked to retire against his wishes. Ralston, the headmaster, gives as his reason that Chips teaches differently than the rest of the teachers. The headmaster says simply that the other masters "obeyed" me and with that he implies that Chips marches to the beat of a different drummer. Chips considers the headmaster's comments and mutters to himself about exams and certification. He wonders what either one matters. He also wonders what difference it makes if the school tries to be up-to-date because Brookfield is expected to run like a factory "turning out a "snob culture based on money and machines."[89] Chips rails on about the schools lack of balance in the curriculum—a curriculum based almost entirely on Latin and Greek or Chemistry and Mechanics.

With this book, teachers-to-be have the opportunity to question what purposes particular curricula serve in much the way that they may question/consider the history curricula highlighted in *Roll of Thunder*.[90] And questioning curricula may lead to questioning many other related arguments (e.g., Once we've asked what purposes curricula serve, we might also ask for whom does the school serve, and so forth). Additionally and almost without fail, students note and discuss the power differential that exists both in the language "headmaster" and "schoolmaster" and that actually exists in the story.

Though Chips was asked to resign, he did not retire nor was he fired. In fact, he became as he said "necessary." And necessary is perhaps an accurate description of the role this book has played historically in perpetuating a "selective tradition" which suggests that particularly privileged members of society should receive a "classical education."[91]

Teachers and teachers-to-be seem to relate to Mr. Chips's situation on yet another level. For example, how often do we hear that the particular methods we model in our classes are simply not being used in the schools where student-teachers are placed or are hired. Supervising teachers feel threatened as well as new teachers in this instance. Chips's story provides the background from which to do a lot of "dissociating" by examining the cultural and ideological dimensions of the text as a "problem-situation for discussion."[92] In other words, to dissociate means (according to Freire's interpretation) being able to distinguish the difference between education and propaganda. The powerlessness that many new teachers as well as experienced teachers feel is not an imagined phenomenon and needs to be a part of class discussions. Additionally, from Mr. Chips's own action represented in the story, student-teachers can discuss political action. Knowing when and how to act in a threatening situation may be easier to deal with when students have been helped to think about the politics of that situation.

Therefore, among other professional readings, we closely examine these words with reference to the role reading and interpreting literature, history, film, theater, music, and so forth plays in the development of racist, classist, sexist, and heterosexist attitudes. Cynthia Brown in *Literacy in Thirty Hours* writes:

> Learning to read is a step toward political participation. But how people exercise their ability to read reflects in part the political attitudes of their teachers. If nonreaders learn to read by writing and read their own words and opinions, then they learn that their perceptions of reality are valid to others and can influence even those in authority. If, on the other hand, their teachers require them to learn the words and ideas in a primer which is donated by those in power, then the learners must accept that experience as more valid than their own. They must accept the concepts of social and economic structure transmitted by the teacher or decide not to learn to read.[93]

I use this passage to talk about reading critically. I suggest that students place the word *critical* along side the word *read* each time it appears in Brown's passage. For example, learning to read critically . . . and so forth. Then I ask them to think of reading critically as reading differently or reading the text of *difference*; that is, deferring absolute interpretation, interrogating power in relations of difference, and including issues of power, conflict, and struggle when we think of difference. I suggest that we think of reading and writing as acts of composing differently, which allow us to produce knowledge, reshaping old understandings and values about race, class, and ethnicity, gender (including role socialization) and sexuality, and teaching and learning and their implied relations of power. Afterward, we reread the passage and discuss/consider how the role of reading if not critical can figure into the development of prejudice—or to making decisions based on partiality. I am not advocating anti-literacy here; I am advocating critical literacy as a way to remake our world.[94]

Again, it seems important to understand the role that books as well as popular media may play in helping to create early impressions of teachers' roles, of schooling, and of the politics related to issues like Whom shall the schools serve? and What is legitimate knowledge?

Judy Mitchell and Don Saker's play *Another Country* provides another literary example in which issues of classism arise.[95] In fact, the play deals explicitly with social class and stratification, people who aspire to higher education, and what their roles are to be. The play is set in England (Eaton). Mitchell and Saker describe the classist nature of the public school system there. They virtually expose public education as "the big lie" by attempting to show that class lines are so deeply embedded that people's roles are predetermined. One student responded to the play by saying: "I grew up in Flint. Unfortunately, I came from a G.M. family so I was not part of the high-bred society. And I knew that. I mean I knew there were certain people that I did not hang out with. I knew what was expected of me." Another responded this way:

> I heard how in inner city schools their [the kids'] parents may not have enough money, but they send their five-year old to school dressed to the hilt because if they didn't, the child would be placed in a lower track. . . . The popular kids in the smart tracks were always dressed well. If you were in athletics, you were allowed to slide off on some a little bit. When you went to school you knew who the crowd was.

Both the students' responses/stories and the literary and professional texts read seemed to open spaces for more of that culture work Freire calls "dissociation."[96] Issues raised here by students and other issues raised in this chapter need to be thoroughly critiqued in teacher education classes—in other words, I perceive that prospective teachers need a chance to say what's right and what's wrong with this picture and how might it look if things were different.

In taking this position, however, I presume many will argue that it is a waste of time to imagine things being other than the way they are; those who do not find value in raising possibilities for other ways of being will argue that what we ought to be about is helping students and teachers-to-be find ways of functioning realistically within the world as it is. They may also argue that preparing students and teachers-to-be for a world we do not have yet leaves them ill-prepared to deal with things as they are. To that I would argue to prepare students and teachers for today and tomorrow we need to teach less narrowly, in less technical functionary ways, and in ways that challenge current practices or the world will never be different. If students and teachers learn to think more critically, using critical literacy skills to interrogate power and to examine relationships between knowledge and truth, then they will be able to make intelligent decisions today and tomorrow. If we create spaces for the voices, languages, and cultures of all students and teachers to challenge assumptions both locally throughout all content areas and in wider contexts, then schools will be a place to do as Weiler suggests, "to reshape knowledge and values."[97]

Although those who argue against practices that challenge tradition may not be willing to argue that things are quite okay the way they are, they may argue that there's no benefit in trying to change current situations because "the machinery is too big," or they might see most any change as simply a trend. I would argue, on the other hand, that teachers-to-be and all students need opportunities to examine and perhaps deconstruct their own assumptions about how things are, whether they perceive them as okay or not, and about women's roles and their situations as teachers so that they might pose possibilities for future otherwiseness.

The reasons both the general public and those in education often give for not seeing the value in a curriculum of critique and possibility are as vast as the possibilities capable of being raised in critical discussions. Additionally, there is the perception that choosing any course or option over another privileges one and marginalizes the other, and I will admit my own complicity in such actions. But that being the nature of exclusionary practices, we might all do well to entertain the otherwiseness of a practice that does not exclude but that finds creative ways to include. For example, although my own political agendas become quite apparent in the readings I choose, the dialogical nature of my classroom (also a political choice) permits students to contest readings of the texts I've selected and those they have selected through discussions that contest my political/ideological views. Those (perceived) contestations, theirs and mine, difficult as they may be, offer rich terrain for critique and thus for posing alternatives. (I suggest "perceived contestations" here to make a point about the nature of my perceptions and students' and to suggest that sometimes despite our best intentions the socialized roles students have learned may mediate against such contestations. In Chapter 5 I thoroughly discuss students' socialized roles and how their social and political positions affect their voicings in class.)

Therefore, although I argue for curricular content and form that allows for critique and possibility raising, I am not suggesting that finding creative ways of meeting what I perceive to be students' immediate needs (though perhaps not specific lessons, at least, how to create classroom conditions for teaching critical thinking/critical literacy) and what they perceive are immediate needs is not also very important and something I value. (In some classes, students' immediate needs may be to find the voice to counter my agenda.) I recognize the tenuous nature of student and teacher relationships and how those unequal relations have helped create in both experienced and inexperienced teachers the need for greater certainty. But this is perhaps the most important reason to argue for creating spaces that value imagining a future in which all school teachers and their work with all school children becomes an opportunity for countering the status quo/the sameness of schooling practices/the socialized roles of both students and teachers and for making culture relevant to their lives.

I share Weiler's conviction that schools *can* be sites of learning despite their being state institutions that seem to reproduce social institutions by controlling the status quo—a conviction echoed in the writings of Giroux, McLaren, Giddens, and others.[98] That's why studying the various ways in which all learners make sense of schooling seems to be an important place to begin an emancipatory project. To borrow Weiler's words again, "Both teachers and students are human beings who create meaning and who can reshape the knowledge and values of the past for their own uses."[99]

I assume that professional readings and research narratives (like Weiler's) alongside literary texts like those discussed in this chapter can enhance if not begin the process of reshaping knowledge and values because readers are invited into more critical spaces where discussions of power and its distribution or questions about gender, culture, and ideology may occur and where life as usual may be contemplated and then imagined as if it could be otherwise. Though my focus here has been on pairing unlike texts, again I do not mean to suggest that such pairings are the only way to educate for critical consciousness. In Chapter 5 I explore schooling narratives that focus on student voice and position as they emphasize the continual process of reshaping dominant, residual, and emergent meanings and practices.[100]

CHAPTER 5

Turning the Gaze:
Student Voice and Position
in Schooling Narratives

"Talk hard."[1]

Frequently in episodes of "Welcome Back Kotter" we saw Kotter, the teacher, in roundtable discussion with students he disrespectfully called the "sweathogs."[2] The interesting juxtaposition of classroom dynamics that, on the one hand, suggested mutual respect, both labeled students and became an acceptable term for teachers to use, on the other. What could be harmful about the loveable Kotter calling students whom he obviously liked sweathogs? And students obviously liked him in return as is witnessed by their frequent visits to his apartment. So what's in a word? Do teachers in everyday life feel the way Kotter seemed to feel when they use unfair labels? Were Kotter's students not victimized at times with the very labeling that seemed so innocent—victimized by the principal, for example? And what about Horshack's laughter? Could his laughter have revealed clues to suggest that sometimes the most innocent words/names are demeaning? Can words convey what actions cannot and vice versa? We and our students may need to be more discriminating when faced with sitcoms that seem harmless enough remembering that nearly all books and media present a particular image of the world. Kotter's practices may, on the one hand, seduce us into seeing him as a progressive teacher, and his language speaks, on the other hand, to that unconscious or perceptual understanding that is much more difficult to change.

Furthermore, what sitting in a circle suggested may have been much more than the mere fact of an upcoming discussion (which,

153

of course, is not a mere fact at all in some classrooms). Examining the social dynamics of holding class as a roundtable may suggest a basis for authenticating student voice and position. In other words, voice has as much to do with mutual respect as simply getting a turn to speak. It has to do with the special understanding that words can get things done in the world, but they can also do more. Words are for expressing thoughts, feelings, emotions; words are for expressing understanding that leads to action; words are for expressing relationship. Communication, then, may be seen as language that regulates relationship as Carol Gilligan writes *In a Different Voice*:

> [Communication includes] the discovery that responsiveness to self and responsiveness to others are connected rather than opposed. . . . [That discovery comes] by sustaining the web of connection so that no one is left [out]. . . . We know ourselves as separate only insofar as we live in connection with others[;] we experience relationship only insofar as we differentiate other from self.[3]

Additionally, to consciously make a place for words (as in a conversation or group discussion) is also, whether consciously or not, to imply that the spaces in between words are important. These spaces often negatively referred to as "silence" can be positively instantiated if we consider what Maxine Greene refers to as the place of consciousness or meditation in which thought occurs.[4] Or to what Ruth Vinz refers in a brief essay entitled "Silences" as the time for constructing meaning. She says, "Sound and silence are both acts of interpreting and imagining. . . . Silence suggests time for fluidity and indeterminacy: both positive strategies for idea formulation."[5] Though at first glance, her ideas may seem contrary to Bakhtin's position on the social construction of meaning as multivocal,[6] relying not on individual understanding but on community, if examined more fully, Vinz's notion may imply rather the necessary moments between utterances in group discussions that signal one's thoughts framing on the heels of another's. It is again then in the seeming contradictory space, the space of both/and, that perhaps a necessary part of sense making occurs—the sort that is born of what Derrida refers to as "differance" or deference or deferring absolute interpretation.[7] In any case, this space for thinking, reflecting, deferring may be critical in the sense that at the very juncture where uncertainty lies, a space may have been created for forging new meanings, practices, alternative ways of being in the world.

Dialogue then, as Freire reminds, is not an "empty instructional tactic."[8] Instead, it may be a vehicle through which to evoke contemplation over good literature as Margaret Buchman suggests.[9] Or the place where student voice is authenticated—where thoughts, feelings, and experiences are validated. For as Greene writes in *The Dialectic of Freedom*, "Without thought or 'freedom in relation to what one does' [quoting Foucault], there is little desire to appear among others and speak in one's own voice."[10]

In other words, I can think, puzzle out, evaluate, try to detach myself from my own circumstances in order to see what obstacles constrain my freedom and the freedom of others; I can name these obstacles as problems; I can politicize them by examining the possible power relations that might interfere and pose alternative arrangements; I can even name those arenas in which it might be important to voice my own and others' grievances.[11] I may not, however, be immediately capable of accomplishing all that I wish to accomplish. Yet without such reflective shuffling back and forth—wrestling with social and political realities in a kind of intersubjective space—I may not garner enough social imagination to reshape even the slightest wrinkle in my otherwise possible world.

Furthermore, the politics of voice and position and who's looking at who has much more to do with status in the classroom than with mere room arrangement. That is, voice and position have to do with "dialogue across differences" as Nicholas Burbules and Suzanne Rice suggest.[12] I may be a white female with working-class roots, but in my classes and despite my resisting particular internalized constructs of authority, nonetheless, students tend to see me as an authority. Here position relates once more to a kind of hegemonic governance—not so much to a rule in the sense of a direct political form of domination, but to a process whereby position is regulated by a "complex interlocking of political, social, and cultural forces."[13]

Discussions of position need then to examine differences both horizontally in terms of race, gender, and class and across hierarchies that exist in schools in order to form a critique that challenges power and authority. Regardless of how teachers see their roles (i.e., whether they see themselves in a traditional authoritarian role or whether they see themselves as a facilitator of dialogue), the political reality of classrooms seems to suggest that students still see their teachers as authority figures. Nonetheless, dialogue, though difficult, may be one of the few approaches available to teachers that, perhaps, momentarily disengages or decenters power and creates the possibility of reconstructed subject positions. As such, dialogue may have the potential to lead to "understanding, cooperation, and accommodation [that] can sustain differences within a broader compact of toleration and respect."[14] If we politicize notions of voice and position that include issues of race, class, and gender differences—in other words, if we examine those constructs in a larger sense according to structures of inequality that exist within the wider society—we may with our students be encouraged to critique power differentials that exist both among members of small groups and across whole classrooms both laterally and hierarchically. Not merely then do important questions like "Who has the right to speak?" "Who feels safe to speak?" "Who has the opportunity to speak?" "Whose ideas will be tolerated?" need to be asked, but also questions like "Who has the right to know?" or even "Who has the right to question?" become crucial. And all are questions that push us to consider the politics of student voice and position. In the following pages I examine student voice and position through literature and other popular media that illuminate such issues through students' perceptions.

THE POLITICS OF STUDENT VOICE

In *Pump up the Volume,* Mark, the son of the new commissioner of education in a small Arizona town, shakes up that system in this anti-establishment movie that shows what happens when students insist on those rights.[15] In the "wasteland" of Hubert Humphrey High, students do not "march to the beat of a different drummer"; they don't march at all. They seem scarcely alive, that is, until Mark, alias "hard-on Harry" arrives. Quiet by day, up to what appears at first to be little more than sexual debauchery by night, Mark becomes the eyes and ears of the school.

Having just left school and friends in New York City, Mark is not adjusting well to suburbia or to his new high school, where both students and teachers lack spirit and where "'yuppiedom' is rampant," to quote Mark. Mark's father's answer to this problem is a citizen's band radio intended to allow Mark to stay in touch with friends back East. After failed attempts to connect with old friends, Mark's loneliness and feelings of being dispossessed lead him to patch into an unused radio frequency at 10:00 P.M. where he becomes his own one-person show—and a voice. As popularity of this pirated talk show grows, Mark becomes both the voice and the listening ear to every lost and lonely teenager at Hubert Humphrey High—what he calls symptomatic of a sick society. With a new girlfriend who echoes his own divestiture, Mark virtually brings down the school and with it the principal who has expelled every student whose scores would interfere with the school's ranking.

In the New Line Cinema production *Pump up the Volume*, the audience experiences with Mark the direct implications of a kind of social sterility mechanism that needs to be explored. As Jenny's story (Chapter 3) of the process of sterilizing, filling, and capping milk bottles suggests, students filled on the pap of multiple-choice "official school knowledge" may resemble capped and sterile milk bottles with no ability to think, make decisions, or question dominant interests.

The autobiography of Rosemary Sutcliff entitled *Blue Remembered Hills* provides another interesting example of a kind of questioning the system.[16] Rosemary, however, is writing about her life as a small child inflicted with arthritis often confined to hospitals. Nonetheless, this portrayal suggests the kind of questioning that older students (especially teachers-to-be) might take up with respect to reading materials/literature for young women that perpetuates a particular form of feminization through sex-role stereotyping. The emphasis on voice here is reflected in Rosemary's raising these issues in a wider forum so that her story/autobiography enters the larger debate on textbooks and imaginative literature and the selective tradition.[17]

Throughout this autobiographical account of Rosemary's formal and informal schooling, she raises the issue of females not having an opportunity to see themselves doing exciting, adventurous things in books. Nearly all of her favorite adventures featured males having all the fun except in a few books like *Emily of New Moon* and *Anne of Green Gables* by L. M. Montgomery.[18] One moment stands out in particular, however. That is, when Rosemary's mother decided that it was time for Rosemary to learn to read for herself (Rosemary's mother had always read to her avidly), she introduced a book about a rosy-faced family who lived next door and had cats who sat on mats. Rosemary's response was that if this is what she would have to read if she had to read by herself, then it would be better not to learn to read at all. She would just refuse to read and her mother would continue to read exciting books to her. How could choppy sentences with boring characters and no plot replace adventure stories from Robert Louis Stevenson, Hans Christian Anderson, and Rudyard Kipling—especially, "Puck of Pook's Hill"—and Greek and Roman mythology? How could she continue to meet the likes of the rosy-faced family when she had fought alongside Beowulf in the dark halls of Heriot?[19]

As Rosemary questions conventional wisdom, she does more. She voices her desires. Rosemary's contestation pushes us to examine the fallacies of primer reading texts as a kind of textual authority. But more, her voice may challenge us to consider questions like, How might such an imposition affect Rosemary who comes from a print-rich environment in which reading is valued and certain texts are privileged by contrast to the child for whom none of these features are in place? Language arts students, English teachers-to-be, seem to find this particular text useful in several ways: for example, as a means of engaging questions related to early reading instruction and a kind of political economy of basal readers, as a statement on student voice and resistance that makes sense to them, and as a site of discussion about the privileging of some texts over others.

Additionally, as *Blue Remembered Hills* is examined with respect to early reading instruction that coincides with language learning and that later may affect one's sense of self, voice, and ability to debate ideas and issues in larger contexts, it may also encourage a class critique with respect to cultural boundaries and limitations imposed by particular curricula. If we examine Rosemary's early learning environment against other early learning environments and her autobiography against, for example, Lisa Delpit's essay entitled "The Silenced Dialogue: Power and Pedagogy in Educating Other People's Children,"[20] we may be led to consider what Mina Shaughnessy argued were the tensions between format and freedom.[21]

That argument, though framed against a situation in which white teachers teach black children, seems to be Delpit's point of contention. Delpit writes about issues of power that are enacted in classrooms: She describes the selective traditions that are presented in textbooks by developers of curriculum who tend to present a dominant or mainstream view of culture. In this discussion, Delpit sends an urgent but explicit message that those in power subvert the potential for those who have little or no power when they do not directly teach the codes for participation in society. Related to linguistic forms, communicative strategies, and ways of presenting one's self, she states that teachers need to explicitly address "ways of talking, ways of writing, ways of dressing, and ways of interacting [because] . . . [t]hose who are less powerful in any situation are most likely to recognize the power variable most acutely."[22]

Delpit's essay appears to become a debate over skills approaches and process approaches. Yet what experienced teachers and prospective teachers might question is not so much the methodological debate, though that may be important, but, instead, they might question the particular formulations of power suggested in the essay as desirable, something to attempt to gain access to, and so forth. Here as in other attempts to clarify issues of power, teacher work is not seen in relation to the wider society (with the exception of noting how particular commodified methods or particular commodified reading experiences over others may offer consumers of those experiences access to the culture of power). In this instance, students might be challenged to question who belongs to this culture of power and where teachers of all races fit in. Students might further question the seeming commodified nature of texts and experiences; that is, how are those texts and experiences valued and in relation to what (Are they valued as marketable commodities and at what price?), and who decides that they are of value? The relation of student voice and resistance to particular learning experiences may also be questioned here.

The latter relation may be important as it relates to children of all cultures because what seems to be missing in both cases (Sutcliff's and Delpit's) is the understanding that not one formula for all children works best—neither one method of teaching reading nor one kind of literature (especially when the most common form of early childhood reading in schools is from controlled readers or books in basal series that not only control the readability but the language and the view of the world that is presented.) If Sutcliff's teachers had recognized her background and wiggled the fit, she might have had better early schooling experiences. If the teachers of the children Delpit writes about had considered their backgrounds and wiggled the fit, their learning experiences might have been more meaningful to them. The problem arises not because of particular methods, but because it is deemed that one method works best in all situations.

But neither Delpit's argument nor Sutcliff's seems peculiar to method. Both arguments seem to deal with content and especially with worldview. You may recall that what Sutcliff objected to was the rosy-faced family who had cats that sat on mats; she also objected to three-word sentences and boring plots. Remembering also then that not only had she been exposed to what might be called adventure literature (perhaps because she had few adventures herself and could experience the world vicariously through books), but also that she herself was arthritic, confined to her bed most of the time, and spent long periods of time in the hospital unable to attend school, it may seem little wonder that she resisted reading about a world that not only would she have difficulty believing existed but also that did not transport her to a more favorable and exciting environment.

In Delpit's case, if what black children are suppose to be familiar with when they come to school is mainstream white culture, then what mainstream teachers, publishers, and so on must be expecting is that the only materials and cultures they will have been exposed to at home is mainstream white culture, regardless of social class, economics, and education. It may be an overlooked phenomenon, however, that perhaps the more well educated a family the more that family will wish to educate children about the particular culture from which they come by making sure, for example, that black children read African stories, and so forth.

And just as Rosemary's refusal to read uninteresting books was marked by her "silence" illuminating a kind of voiced statement of resistance,[23] Sarah's silence in *Children of a Lesser God*, though not only a statement of resistance, also illuminates a whole range of feelings with respect to language, speaking, and authentic voice.[24] Sarah is deaf and refuses to learn to speak except through sign, which she believes is the only language she needs (she believes hearing speakers make fun of nonhearing ones). As a text for study, what this film may reveal is the way in which society tends to expect those who are different to change to meet particular criteria that someone else establishes. In this instance, the particular change is teaching those who sign to learn to speak in order to communicate with others rather than teaching others to sign in order to communicate with those who are deaf (even her mother never learned to sign). In the movie, sign language seems valued only in that it acts as a vehicle of communication between student and teacher. The school's and the teacher's (Jim Leeds) philosophy is that deaf children need to learn a total system of communication—signing, speaking, lip reading, or they will be disenfranchised. In one scene at a party where Jim was the only hearing person; however, he seemed disenfranchised in contrast to the communicative abilities of the deaf children.

As the story unfolds, Sarah (who was a student in the school and is now employed by the school) and Jim become lovers, and Sarah begins to think Jim doesn't really want to help her; rather, he wants to change her. Sarah believes that part of his mission as her friend and lover is to make her like him. In a moment of anger and resistance, she tells Jim that he will not be capable of entering her silence and knowing her unless he learns to speak her language—unless he learns to sign. Though Sarah's resistance may be seen as personal, it tends to evoke a critical response from student-teachers with respect to the political motivation for teaching/changing others.

That the relationship is both male/female and teacher/student (not that Sarah is literally in Jim's class) seems to offer students a particularly familiar lens through which to critique personal relations and subsequently by extension to classroom relations. Sarah's comment that Jim wants her to learn to speak so she'll be like him invites readers of this film text to consider the various political formations in both personal and professional relations in which dominant/subordinate binarisms exist.

Teachers-to-be seem to recognize almost intuitively that their years of education have been almost a process of colonization. Teacher-educators especially seem to run the risk of being thought of as colonizers because we tend to want prospective teachers to teach the way we teach, to value what we value, and in short, to be like us when they graduate.[25] In fact, I have had graduate students come to me for advice asking what they need to study in order to "look like me" when they graduate. This mirroring effect is in some sense what Gilligan suggests is responsible for our coming to name "the other" in relationships.[26] Reading the passage from Gilligan and interrogating the idea of seeing all that does not resemble us as the other seems to help teachers dig into this film and work through some of the less obvious tensions.

At this juncture we also discuss how telling stories as they spin off films we view and books we read often reveal painful experiences that begin to help us honor each others' otherness. As one student said (and a lot here depends on how much any person is willing to share of herself or himself at any particular time), "sometimes knowing someone's pain makes them seem more real." At least it makes us seem more multidimensional, and it reveals to others and ourselves many of the experiences we've had both positive and negative that form our identities and show us what we know and can do. And that as Raymond Williams says when he describes the philosopher Vico's response to Descartes is the "criterion [for] . . . full knowledge." In other words, "We can have full knowledge only of what can ourselves make or do."[27]

Perhaps then in terms of teaching and learning, what most needs to happen is something that will draw out or bring forth from what Louise Rosenblatt has called the "deep well-spring of cerebration,"[28] what we know and can do from experience so that as teachers/learners we can help students build on that. I perceive that the sort of narrative work expressed here can enhance those moments. And I assume that conjuring up the imaginative flow of juices that seems to occur through aesthetic endeavors brings about that narrativization more readily. One is perhaps more apt to share any experience (painful or joyous) more honestly (at least as honestly as that person is capable of knowing/doing at that particular moment) under the gentle sway of literary subject matter. And critical readings seem to add dimension and texture to conversation that in the best of all possible worlds may evoke critique that moves students/teachers-to-be closer to *their* desired goals (and perhaps mine for them).

From this point, prospective teachers are encouraged to ask "Whose purposes does Leeds' teaching or any teaching serve?"[29] (The one student in Leeds's class that he can't get through to is also like Sarah—resists accommodating others to serve their needs.) The movie does not end with Sarah learning to speak or Jim learning to sign as one might imagine from the many movies/stories that resolve with the couple living happily ever after. Instead, Jim and Sarah decide to try to negotiate a place to meet that is neither in silence nor in sound.

Not unlike Sarah's silence that voices her resistance, Jerry Renault (in Robert Cormier's *The Chocolate War*) provides another example of student resistance when he refuses to sell chocolates for a school fund-raiser.[30] Though, Jerry's resistance begins as a part of an initiation rite ordered by a gang, it ends with Jerry's resisting on principle nearly everything his Catholic high school represents. Even so, Jerry's resistance may be construed as personal rather than political.[31] Student-teachers may find the difference in personal resistance and that which is political by comparing *Roll of Thunder, Hear My Cry* to *The Chocolate War*.[32] If students compare these books they may come to understand that resistance can be both personal and political at the same time. For in Mama Logan's case, helping children learn about African history can easily be perceived as personal, yet it is also political because she is resisting the white power of Harlan Granger and the school board. In Jerry's case, it may be true that he doesn't want to sell chocolates, but in not selling them he takes on the powerful arrangements operating in his school both in terms of the gang he resists and Brother Leon. What is perhaps more important to question than whether resistance is political or personal is what is the ultimate effect of that resistance? Mama Logan was fired, but she stood up for what she believed. Jerry was badly beaten up for daring to disturb the universe at Trinity High. Yet in neither case did anything change, the powers that be continued on.

Examples like this may lead inexperienced and experienced teachers to think that resisting bestowed curriculum or standing up for personal freedoms is of little consequence. Indeed, experienced teachers often have their own tales to tell about resisting and losing. Therefore, it seems especially important to tackle issues of resistance critically by raising questions that lead to a consideration of the price we pay personally, morally, and ethically when we don't resist powerful arrangements that enact the unconscionable.

In distinguishing forms of resistance, Giroux also raises similar questions. Because it may be the effects of resistance that help us clarify what price, Giroux's commentary relative to naming political projects seems an important angle to consider. Therefore, I often include the following passage from *Teachers as Intellectuals* to help frame discussion related to resistance and cultural and ideological dimensions of teaching. Giroux's explanation includes the way in which resistance is often taken up (which may, of course, relate to its overall effects). He writes that "on some occasions [resistance is] seen as a cynical, arrogant, or even naive rejection of oppressive forms of moral and political regulation."

Furthermore, he suggests that resistance as a form of counterhege-
mony "implies a more political, theoretical, and critical understanding [of] the nature of domination and the type of active
opposition it should engender."[33]

Resistance to domination appears to be what is behind Annie
John's erasure in the novel *Annie John* by Jamaica Kincaid.[34] This
story details Annie John's formal and informal schooling on the
island of Antiqua. At the end of a long illness that seems to mark
Annie John's feminist awakening, she literally awakens to find
that in her delirious state she has erased from her family portrait
all the faces of the people in her life who have attempted to make
her what they thought she should be—who would have made her
exactly like all the other girls growing into women on that island,
groomed to be feminine and subservient (terms used almost syn-
onymously in the book). Her erasure seems to erase the possibility
of standardization, as it signals the beginning of a new life. She
leaves her family to pursue a career—albeit a career in nursing.
One might argue that the socialization process could not be so
easily or completely erased because Annie John moved to escape
one caretaking role directly into another.

Students might contrast this text with the movie *Pump up the
Volume*[35] to discuss whether Annie John's resistance to domination
would be capable of helping to put an end to domination. Students
might consider whether or not Annie John served as a role model
for any of the other females on the island and whether or not her
leaving could have given them strength to follow their own pursuits.

Although *Pump up the Volume* does appear to be an anti-
establishment film resisting domination on a larger level, the text
lends itself to other relevant questions as well. That is, in addition
to illuminating problems around issues of self-determined thinking and voicing one's resistance, it tackles the standardization
issue. In the film, standardization is addressed on several levels: It
seems to represent a kind of monolithic voice or discourse that
implies a unified structure with a single purpose, and in particular,
the issue of test scores and school rankings can be problematized.[36] Though the testing issue is one that teachers are familiar
with, the real issue here may be that of the school's standards and
how those standards tend to structure inequality while carefully
maintaining social classes.

As one teacher recently reported in conversation, "Every time
I give a test, I feel like I am sentencing some kids to the streets."

What she may be suggesting is that the very tool she uses to measure her students' learning tends to be the same tool that ensures their destinies.

A selection from children's literature, *First Grade Takes a Test*, by Miriam Cohen illustrates this point.[37] To Anna Maria, a first-grader, the multiple choice questions on a standardized test are easy. But when the scores are in, Anna Maria finds herself in a precarious situation. She has been reassigned to a special class [I read as gifted] due to her test scores. The remainder of the book is dedicated to Anna's clever finesse as she arranges her return to her original classroom. Cohen attempts to reinforce to her readers through Anna's experiences that tests do not measure all things.

Imagine a child's experience reading this book. Though Cohen shows Anna's strength in dealing with her situation (not wanting to be moved to a special class)—in overcoming her obstacle— what readers may be impressed with is an early fear of what tests can do and how tests can virtually lock them in or lock them out. Whereas Anna Maria contested the results through cleverness, she quickly realized that her voice carried little weight against the more powerful voice of the test scores. She could not simply state that she did not wish to be moved to this special class, but instead had to use finesse to rejoin her regular classroom.

But perhaps more important to consider/question here than the issue of test scores is the issue of texts that seem to participate in some kind of ideological regulation.[38] How words, images, and experiences are taken up in the mind of a reader/viewer seems to be an important topic of inquiry for experienced and inexperienced teachers. What meanings readers make of Anna's experience—that is, whether they focus on Anna's strong will or whether they see how important her family and the school feels it is for her to be moved to a program for gifted and talented children—may affect not only how they view themselves but also how they view what school, parents, and society values. As Maxine Greene reminds us in *Teacher as Stranger*, "The function of art is to make people see. What they see and how they see are greatly dependent on the way the materials of a given work are formed."[39] And I would add that how art is seen may be equally dependent on how issues represented through that art are taken up both in one's intersubjective reality and in one's sociopolitical reality. In other words, even though children may understand the difference in reality and a representation of reality, in actual school settings how often do children see other children taken out of regular classes and sent to special classes (either for remediation or enrichment) and how often do they see those same children having no control over their own destinies—no say in the matter? And the issue of special classes marks perhaps one of our most needed both/and constructs—in other words, classes that no longer exclude through tracking but that help children with difficulties and enrich them all in the same class. It is possible that the same child can have both needs.

Several readings from Feinberg and Soltis's *School and Society* text provide anecdotal material that may help teachers and teachers-to-be critique films and texts that deal with the standardization issue.[40] For example, the dialogue of four teachers in the excerpt entitled "The Roots of School Failure" raises questions about what constitutes school success. Additionally and perhaps more directly linked with questions of success and class reproduction is an excerpt entitled "Social Reproduction." From the latter we have a critique of school and society close to that which Mark in *Pump up the Volume* recognizes and plays out in his evening talk show:

> . . . what do we actually do to the students in the institutional setting of an ordinary school like ours? We train them to accept unquestioningly life in a mindless bureaucracy, that dominant form of institutional life in our society. We blunt their creativity, individuality, and interest in learning by lock-stepping them through a system designed for monotonous mass production. We encourage competition, discourage the cooperative use of knowledge, and stress the selfish possession of it. The students repeat what we tell them, and the measure of success is a grade that can be "banked."[41]

Regardless of the particular focus, all cases in this chapter provide material for helping teacher education students critically and reflectively examine schooling issues. When paired with books, poems, paintings, and films, critical texts may help tap imaginative possibility. Though the cases presented in the Feinberg/Soltis text are greatly more contextualized than some readings, when paired with movies like *Pump up the Volume* or the television classic "Welcome Back Kotter" that dramatize pressing educational issues like the politics of student voice and especially position, both the critical text and the imaginative text may come to life.

By contrast to the measure of success in the *School and Society* passage, Jesse Stuart did not measure success by the degree to which he could perform what teachers had taught him or what his own students could repeat. His autobiography *To Teach, To Love* is his own story of schooling—both from the perspective of a student going to school and then as teacher learning what it means to be a teacher.[42] The son of relatively uneducated parents and a first-generation college graduate himself, Jesse seemed to have a special understanding of what students growing up in small towns saw as purposes for attending school. Although many academic pursuits often seemed meaningless, creative writing seemed to hold a special fascination because he (and later his students) seemed to use writing in a way that helped them to make sense of their everyday experiences. Writing seemed to be a way to make what might seem mundane to others unique and special. Writing was a way of expressing through words the feelings that were attached to lived experiences.

This book easily pairs with Eliot Wigginton's *Sometimes a Shining Moment*.[43] Both authors suggest writing as a means of helping students explore their own experiences as well as the experiences of others. And both authors see writing as one place in the curriculum to help students recognize their potential. Additionally, they stress the importance of students writing for audiences other than teacher—in other words, taking students words into the world through some kind of publishing experience—as a way of helping students take ownership in their work and as a way of motivating them to continue to see themselves as having a voice or participating in a kind of cultural production.

It is the latter purpose for writing that prospective teachers might need to explore in greater depth. Many fine (professional) writing texts suggest the very same things that the authors of these books illustrate contextually—that is, having genuine purposes for writing that student's name, having audiences beyond the teacher, publishing, and so forth. Yet besides the fact that writing texts are largely decontextualized in terms of illustratively creating the world of the writing classroom and beyond, few address the issue of what it means to write and send that writing out into the world as a part of a wider cultural statement or debate. That, of course, has not been typically seen as part of the purview of schooling. Functioning as a part of the wider society is something reserved for adults, and those adults who have a say in how society regulates particular relations are a privileged few. Occasionally, a student passes through who shows promise, but usually that promise is not measured by how well the student speaks out against or confronts the status quo but on how well he or she is perceived to be capable of perpetuating it. Taking a stand that is out of agreement—that goes against the grain—not only goes unrewarded but also is likely to be penalized. And this is where teachers might want to explore the potential of writing as a form of cultural production.

Where schools have traditionally been in the business of reproducing the various social systems that in are place, we might explore the uses of writing, then, to begin a reconceptualization of those various systems. Philosophers' words have long explored systems of thought by reconceptualizing and expressing in new ways age-old ideas. Scientists have done the same. Fiction writers create worlds sometimes through replication, sometimes through a fantastic re-presentation of futuristic visions. Artists attempt this on canvas. Yet regardless of the medium, people not systems write tradition; we alone can practice the actors we are. So for teachers to understand the importance of working in ways that authenticate students' voices, the idea itself of what that voice is capable of and what that capacity means might need to be explored. Furthermore, in agreeing that a student's voice is legitimate, we are also agreeing that student experiences are legitimate and that not just their voices and their experiences but our legitimation of them are a part of a wider cultural struggle.

Perceptions of identity come together then with issues of voice and position when taken up in the context of historical and positional differences. Therefore, we need to create analytical spaces for understanding ourselves and others "as subjects of various struggles in history."[44]

Student-teachers have often related the hierarchical positioning of students to teachers and teachers to administrators, and so forth through a kind of worker analogue especially using terms like client/agent as markers of the worker/boss relationship. In Ford Maddox Brown's painting entitled "Work,"[45] Brown has conceptualized on canvas various classes of workers as a homogeneous community. Teachers-to-be seem to benefit from a reading of this canvas[46] that asks them to explore the language of "work" and how it is symbolically cast in terms of the absence of social classes—the absence of difference.

The irony of the painting itself is that Brown's recording of work may have actually embodied his vision of the world (allied with Pre-Raphaelites and against the backdrop of industrialized England), though the title "Work" seems to suggest the contrary (i.e., the word *work* in itself begs questions of positionality and value like Whose work? and What kind of work is regarded as work compared to management? etc.). Nonetheless, by examining the painting along with Mohanty's argument about attempts to normalize pluralistic societies in the essay "On Race and Voice,"[47] students may be encouraged to question the relational contexts in which both the work and the worker are cast positionally and how that positioning engages power and limits authentic voice/discourse in any community.

The particular passage by Mohanty that targets this concern describes the central issue as one of not simply accepting difference but of "the kind of difference that is acknowledged and engaged." Reading this passage against Brown's painting seems to evoke a critique that problematizes both Brown's homogeneous view of workers and questions what and who is valued in this regard. Mohanty says that when difference is seen as a kind of benign diversity instead of "conflict, struggle, or the threat of disruption, [it] bypasses power" as it overlooks history in an attempt to become a harmonious community. Likewise, as Brown's painting seems to depict all workers in a kind of a benign pluralism, it fails to acknowledge not only the differences in struggles within individual workers' lives but across workers in the workplace both laterally and hierarchically with and against management. When we examine difference within hierarchies of domination and resistance, a reading that suggests harmony may not be possible.[48]

POSITION: WHO'S LOOKING AT WHOM?

"What is it you want me to say?" defines a student speaking from a position of marginality. Students seem to know through many years of enculturation that the valued position in any schooling situation is the school boards', then the central office administrations', then the principals', then, finally, the teachers'. They may have, as Foucault suggests, a kind of transcendental anonymity when it comes to speaking/voicing that reveals their positionality. Foucault describes this negotiation between the speaking subject and her or his position in terms of an "enunciative domain" that refers "neither to an individual subject, nor to some kind of collective consciousness, not to a transcendental subjectivity, but to . . . an anonymous field whose configuration defines the possible position of speaking subjects."[49] Therefore, negotiation between voice and position seems to replace embodiment and is institutionally based.

How, then, is tradition and privilege responsible for this disembodiment? As Barthes describes it, it occurs in the "neutral, composite, oblique space where our subject slips away, the negative where all identity is lost, starting with the very identity of the body. . . . "[50] That is, the student embodied in experience is not taught to value experience, to value the subjective, to value the cultural knowledge he or she brings to the classroom. Instead, the educational/socialization process has taught students to leave the "I," the "me," and the "we" on the doorsteps of their homes. In school only "objectified" knowledge is valued, not anecdotal situations, not relations grounded in personal experience, and not presence but the absence of it. And students' own participation in disembodied positioning tends to justify its exclusion.

As the either/or dichotomy rears its ugly head once again, students are caught between seeing themselves *either* as grounded in "fact" and "theory" *or* steeped in experience. Because students have not been taught to value connections to experience that would perhaps help them understand that theories can grow out of "real" world experiences, they may not understand how to see new information they learn in school in relation to previous experiences in other contexts. They may not recognize the relationship between knowledge and experience. And perhaps as a result then of their inability to value what has not been legitimated as valuable, students see information as knowledge, not something to be turned into knowledge as it is construed against one's background of experience.

The student-teacher relationship as Freire conceives it may be the way in which to deconstruct this positionality and the relationship of knowledge to experience.[51] Out of a space created for freedom—for imagining new possibilities, a "becoming space" as Derrida named it,[52] is the potential to form a new contract between students and teachers. The new contract is conceived as lateral rather than hierarchical (teacher-as-learner and learner-as-teacher, a partnership of coinvestigators) and is not only based on a dismantled power differential, but it is also based in a new conception of knowledge—a revaluation of knowledge.

That is, in the new student and teacher or teacher-learner relationship, the learner, previously disenfranchised, is reinvested as the subject who Barthes reminds us "slips away" in a positional relationship.[53] Barthes's statement may also serve in this instance as a warning of the potential flux involved in new relations that reconfigure old relations of power. And we may heed that suggestion by considering all change involving language and what may be thought of as systems of valuation as social processes—not processes that remain fixed but what Raymond Williams calls "activity."[54] Under the new valuation system Freire posits (student-teacher relation or conception of knowledge), learners become the subjects, fully present in their own learning, meaning that the learners' experiences finally may be valued as legitimate sources from which to form new knowledge.[55] Under a (re)vised formulation (one that continues to be formed), it is not assumed that knowledge can be transmitted, passed down; rather, it is socially constructed in an ongoing process of sense making vis à vis experience. In positionality, the "banking" method sees students as the object of this received knowledge, as, indeed, filled with knowledge. In Freire's conception of the teacher-learner relationship, dialogical inquiry or learning through conversation and investigation replaces the banking approach. Moreover, in this newly conceived relationship, which may make possible the dislocation of position, teachers learn from students as students learn from teachers.[56] What I would like to suggest here, which may extend both Williams's and Freire's concepts, is that as a process it must be under constant negotiation, constant (re)valuation, always already being and always already becoming as experience is narrativized and meaning making is engaged. Then the new partnership may truly become a partnership because it is always already being negotiated between learners and teachers. In this sense, negotiation does not have to replace embodiment but may actually become an embodied activity. Furthermore, if we understand relationships as unequal relations that must work through struggles, conflicts, pain, and other markers of difference, then what is coinvesitaged may also be the relations in question so that what is valued both envelopes the personal and becomes a broader political project of valuation. What needs to be remembered here, however, is that in this country, at this particular moment in history, although we may be experiencing an interruption in the social order through which some teachers are able to form new relationships with students, the system itself has not undergone a rupture or break that would allow us to say that from this point forward we will act in this particular way. Teachers are not generally today as yesterday rewarded for being different. Their efforts to resist tradition or the status quo that is grounded in dominant interests, is, indeed, often trivialized as uncharacteristic of good teaching; therefore, teachers engaged in even covert forms of resistance are often penalized by administration and sometimes ignored or excluded by their peers.

If we can draw any encouragement from this, it might be to consider that the Brazilian tradition from which Freire writes "has not been to exchange ideas [either], but to dictate them; not to debate or discuss themes, but to give lectures; not to work *with* the student, but to work *on* him [or her], imposing an order which he [or she] has had to accommodate."[57] Freire states further that the existing system, one that gives "student[s] formulas to receive and store . . . [but does] not offer him [or her] the means for authentic thought, assimilation . . . re-creat[ion] and re-invent[ion] . . . could not prepare [students] for integration in the process of democratization."[58] If these methods, approaches, and so forth sound familiar, it is because they are. These, in fact, are many of the very traditions on which American education rests, if not overtly then covertly, if not stated as principles then accepted as values and traditions—even as we claim to be a democracy. Yet these are the traditions that create position.

On the last pages of a chapter entitled "Education as the Practice of Freedom" (in *Education for Critical Consciousness*), Freire makes problematic our notions of democracy as he discusses what he says Aldous Huxley calls a way to "dissociate ideas" by defending democracy rather than subverting it. He says that we subvert democracy when we make it irrational, when we make it rigid in order "to defend it against totalitarian rigidity," when we make it closed rather than open to possibilities out of insecurities and fear, and when we make it "an instrument of the powerful in the oppression of the weak."[59] On the other hand, we defend democracy when through education we practice the "art of dissociating ideas."[60] As Pagano and Grumet have often conceived of teaching in terms of art,[61] here Freire makes a similar association. As I have suggested in this text, we might use films, advertising, television programs, literature, music, and so forth as an "antidote to the domesticating power of propaganda."[62]

For example, as students' projects in one class examined gendered categories to practice Freire's "art of dissociating," one student examined perfume advertisements and wrote this:

> Perfume advertisements are among the most exploitive. . . .
> They sell sex and women's bodies. . . . One example of this is
> how a woman may not believe she is physically attractive. The
> ad reinforces this idea, but says "you can become sensuous
> with this perfume." [Others] sell fantasies, rather than perfume. . . . The nonverbal . . . becomes a means for drawing
> attention to verbal messages, but it [may] also become the message. In an ad for Masquerade perfume, the fantasy here is not
> quite obvious. The men and women are masked, providing
> them with total anonymity. Both are leaning against the railing;
> they can lose control and go over the edge at any moment. The
> pair is in a passion-consumed embrace, but if one examines the
> scene more closely she will see that the man is in complete control. He is active; she is passive. The man is removing the
> woman's clothing as she clings to him, tilting her head back,
> mouth open . . . [H]ers is a position of complete vulnerability.
> What this advertisement advocates in its subtle way is female
> submission, male domination. It is a mock-rape scene. In addition to the troubling foreground is the background scene—a
> roomful of people are sitting idly by as though nothing out of
> the ordinary is taking place. The ad helps to affirm the misconception that women want to be and fantasize about being
> raped.

In this instance, the student seems to begin to "discover the difference between education and propaganda."[63] Freire ends his discussion of education that teaches the practice of freedom by saying, "At the same time [students] are preparing themselves to discuss and perceive the same deceit in ideological or political propaganda, they are arming themselves to dissociate ideas" in order to defend democracy.[64] (See Chapter 7 for an example of how I use particular popular music as an opportunity to examine issues of violence against women.)

In a dialogical teacher-learner relationship such as that described by Freire, where education becomes the practice of freedom, the teacher, Pagano says, "has the power, in her gaze, to give one back to oneself; she has the power to subvert the father's text."[65] Therefore, in a space created for practicing freedom, if the teacher teaches from a new position, she or he may be capable of

acknowledging experience as the basis of knowledge, thereby subverting patriarchy and positionality. In the following passage,
Pagano articulates that cultural (re)positioning in terms of desire
(what Kristeva calls the primary drive toward "split-unification"[66]):

> Through this relationship students become participants in a cul-
> tural conversation. The teacher helps to initiate the student into
> that conversation. Teaching and learning unfold in the register
> of desire. Knowledge in the register of desire becomes a search
> for acknowledgement, for finding and forming oneself in the
> representations with which our world is written.[67]

Thus, it seems that position is located in power and knowledge,
and dislocated or relocated position is situated in experience, in
narrative, in the "representations with which our world is written." The narratives in this text are some of those representations,
both the stories told by other historians in another place and time
and those told by student historians who shape their worlds with
their words.

Within Sherwood Anderson's account of the committed men-
tor-teacher is an example of such a teacher-learner relation. In one
particular scene we see Kate Swift's passion as she attempts to cul-
tivate the young writer, George Willard. She reminds George that
in order to be a writer he will have to know life not just words.
She adds that he will have to know what people are thinking not
just what they are saying. And in this particular passage, connections are formed as Kate Swift attempts to bring George Willard
into the conversation.[68]

By contrast, in a particularly negative student-teacher relationship in which the hidden curriculum is perceptively understood, we see Benjie as he crosses his arms, sits back, and eyeballs
the situation in quiet resignation. *A Hero Ain't Nothing but a
Sandwich* shows how perceptively students understand where
they stand in position to both the school and the society. That is,
whose gaze is focused on whom?[69]

Alice Childress's novel opens with Benjie, a young black student, who has a serious drug addiction. Through a series of narra-
tions, this Harlem tale reveals itself in the idiom of the streets.
Our knowledge of Benjie's school life is presented from several of
his teachers' perspectives and from Benjie's viewpoint. It is from
Benjie's perspective, however, that we learn the hidden agenda of
his English teacher. Here we see the stereotypical banking teacher

who is the only authority in the class, the one with all the privileged right answers whose primary job it is to deposit knowledge through intimidation.

In one particular scene we get Benjie's take on the situation. Benjie says that he hates school; he even feels bad walking in the direction of the school—forcing himself to go where he does not belong. He says school teachers are "hard-eyed" people with "talkin" eyes who say one thing while their eyes are "screamin" something else. Benjie says that teachers will say open your books and turn to a certain page to read and this really means that they're not interested in hearing how good you read; instead, it means they want to show that you can't read at all, to call attention to your failings, inadequacies, problems. Benjie is clear about that hidden message as he iterates that teachers say one thing, but their eyes "be stonyin" on you saying another. His response to this treatment is silence.[70]

In *Education for Critical Consciousness*, Freire calls this teaching for a "culture of silence."[71] As in the *Hero* text, when students are subjected to language as well as values that make them feel as if they know nothing, silence may abound. To the teacher it may not appear that Benjie is thinking at all, yet I suspect that the ability of students to read through the masks of many teachers suggests their potential as thinkers, even critical thinkers. In this book it is not difficult for student-teachers to begin to understand the differences in the meanings students make of schooling and those teachers make. One particular assessment of this phenomenon may be revealed by asking simply what teachers think is happening in the classes represented and what students think is happening.

When we ask that question in my classes, I am almost always taken aback by the variation of answers none of which usually match what I think is happening. During one term, I asked students to keep a double-entry notebook,[72] and I gave them five minutes at the end of each class to write a sentence or two in the right-hand or observations column of their notebooks about what they thought had happened in class that day. Before coming to class again, they were to write in the left-hand column their personal reflections/connections to what they had written in the right column. We always began the next class by having a few volunteers read from both the observation side and the personal side of their journals. Across-class dialogue almost always occurred, but what most amazed all of us was how differently each of us interpreted what class was about (despite the risks associated and despite the extent to which students were willing to write honestly in their journals).

I valued that activity because it taught me a lot about what students perceive are hidden agendas in every classroom. But even though I valued that information, I have not continued to require journal keeping to that degree each term. For one thing the most common criticism of the class was the burden or "tyranny" as one student put it of keeping two journals: I had them keep a response-to-reading journal as well. At times, I have collapsed the two, asking for both the classroom-finding journal and the reader-response journal in one notebook.

When I do that, however, I feel almost as though students see the collapsed journal as another hidden agenda (my wanting to know what they think about class without my really saying so because many students still can't imagine that I think I could learn from them and believe that my argument is just a cover). In fact, occasionally a student will announce that perhaps teachers use reading journals not as I have suggested—as a place to think out-loud about their readings and as a springboard for class discussion—but as an unacknowledged agenda in journal keeping; that is, checking up on students' reading. Consequently, I never grade journals and I don't even read what students request that I not read. I do this in an effort to reduce some of what I discussed initially in this chapter as the effects of position on voice.

When I have discussed what students perceive to be hidden agendas in our class in connection with this particular text, *A Hero Ain't Nothing but a Sandwich*, I am quickly aware of how often students resist even fairly common schooling practices today—practices like journal keeping, reading aloud, sometimes being read aloud to. Many teachers-to-be have recalled situations when their tentativeness at reading aloud was misconstrued in one way or another and became an instrument of their own failure. For example, one student could read but simply had a problem with pronunciation so the halting speech was perceived as an inability to read. Another mentioned not liking to stand up in front of the class because other kids made fun of what she perceived was the way she looked; therefore, when she refused to stand up and read, she was sent out of the room and given a low grade on reading. She remembers this experience and tells it with pained expression saying, "I knew how to read, I just didn't want to stand up at my seat to do it."

Another student asked why she didn't just tell the teacher her problem in private, and Mary responded, "Because I didn't want to sit and read and be singled out then for getting to do this reading-aloud thing differently." One might think that Benjie and others who refuse to participate in a system that seems to delight in parading one's difficulties/struggles in front of others is a smart thing to do. However, Paul Willis's British study, *Learning to Labour: How Working-Class Kids Get Working-Class Jobs*, suggests otherwise.[73] He suggests that though students' reading of school and of particular teachers' intentions may be accurate, it serves, nonetheless, a socially reproductive function along class lines.

Childress's text seems to bear this out in Benjie's character. In other words, because of the ways in which schools are structured, the kind of thinking that pushed Benjie into silence may have also pushed him back into the streets.[74] This particular passage from John Ogbu ("Class Stratification, Racial Stratification, and Schooling") draws on Willis's cultural reproduction and resistance theory.[75] Juxtaposed with *A Hero*, it seems to help teachers-to-be politicize Benjie's story and produce personal connections that have political relevance: "Working-class and minority students reject school knowledge and meanings because they seem to understand that the kind of education they are receiving cannot solve their collective problem of subordination."[76] Ogbu says that when these kids either consciously or unconsciously reject school and turn to the workplace or the streets for legitimation and support in their resistance to white culture, they become a part of a counterculture that makes it virtually impossible to succeed in a dominant white man's school or society.[77]

Here I challenge students to question further why working-class and minority students seem to reject school knowledge if, indeed, they do. I encourage them to think further about what accepting it might mean. For example, what if what they accept perpetuates an interpretation of history that leaves them out, a history that is interpreted through white male privilege, and if acknowledges their history at all, acknowledges it in terms of compliance with their own oppression? Or I encourage students to ask whether or not it matters if working-class and minority students accept school knowledge. Would the results be different if, for example, black students accepted standard English forms? Would they immediately gain access to the "culture of power"? Would this mean having to "act white" in order to belong to this culture? And what does acting white mean? And what is deemed more desirable about mainstream culture that makes it worth it for a black man or woman to act white? Instead of perpetuating such unconscionable attitudes, shouldn't schools be the particular sphere in which such outrageous thinking is contested? These and other questions tend to help students politicize educational prospects for minority students and may suggest that there may be perhaps a more historically grounded cultural struggle operating here?

Telling the story of Weis's study *Between Two Worlds: Black Students in an Urban Community College* seems to help make that connection.[78] For example, Weis suggests that black students may not consciously reject school knowledge. She says that students participating in her study said that they saw getting an education as a means of escaping poverty. The behaviors she observed, however, tended to discount their statements. In other words, they were excessively tardy; they seemed not to care about schoolwork, and they did not persevere when things were difficult.

Though Weis is referring to particular participants, the tendency to generalize to a we/they construct is especially problematic here, and students are encouraged not to generalize. The "they" when referring to black students may be useful only when relating it to a collective identity that grows out of a collective struggle—an identity and struggle clearly different from that of mainstream or working-class whites.

A Hero Ain't Nothing but a Sandwich depicts black minority struggle as different from the struggles of working-class whites and also suggests struggle relationally between hierarchical structures of schooling and the black community from which Benjie comes.[79] In that way the book is related to the movie *Teachers,* through student to teacher hierarchical positioning that can be seen especially in the portrayal of the character Ditto.[80] Ditto is the nickname (given by students and adopted by teachers) of a teacher whose only contact with students is through the ditto master. Daily dittos are placed in a basket on his desk. As students enter the room, they pick up the ditto sheet for that day and work until the end of class. Ditto, the teacher, sits with his back to the group (perhaps a profoundly symbolic move in itself) and reads the newspaper in complete silence. Students perform their daily ritual passively and without question. This extremely sardonic commentary on a teacher teaching ends ironically when Ditto dies of a heart attack but is not noticed for days simply because he remains in exactly the same "sleeping teacher" position anyway.

The "commodification" question is also illuminated through the character, Ditto, and relates to how teacher-student position seems both to depend on and to perpetuate a redefinition of content and of the learning process itself. That is, according to Wexler, "unlike earlier emphases on the classroom as a micro-community, where social and civic learning takes place, what is now most important about effective education is the amount of time on task."[81] What students may be led to question here is where and how this redefinition of schooling practice occurs and where and how it is located within larger historical movements/processes. As prospective teachers take up the issue of what is commonly referred to as teacher deskilling (Ditto may have exemplified a version of a deskilled skilled worker,[82] but if we do not want to consider teachers as skilled workers then why continue to refer to their deskilling), they may further be encouraged to think about how students' own abilities are derailed when they have a teacher whose job seems to be surveillance.

By contrast, John Williams's novel, *Stoner*, is the story of how resistance to domination helps replace fear and begins to help John Stoner feel more comfortable expressing himself.[83] Set in the Midwest, *Stoner* is the story of a young man who attends college to study agriculture and falls in love with literature. After deciding to teach, he remains at the university through graduate school and is offered a faculty position after graduation. This schooling narrative is particularly rich with images of student-teacher relationships that display position and resistance in response to subordination.

In a relationship in which students are placed positionally with teachers, voice is denied as is literally the case in this portrait. Stoner's reaction to Archer Sloane's threatening voice and position is fear. Stoner, frozen in his seat, cannot answer, and Sloane makes it clear that he has the "privileged" right answer. Here students see Freire's banking teacher,[84] the only authority in the class, the one with all the right answers who deposits knowledge through intimidation.

The movie *Educating Rita* seems to epitomize the teacher-learner/mentoring relationship—at least, on the surface. That is, Rita learns from Frank and Frank learns from Rita if that is all we take a mentoring relationship to mean.[85] We may not, however, be able to say that their relationship is the precise student-teacher relationship Freire describes; albeit it does appear to be a relationship in which "the one-who-teaches . . . is himself taught," and they do appear to be in a relationship in which each learns from the other.[86] However, this seems to happen more out of Rita's insistence on being taught than on any negotiated joint responsibility for teaching/learning or curriculum.

Further, they do not appear to be critically coinvestigating the role literature plays nor reading it against the world, for example; rather, in Rita's view it is the "body of knowledge" through which she will learn social graces and become a "fair lady." The allusion to Eliza Doolittle and Henry Higgins is perhaps no accident as Rita's literacy narrative unfolds to reveal a kind of colonizing of Rita into the world of words and academic relations.[87]

Currently a hair dresser, Rita wants choices; she wants to cross boundaries or, at least, to dislocate them, and she believes education will provide those choices. For example, she wants a baby, but she secretly takes birth control pills so that she can have a baby when she decides (unfortunately, her husband burns her books when he learns of this). On the one hand, she is passionate about things that matter; on the other, we find her worried about learning social graces that will remove her uniqueness and make her like the status quo.

She returns to night school through the open university system. Her first encounter with her tutor, Frank, the teacher responsible for open university enrollees, is to barge into his office to discuss her enrollment. She is eager to learn, to read, to grow intellectually. She is also eager to abandon her working-class culture, which she believes can be accomplished through education.

Initially, Frank resists helping her become like everyone else—students who parrot back information on tests, who don't think original thoughts, and who have abandoned any uniqueness in the course of trying to fit in. But therein lies the contradiction with Frank. He seems to have the creator complex; he wants to "make" something of Rita. According to Frank, Rita is like clay to him—eager to learn, curious, eager to be formed.

Rita, who finally crosses enough boundaries to fit in with

some of the other students, decides to go away to summer school with a group of them. When she returns, she is way ahead of Frank. And Frank, in the traditional creator mode, takes credit for that too by confessing that he has created a Frankenstein—a thoughtless, culturally literate blend like "hollow men" and "dead poets." Rita gave up what Frank perceived to be her real life/her working-class life, which to her was no life at all, for a life of what he called hollow, intellectual pursuit.

What may be examined in this film is the nature of mentoring relationships and whose investment counts more. In other words, where does mentoring leave off and traditional teacher-pupil roles begin? And, how, in this most unequal system can equality between teachers and pupils occur? Is it possible to be different and not be in a relation of power? In the particular film, Rita got what she wanted; Frank regretted giving to the point that Rita outgrew her need for him (another issue that needs to be problematized). Rita lost her cultural rootedness, but she grew intellectually. What may be learned is that teacher-student relationships are special but tenuous relationships and that education is more than learning to read literature; it is also about valuing culture.

Students and teachers viewing this film may come to further understand the importance of an education that incorporates the stories of those who study not just the dead authors of "enduring" literature. This movie may also help to illustrate that sometimes the meanings students make of schooling do seem to exist because of the particular ways in which we teach, but other times meanings seem to be grounded in the particular perceptions students have about the purposes of schooling that may or may not have arisen solely because of how or what we teach. What may be important to question here are the differences in the ways teachers and pupils perceive those purposes, understanding too that sometimes one's perceptions and attitudes far outweigh any conscious effort on the part of either student or teacher and may exist despite the kind of relationship they themselves enjoy.

Another example of nontraditional student-teacher relationships can be seen in the novel *Journal of an Aleutian Year* by Ethel Ross Oliver.[88] This book is the account of a teacher's year long experience on Atka, a tiny island in the Aleutian chain. Through Oliver's portrayal of the circumstances concerning the Aleutian Islands during the second World War, she presents a rich picture of native life. She tells the stories of many who endured inhumane conditions in Japanese work camps. In the course of sharing what she learned from the people of Atka, Oliver describes a number of special teaching experiences.

For example, both she and students left the classroom to dig clams when the tide was out or to hunt deer, usually without actually participating in the kill. Or Oliver brought local people into the classroom to teach particular skills such as basketweaving in one instance. As students taught her the customs of their island, she taught them many things about the customs of other people in other areas. Through simply interacting as people who shared a mutual respect for what each had to offer the other, unique relations were formed.

Journal of an Aleutian Year compares with the film *To Sir with Love* in terms of the development of mutual respect, though not until late in the script of the latter.[89] The teacher, played by Sydney Portier, never planned to become a teacher, and his teaching style suggested initially that he thought teaching was simply a matter of giving instructions and having them followed. Students seemed to sense his lack of interest, and consequently, they resisted every assignment, playing the kinds of tricks that students often do with substitute teachers. The turning point came after a particularly offensive prank when both students and teacher seemed to realize that relationships depended on mutual respect.

From that moment on students and teacher set the curriculum together, planning field trips to parts of the city with which they were unfamiliar, to museums, and so forth. Though it may be problematic that visiting museums, for example, seemed to legitimate privileged art forms (but I do not perceive that this has to be case, for one can critique art forms in museums as readily as any other art); nonetheless, students became interested in their own cultural backgrounds, mostly working class. Students began to appreciate their personal histories (though heretofore they seemed not to understand that working-class families have important histories), and as a result self-esteem seemed to improve.

Student-teachers discussed this film against an essay entitled *Making History* that suggests ways for students and teachers to investigate their personal histories.[90] The essay suggests the following activity as a means of creating a sense of cultural/historical connectedness. The activity begins by asking students to remember and write about a time when their qualities, capabilities, and expertise were not only recognized but also acknowledged thus validated in some public way—a time when they felt a sense of inner strength. Before students write they may need to jotlist some of the factors, internal and external, that led to feelings of accomplishment and a sense of inner strength and confidence. Teachers should help students to recognize also that these moments do not have to be extraordinary or once-in-a-lifetime experiences; rather, such moments may occur in some everyday experience such as helping or being helped by a friend or family member. The following questions may also help students to visualize or re-experience the moment: What was the situation that created the particular feeling or sense of accomplishment/inner strength? Students are asked to be explicit describing in detail the setting in which this moment occurred. Also, were there other people around? What time of year was it? What else was happening in your life at the time? How did the other events make you feel? What inside you prepared you for this moment? Were others involved, and if so, how? How did you express your feelings to them? At the end of this writing task, students are asked to examine the writing and share their experiences with peers if they feel comfortable doing so. Then, as a class, discuss the factors that can lead to gaining inner strength and self-esteem from understanding our connections to other people and to our histories.[91]

We tried this activity as a class. During the conversations that followed we discussed one notion of "cultural capital"[92] as the cultural awareness that one can gain about his or her own history when deliberately taking stock of those moments some have referred to as transformative. I use transformative here not so much in the sense of life-changing but in the sense of recognition that makes us somehow different than we were though not yet fully evolved, rather still becoming—emerging. We talked about the idea that students in *To Sir with Love*[93] seemed to have increased self-esteem because of an increased cultural awareness and understanding. The concept of "cultural capital" described here suggests that such awareness produces the possibility if not the capability for individuals to act autonomously.

Questions students raised with respect to the activity and to the representation of cultural awareness in the film seemed to suggest an understanding that taking stock of one's culture informs an awareness of one's class and brings a kind of appreciation for it that is often absent or, at least, displaced without the acknowledgment or legitimation of culture first. Here subject positions seem integrally related to the understanding of subject histories and to what became, in the film, a legitimation of identity and voice.

In *To Sir with Love,* when students thought more highly of themselves, they ceased some of the resistance that interfered with opportunities for meaningful learning that related to their lives.[94] They began to learn skills that could lead to democratic participation. They learned what June Jordan and others have called *code switching* or what Jordan refers to as the difference between picnic language and formal dinner party language.[95] Jordan says that realistic language or what I have often referred to as authentic language can be used anywhere: to describe art, to debate, to express anger or love, to converse with friends at church or the local bar and grill. She says the structure of ideas reveals the worldview of the speaker and how and what the speaker values, and the way the speaker strings words together to represent those ideas reveals the speaker's consciousness; syntax, she says, equals voice. Jordan states explicitly that authentic language, language that carries the speaker's voice, contains the presence of persons and is motivated by the desire to "say something real to somebody real."[96]

This passage is embedded in what Jordan and her students derive as rules for Black English (Jordan says she had never taught anyone to write in black English so she and her students negotiated the rules of written black English together). That derivation evolves from a discussion over Celie's black English in Alice Walker's *The Color Purple.*[97] After the black students in her class reject their own language written in Walker's text, and after Jordan explains that students are not accustomed to seeing "realistic" black English in print, together they embark on a project to understand the rules/codes of Black English Vernacular (BEV) and to understand how to write what they speak. This effort had its greatest effects on a student in the class, Willie Jordan, whose unarmed brother, Reggie, had been killed by the police. Willie wanted to write something to publicly express his outrage, and he wanted to be taken seriously.

As students learned to translate their own spoken words into written BEV, they became aware that the Standard English they had attempted with difficulty to learn was immersed in abstraction or with "nothing/nobody evidently alive."[98] They discovered then that their own person-centered assumptions growing out of an oral tradition helped create their difficulties in adopting prescribed standard patterns of speaking and writing. Yet learning to switch codes from spoken to written using the rules of black English they'd derived made it possible to communicate effectively in their own language—as Walker had done.

Moreover, Jordan's students learned that public participation required the ability to critically discern information; that is, like what the circumstances really were that surrounded the police shooting that resulted in Reggie's death. And my own students, teachers-to-be, were encouraged to think about their own capacities to make good decisions and how that capability seems more necessary today than ever before. As one student reminded us, according to Bruce Springsteen in the song "War,"[99] the leaders we follow blindly will likely get us killed.

Interestingly, and perhaps owing to a selective and single-minded vision of society, in the broad sample of schooling narratives studied for this project, few narratives authenticated student voice or showed teacher-learner partnerships in the Freirean sense (learners teaching and teachers learning)[100] or students' in positions other than subordinate ones. If books and films are held up as mirrors to society, then the works presented here may suggest that no amount of human agency is capable of breaking down the structural barriers that inhibit political participation by all members of a society. However, if we consider Bill Nichols's notion that movies are more than a mirror image (they represent shifting scripts that can be [re]written) and we extend that to literature and other aesthetic materials,[101] we might begin to see possibilities for cultural production—humans with agency to (re)write their cultures even within structures of constraint.

Despite the difficulties, without helping students who are preparing to be teachers begin to think about their roles and social responsibilities as they extend beyond the walls of their classrooms, they may not realize their own potential for political participation in the project of teaching for change, teaching for freedom. Reflection on these and other materials may be a place to begin such thinking. June Jordan sums it up well in the last lines of her essay. She writes, "Justice may only exist as rhetoric. . . . [I]nequality and injustice are serious problems . . . [and] people are perpetually short-changed by society. Something has to be done about the way in which this world is set up. Although it is a difficult task, we do have the power to make change."[102]

In Chapter 6 I illustrate through story vignette the particular struggles prospective English teachers who participated in responding to the materials in this text shared as they remembered schooling experiences and attempted to construct new images of teaching.

CHAPTER 6

More Stories

Stories are our tools for world making. When teaching and learning focus on world making, narrative may hold limitless possibilities. Narrative is more than a way of knowing; it is a way of knowing that we know something and that we have a right to know. It is not necessarily knowing that is filled with certainty, but it is, at the very least, knowing we have the right to puzzle over situations in a quest for understanding. It is a way of bringing to the surface what was once inarticulatable. And finding ways of helping students share their stories is what this story is about. Locating our own stories, then, is key.

When I was a child, stories meant two things in my house. They were either lies or they were stories accepted as tall tales. If I were suspected of telling an untruth, my mother said I was telling stories, fantastic stories at that. You know, "you're storying or you're a storyteller." Some of these qualified as tall tales, but I usually made them up. Yet if I had not heard them from someone else first, in my house they were fibs told in order to conceal some truth or to perpetuate some untruth.

The other use of the word story was when my father who was a great teller of tales told us stories—ghost stories, stories of supernatural occurrences that he swore were true. We now call these folk tales. Or when I followed my mother from room to room and she told me stories that were the home-rendered versions of some of my favorite books or Bible stories extended to a contemporary setting told primarily to teach some lesson. All were the finest stories.

Yet when I analyze the thinking that produced these stories, I find there is little difference in the fib, the folk tale, and the adlibbed versions of story books and rhymes. All were fictions, all created for specific audiences, and all for very specific purposes. And frequently those purposes differed little. Most were devised for the purpose of getting and holding the attention of someone.

My mother's stories held my attention for hours. My father's stories kept the attention on him for hours and held our attention—my mother's, my sisters', any guests' who might be visiting, and mine. And my stories that bordered on fantasy usually had the same effect.

Stories were engaging; they drew me into a world—a fiction world, sometimes a better world, but always a world that let me take part. A world where I was a player right alongside any of the best characters. From inside this world I could see things more clearly, things that connected the past with the present and made the future not nearly so distant. Not nearly so impossible.

Early in my schooling experience I was typecast as a candidate for making someone a good wife and perhaps getting a job in an office. Not that there is anything wrong with either, if those are the choices one makes. I had not, however, made those choices yet. Circumstances beyond my control brought me face to face with discrimination. And because of that discrimination, my future looked bleak.

Being female and poor seemed to have earned me two strikes. I was tracked into the general not college-bound program at my school and my choices were immediately limited. Because I was fourteen I did not know what I wanted to do for the rest of my life. All that meant to me then was that I had more free time because I didn't have to study. Many have an idea of where they want to go, what they want to do; I did not or at least I didn't think I did. It was not until my junior year that I began to think about college. Because of my socioeconomic status, however, no one ever counseled me except to suggest the technical orientation. Therefore, by the time I knew I wanted to go to college, it was almost too late. I had taken no college preparatory courses except English, which I chose; my parents could not afford college, so they did not protest.

Because of early experiences with reading and story, my enchantment with literature fueled a desire to overcome my lack of preparation, and I became determined to work my way through college attending tutorials or whatever it took to catch up. I learned to read at a very early age. Though I don't remember learning to read, I believe now I learned to read by being read to. My mother used to say that I was reading from memory; I now know that reading from memory is really reading—it's the earliest reading a child does.

Almost my earliest memory is a reading one. Perhaps that's because I was showing off; at least, that's what my sisters called it. I was three years old, and I distinctly remember sitting in my red rocking chair, paint peeling off, wearing bluejeans or dungarees as we used to called them, cuffs turned up, white sneakers, and a white tee-shirt. One of my dad's friends, Mr. Christy, came by after work and my dad, who loved to brag about his children, asked if he wanted to hear me read. Mr. Christy, of course, did not believe that a child my age could read, but I proceeded to read one of my many Golden Book favorites, *Henny Penny*.[1]

My reading abilities advanced rapidly, however. I was fortunate that my older sisters had gone to school at a time when they had to buy their books. These lined the bookshelf in the hall outside my bedroom. I feasted on *Little Women, Little Men*,[2] and all the anthologized literature the shelf held. I learned everything from books. One particular memory associated with these old books was the thrill of finding a moldy page from one of my sisters' pressed prom corsages.

In the midst of all this literature (mostly by dead white men) were other stories, perhaps richer stories just waiting to be told. And like Eudora Welty, I was always on the look-out for a great story.[3] Stories were a part of my life, a part of what taught me to appreciate the storyteller's or writer's craft, a part of what taught me to appreciate my working-class parents' gifts. With little formal education, each in his or her own way taught me the power of narrative.

Focusing on one's early schooling experiences, informal or otherwise, and examining beliefs about those experiences is something few teachers-to-be contemplate, let alone undertake. By looking backward, reflecting on the past, and then projecting oneself into the future imaginatively, reconceptualization begins.[4]

Not only did pairing literary texts with more traditional ones give rise to pressing educational questions, but it also evoked a reconceptualizing of school through reflection on the past and projection into the future. Both students' narratives and the narratives drawn from aesthetic texts dramatized schooling situations; they seemed to create the expectation that anything could happen. Unlike their textbooks, literary texts were not seen as a particular body of knowledge designed to prepare them for teaching, and because the range of literary texts examined did not represent what they had come to think of as "the literary canon," these more imaginative texts seemed to re-create a wide range of possibilities. The stories told and the stories read seemed to decrease the separation of "words we read and the world we live[d] in."[5] Following are some of their stories.

THE STUDENTS OF TE326:
TEACHING REMEMBERED AND
UNDER CONSTRUCTION

The latter part of the heading of this section was given to me by one of my graduate students, Sue Allen. Like the sense of this chapter and a lot of this book, students voices reverberate with stories that illustrate what looking back and looking ahead means. Part of what it means in teacher education is an attempt to examine what it is we liked and what we didn't like about our past schooling experiences and where we might go from there. After many years of teaching I made that deliberate journey and discovered much that I would not want to repeat but also many things that I liked that I wasn't doing. One of those things was the deliberate use of autobiography to help narrate and critically analyze the stories of our lives. I discovered too what a rich curriculum could be developed through autobiographical sense making. As I suggested in Chapter 2, when we actively theorize our own life experiences—taking the "homecomer" perspective that Greene suggests and making the familiar strange—we begin to understand how it is that we both shape (as memory is observed through interpretation as Ulric Neisser suggests[6]) and are shaped by our past experiences. Thus I owe much to my students for sharing their words, their lives so openly in the press to help me understand how to teach. Leo Tolstoy wrote in his diary in 1857 on the eve of starting the first free school stripped of all existing institutionalized educational practice that our pupils should teach us the "art of teaching."[7]

Almost all of the students in TE326 were just a term away from student teaching. Because our program offers several ways for a student to receive a teaching certificate in English education, students came to this class with a range of field experiences. Their experiences vary from year-long mentorships with teachers in one of the local middle or high schools in one of the programs to an intensive field placement for a term in another program to only a few hours a week in a classroom for students in a more traditional program. The latter fulfills arranged-hour requirements for some of our English education courses through the Department of English.

Many of the students in this class have been in several of my English education classes before. Because there are only a few of us who teach English education courses in the English Department, I seem to have the same students over and over again. Therefore, the perceived ease with the curriculum in TE326 and students' vaaried capacities to reveal sometimes painful experiences may have more to do with familiarity than with course structure or materials.

The content of this course is not specifically designated except by description and that description, albeit a methods course, more generally becomes a course in which to extend opportunities for practicing methods learned in, for example, the teaching of reading and language study, the teaching of literature, the teaching of composition, and to take curricular issues farther relating them to cultural and sociopolitical concerns in the wider society. Hence some of the stories of curricular concerns told here are told during discussion and some are told in the course of students teaching a lesson that involves reading and writing and is perhaps accompanied by language study.

It has been my desire to allow students' stories to stand on their own. However, in order to contextualize briefly each response without restating previous discussion respective to particular texts, and in order to eliminate the possibility that I might inadvertently begin to deconstruct some of the students' responses or in some way rank them according to what I might see as more or less reflective responses, I will as briefly as possible simply describe the context for each student's response (context follows response/story).

Looking Back

Actually, when I was in high school, we had corporal punishment. If you misbehaved, you had the choice of getting detention or getting a couple of paddles. I don't know whether it was a very small town or what, but everyone knew everybody else, so the corporal punishment thing was no big deal; it was like a joke. I mean everybody would laugh. It hurt, but it wasn't any type of motivation for better behavior. Sometimes, you would do stuff, just so you could get paddled and get the attention, being in front of the class.

Jeff's story is told in the middle of a book talk given on *Nicholas Nickleby*[8] when the discussion centered around issues of corporal punishment.

I was in a group of friends; the other girls didn't excel in school at all. When I found myself doing well in English, that's okay. But I had another friend that did well in chemistry; she was always shunned. Because that's not what girls do; guys do that.

Lisa's story is told following discussion of gender issues related to career choices. The context for this discussion is the reading of a chapter in Weiler's *Women Teaching for Change*.[9]

We were doing writing assignments. There was this girl who wrote about her boyfriend. Her mother and father got really upset. They said, "You have no right promoting these types of things, or anything personal from my daughter. You should be talking about things related to school."

This story emerged one day before class began when two students, Rachel and Todd, were talking about an experience Rachel had in her field placement the day before. Rachel was in an intensive field experience for the term so she had built some rapport with students in the class to which she referred. As a result of her story, class that day became a discussion of public/private issues in writing and how that is related to "official school" curricula. In other words, her story became an opening into a conversation about challenging textual authority and tradition and who decides what is or is not "appropriate" for school.

When I was in high school, we used that first five minutes as some meaningful way to begin the class, like some sort of grading activity, or some assignment put on the board, or a quote from something. And when we came in, we'd either do our reading or look at that quote. Those were meaningful ways to begin the class. I really enjoyed that. And I thought it was a very good time saving technique.

After reading to students from McNeil's *Contradictions of Control*[10] on the use of particular content and teaching strategies that

McNeil suggests are more for purposes of classroom management than meaningful learning, Todd offers this story. Prior to my reading of the McNeil passage, we had two book talks: *The Chocolate War* and *A Hero Ain't Nothing but a Sandwich*.[11]

> In one TE class we studied how knowledge varies according to social class. And we learned the way the curriculum is in the schools in the lower working class areas. The structure of the courses is to focus on skills and worksheets and never challenge their students to think. Therefore their test scores were lower than those in the upper class schools. In those schools students were writing and doing really creative projects.

Chris's story follows Todd's.

> The opposite of that is we can talk about the inner student and making the classroom a more active place for their learning. But this other thing comes to mind—a thirst for knowledge. I just started acquiring it myself, but I never had a thirst for knowledge in high school not even in my undergraduate training. I did what I had to do to get through. But when you talk about engaging the student in the classroom, what is the boundary, what is the step-over to that thirst for knowledge?

Hal is commenting here about the boundary crossing he saw students doing in Mike Rose's book *Lives on the Boundary*, which we read in connection with seeing *Stand and Deliver*.[12]

> There are many social factors in addition to teachers that influence the agendas with which students enter and leave school. I had no genuine desire to concentrate on my French lessons, because I believed in my lifetime I would never have the money nor the inclination to go to France. I did not believe that French people would treat us any better than Americans.

Elizabeth's story follows Hal's.

> Before I came here, I attended another college for two years. We realized that most of the materials we had in the books were materials that had been collected by somebody else (not by people in Kenya). Most of the books that we study in our schools have been written out here [America]. Then we realized that our

customs are dying. Now, we have started a project of collecting all of our traditions, customs, and history.

Helen tells this story after several students present a lesson on recovering historical traditions according to the foxfire program articulated in Eliot Wigginton's *Sometimes a Shining Moment*. At this point in the course, we have read Wigginton's book, heard a book talk on *To Sir with Love*, and completed the writing activity in *Making History*.[13]

> I understand about remedial. I'm not real bad in math, it just takes me a long time to do math, so I scored really low on that placement test. But you can make up that test using as much time as you want. So I went there to make it up. Not that I needed math in my curriculum. I just wanted it on my record that I could take 108 if I had to. The person is laughing at my low score, he said, "I wish they wouldn't even let you take this re-test; you should just be put in a remedial math class." Then he said something like, "It's the one-credit class that meets every day, a stupid section for all you that are too stupid to place in anything else." I felt so bad that I didn't even take the re-test.

Mary's story surfaces in a discussion on tracking around the reading of Jesse Stuart's book, *Mr. Gallion's School*.[14] This autobiographical narrative is one of Stuart's experiences in a school he'd taught in twenty years earlier and to which he is now returning to be the new principal. The books deals mostly with his successes at helping children who had been tracked into remedial classes discover their intelligence and talents and find self-esteem.

> There was one guy in my school, so intelligent, he was like the kind of kid in elementary school that got all A's and 5's in citizenship. Maybe he wasn't that bad, I just remember him getting in trouble a lot. Maybe he just needed a little extra attention, but he got put into remedial from junior high on up, to stifle him. The remedial class was like a punishment. I've seen that lots of times before. That was sad. If anything, he should have been in the gifted program.

Mark also offers his story in response to the issue of remediation.

> I never knew what it was like to be totally captivated or enraptured with the material when I was in high school. I hated high

school. I hated my classes. Nothing ever motivated me to do any work. I just showed up. I was just there, turned in crap that I had done over night, the night before it was due and that was it.

Lucy offers this story in a discussion that actually takes place during a writing lesson Mary presents to the class that is to include discussion of dialect. She leads the class in what she calls a whole-class composition in which students in groups of three are asked to complete a topic fragment (each group's fragment has to build on the previous group's completion); for example, (1) My mom, she knew Aunt Hattie Lacefield, in them days and she was . . . (2) My life was changed, again, when my old man . . . (3) That's what I hate about the dad-gummed oil . . . (4) She done what she could and lived as a . . . , etc. The conversation evolves, however, into more a discussion of student involvement than dialect. Prior to this we have read or heard book talks on *Sometimes a Shining Moment, To Teach, To Love, Mr. Gallion's School, To Sir with Love*, and we have read/viewed *Lean on Me* and *Stand and Deliver*.[15]

Projecting into the Future

> What I'm hoping for is to prepare inner-city students for college. Even, if they are in remedial classes, I want them to have attained a literary background as though they were in college-prep classes. I want even my remedial classes to read *Beowolf*. And, to have the basic understanding for the most popular literature classics. But, not only that, I want them to be able to write. I am not saying give up our culture. I am not saying it's wrong to speak black English. I am not saying that. But, in this society, to get a real job, to go out in the world outside of _____, I want them to be able to do that. And, they cannot do that with black English.

This story of how Kathy hopes to teach someday becomes a part of our discussion of *To Sir with Love* and Jordan's article, "Nobody Mean More to Me Than You and the Future of Willie Jordan."[16]

> I know there is no way as teachers, if we have thirty-four students in our classrooms, that we can give each individual student the attention that they need. So what do you do? You want to be this great teacher, but you have all these students. I don't know what the answer is. Less populated classrooms, I guess.

Terry's story is in response to Ashton-Warner's *Teacher*.[17]

I think I am going to do a lot of small group work. I think they will probably benefit most if we do it in a small group situation with me walking around checking what they are doing, figuring out where they are going.

Martha's story also follows the reading and discussion of *Teacher*[18] and a lesson presented by a team of students on integrating reading and writing in the language arts class.

All your life you're going to be a teacher so you'd better be a lifelong learner. Probably five or ten years from now everything we are learning, everything that we think is so great, so new, is going to be obsolete. Again, you'd better be constantly learning, and reflecting, and assessing. Whether that ideal of being a lifelong learner, so to speak, and learning new ways of doing things so that you can pick and choose becomes a reality or not, it's the ideal we strive for.

Anne's story is told within the context of a discussion that helps bridge a short passage by Paulo Freire in *Pedagogy of the Oppressed* and discussion of *Educating Rita*.[19] The gist of the conversation is on the role of mentoring in student-teacher relationships.

I've been considering and considering career choices a lot. It's as much what we're up against, not just in the schools but politically, too. In some ways, I really don't feel as if I have a choice.

Ellen's story is also is response to Weiler's *Women Teaching for Change*.[20]

Reconceptualizing

I went to visit the school where I'll be doing my student teaching. I'll be teaching grammar and American literature. In the grammar courses, day after day all they do is a Warner's lesson. They don't use journals. They don't do any writing. The tests are all objective. It was funny! One teacher said, "Oh, I might have to write up a test!" Another, "You didn't have time to do a machine score test?" They do have one part of writing, they have vocabulary words. I was in there while she was giving the test. All she did was say the word, and they wrote it down.

Karen's response is to our discussion of Ditto from the movie *Teachers*.[21]

I'm in a class right now that is not tracked; we have special ed with everybody else. The only reason I knew that there was a special ed person in the classroom was this adult helper. He [the student] would not participate at all the first week I was there. Then the second week, I think it was because both my cooperating teacher and I gave them opportunities to work in groups and work with people and not feel less because he couldn't live up to expectations. Maybe in some classes we are doing everything we can to incorporate everybody. We tell them if you have a problem, come to us for help because we can't read your mind and determine if you need help. There are going to be people who slip through, I'm not sure how much I'm willing to do to stop them. I'll do everything I can within the community of the classroom.

Sarah's story is in response to Martha's book talk on Rosemary Sutcliff's *Blue Remembered Hills* and a discussion of Michigan's new plan referred to as "inclusion" by which all students with special needs are included in regular classes and are given an aid.

We make the assumption that good grades are inherently good. That may not be exactly true. That's one of the problems I'm dealing with: where is my right? If it is on the student's agenda not to learn, where is my right to intervene and try to push my way into that student's agenda and change it. When I was a senior in high school, I determined it was not my agenda to pass math, and I didn't. I think it would have been a lot worse if my teacher had intervened and said, "What's wrong with you? How can I reach you?" That's the problem I'm dealing with: school success may not be inherently good in itself, yet that determines how good we are with our students . . .

Hal's story is offered in a conversation about grades begun during the reading and subsequent discussion of *Mr. Gallion's School.*

In my field experience, all they do basically is copy notes off the overhead to get credit on them. So what I did was some writing assignments, something different. They loved it, and asked, because we had time left, "let's do something else." So we decided to play win, lose, or draw. They structured it out, how much time, etc. It was like a 180 degree, the complete change in motivation.

Mary tells this story also in connection with the discussion on the foxfire lesson.

On Monday, we had a write around, where you sit in a circle and start a story and pass it. It worked out really great except three people wrote incredibly gross stuff on the story (all blood, guts, etc., stuff that really had nothing to do with the story). _____ and I were really upset; a lot of students were upset too that this was happening. We weren't sure how to deal with it. I went back on Wednesday, had them get back in a circle and take ten minutes to freewrite about what things happened with their write-around, how they felt about it, and how they reacted to it. And the guy who really screwed up, I couldn't believe it, said: "I apologize I was trying to have a lot of fun, but I ruined it for a lot of people." Everybody got real quiet. Then they started giving all kinds of suggestions. So that was really an interesting way of handling it. It was all peers.

Jeff's story is also in response to Mary's whole-class composition activity.

In *Stand and Deliver*, Mr. Escalante stressed the philosophy that students would rise to the level of expectations. I was thinking about that the other night when I was writing in my journal, and it amazed me. I do not remember ever hearing that line in high school or any school, just in a few classes here at college have I ever heard that. And that is why teachers should be teachers. I mean that is what it is all about.

Lucy's response follows a discussion of *Stand and Deliver* and *Lives on the Boundary.*[22]

People think you are touched by God or something and that's how you are intelligent. But it's not. Anybody given the right circumstances, situations, and the right amount of encouragement will be able to do something. There is so much social pressure; we should be caring and compassionate and allow students to open up, give them an environment where they can take risks.

Mark's story also becomes a part of our discussion around *Stand and Deliver* and *Lives on the Boundary.*[23]

The people who are set in their ways aren't saying let's stay set in our ways, they are saying the way I was taught was great. Like we are saying the way we were taught is so great.

Sharon's comment follows a conversation about teachers telling teacher stories referred to by Herbert Kohl in *Growing Minds and Becoming a Teacher*.[24]

> I think you have to decide if you really want to be a teacher. When you decide that, you know you really want to do it for the kids. Most of the feedback I got while student teaching was negative. I didn't care, because, I knew it was working for the kids, and that was what I was there for, regardless of what Michigan State thought or the people that had been there since the first brick was installed in the place. If they see that it is working for the kids they will come around to your way of thinking eventually. They saw me sitting on the floor with thirty kids all around me pretending that we were in a cave. They thought that was really strange. But it was working, the kids' writing was great after that. You can be bold and daring. You can take chances because you want to be there.

Mary's story also follows our discussion of *Growing Minds*.[25]

> You need to know the why behind it. Why something succeeds. If you can explain why something worked well, no matter how screwy it looks, they'll believe you if it is for the benefit of the kids. Or if you really screw up, and you know why, then you can go back and change things, and make it better. The why is really important, I think.

Steve offers this response to our discussion of the role of theory in teacher preparation. Actually, our discussion on the pairing of literature and more theoretical readings occurred one day following the reading and discussion of a brief passage from Jo Anne Pagano and an article from Lenore Weitzman to help us talk about some of the socialized conceptions we have come to think of as common sense that Weitzman suggests we may learn from fairy tales and children's literature—conceptions especially related to gendered roles and expectations of teachers.[26] Besides some well known children's classics the other imaginative text that entered our discussion was Pat Conroy's *The Water Is Wide*.[27] One of the students had become more than a little disgruntled with all the theory we discussed and wanted to know why we were reading so much literature and seeing films in a teacher education course that was suppose to teach them what to do when they did their student teaching. Though I had initially covered my reasons for developing the course in this way, an office visit from the student revealed her concern. Although she was too nervous to say anything at first, unfortunately for her (and I completely understood her concern), she was one of the few students who had slipped by in our efforts to advise students to take the other methods' courses prior to this one because we wanted this course to function as more of a capstone/critical curriculum issues course.

> If you really fire kids up though you give the next hour teacher a big burden. Last spring term, I taught just two days a week in someone's class. The regular teacher who had been around twenty years had the kids the other three days. By the end the teacher said, "I'm really tired of your antics; I've got to deal with these kids when you're not here."

We studied Ashton-Warner's *Teacher* in connection with reviewing process methods of teaching reading and writing covered in previous classes. Terry's concern here is frequently expressed because students still see that many classes are taught in very traditional ways.

> I am watching a class right now, and the teacher has absolutely no control. She told me she never taught seniors before; she always taught freshmen. She has classified them as remedial. She treats them like that, and they are just terrible. I don't think she is even aware of what is going on in the classroom. That scares me. It's just the pits taking over a class when the other teacher had no control.

Julia's response captures another extreme, however: the opposite of tight control. It occurs within the context of our discussion of the movie *Lean on Me*.[28]

> There's this one ninth grade that is reading *To Kill a Mockingbird*. They are kind of into it, but the teacher loves the book so much that she stands up there and wants to do all the talking. There is this one kid who reminds me of my teen-aged brother; he just wants to talk and discuss. I could see that the class at first really wanted to discuss the book. But she just wanted to

lecture, she wanted to share her knowledge. Suddenly, they are all tuning out—staring into space—and she is still up there talking. At the end, she says, "My throat is so sore, but I just love that book."

Lisa tells this story in response to a discussion of *Dead Poets' Society*.[29] The conversation has turned to teaching styles and students are debating the merits of Keatings' lively though romanticized style compared with the more familiar lecture model of teaching canonical literature.

> In my field experience, half of the class is remedial and half is regular track. I asked my co-operating teacher what those remedial kids had to do to get into the next class. She said, "Well, they don't really." I said, "Is there a test they can take, paper they can write, something they can do?" And she replied, "No that would just hurt their feelings." It's like a permanent stamp on them. I'm shocked every time I go into that class.

Sarah's response is to a discussion around the pairing of an article on the politics of tracking with a book talk on *A Hero Ain't Nothing but a Sandwich*.[30]

> We got this sixth grade class, and my teacher told me, he stood right in front of the desk and said: "Now! this is a sixth grade class and all the good kids and all the smart kids have been tracked off to the good classes, so don't expect too much." So I started my poetry unit, and I wasn't using the book. He said, "I think you're losing them; I think you should be using this." I said, okay! Then I looked in the book, it had poems about a tree house, you know, cute little poems, like by Shel Silverstein. They didn't want to hear about a tree house. So I brought in Whitman, and we did "Oh Captain, My Captain." We did it with a picture and we talked about the symbolism, and drew it all out and everything. They really got into it. The next day, they came back with their own pictures and poem. They said, "Listen to this poem, what do you think of it?" Then they wanted to know what their book said about poetry. This teacher with his worksheets hadn't really noticed these students as people. It was just amazing what these kids came up with.

Jeff's story continues the tracking discussion.

There is hope. My mom is the director of gifted and talented at
_____ Schools. She is doing some wonderful things
with kids. They target, I don't want to say track, gifted under-
achievers. They want to target them and get them out of doing
the basic fill-in-the-workbook stuff. They want to get them
thinking critically. Some are so talented that they can do wonderful things.

Mary offers this response in contrast to an anti-tracking position
taken up by some members of the class after reading the Giroux/
McLaren article. Her response occurs within the context of a discussion about students are who regularly removed from their
classrooms to attend either remedial programs or enrichment programs; I had read the children's book *First Grade Takes a Test* to
the class.[31]

After working in the _____ school district for the
better part of a year, as a student-teacher and then as a substitute teacher, believe me the _____ schools are tracked.
Many teachers, coordinators, department heads may suggest
that the schools are not tracked. But after subbing in practically
all the language arts classrooms in both the high school and the
middle school, what I found is that they like to target talent,
especially that of the community leaders' children.

My research assistant, Rashidah, gave this response to Mary's
comments.

Today the regular teacher was gone. So we had a sub. She had
left notes that we could either have the students read quietly or
we could read aloud. Like I said it's an inner-city Flint school
and it's 99 percent black. I asked them what they would rather
do, so one of them said for me to read it. So I started reading it.
I read maybe a page or two, and I felt so incredibly stupid,
because this is a story about a white middle-class family, and
this kid who likes this girl, and his parents wanted him to shave
off his mustache, and he wants to drive his father's car. I
couldn't even finish it. I felt so stupid, in front of these kids
reading this story.

Mark's story follows Rashidah's comment about subbing. Both
responses occur within the context of discussion on tracking and
meaningful school experiences.

We need to always have an open mind with students. Just yesterday, we were in this class with both regular and remedial students. My teacher told me at the onset to try to pick out the remedial students to see if I could. And I could. I could tell by the questions she asked them: "And how do you feel about" (she asked the lower track students the same questions in slow motion). They could also see that they were the "dumb" ones. And I could see a big danger in this model of teaching. I don't have any experience with lower track kids, but I had a friend that was in the lower track all through school. It was a big leap for her to go to college. I could already see the problems these lower track eighth-graders were having and going to have believing in themselves. I always looked up to my teachers, and if I had a teacher that talked really slowly, I would feel bad.

Terry's story also emerges out of the discussion on tracking.

It is important to me that things are meaningful. We ought to be able to apply what the teacher does in class, outside the class, outside the school, and not just on the final exam. But do you think that this hands-on stuff is the best way to write? Do you think you can learn as much from doing as you could from a good discussion, or by hard brainstorming, or even a good lecture?

Jane's response follows a foxfire lesson and discussion of Wigginton's program as an example of the kind of experiential curriculum Dewey proposed.[32]

We did a lot of neat stuff with drama and acting. My students wrote their own play and produced it on stage, did all the costuming and stuff. The kids would go out and memorize their lines even though they were not being graded for this. It wasn't until afterwards that we found out that we got our students from the remedial reading class. I was amazed when I found out because I just assumed that they were regular track eighth-grade students so I aimed my lesson at that and they rose to the occasion and performed really well.

Mark's story response follows Jane's and spurs continued discussion of Dewey and his notion of art as experience.[33]

I think what we got to realize is what exactly do terms like *remedial, learning disability,* and others mean. A lot of times, students are assessed on the most demeaning things—it's largely social and economic class. Because the administration figures kids from the lower class aren't going anywhere so they track them toward shop, etc. One of the students we had seemed brilliant. But according to test scores and teachers, he was just a remedial student.

Jeff re-enters the discussion on tracking as he circles back to his previous story and focuses on a particular student.

It's weird what you don't find out from tests. Sometimes doing well on a test just proves how well you can take that particular test. I was told not to even apply for Michigan State because my ACT score was so low. Yet I graduated with honors. And then I got into a setting where it was more important what you thought and how you critically approached the material than checking off little boxes and circles. Here we don't need to get so uptight; you can just take your time.

Sharon's comments on the testing issue arose when we discussed standardization in *Stand and Deliver*. At this juncture, though we didn't view *Pump up the Volume* in this class, students who had seen the movie brought it into our discussion.[34]

One thing that bothers me because of the low status and respect is that a lot of people who would make excellent teachers are not even considering the field. Well, I have very low respect for some lawyers I know who have no integrity. I have a lot of low respect for people going into the medical profession—especially because of medical students who cheat on their exams. Someday I might send my kids to some of those doctors.

Julia's story is told within the context of a discussion from Weiler's text.[35]

ABOUT STUDENTS' STORIES

Though I've attempted to withhold judgements about students' stories by refusing to analyze, I realize I am guilty of judging by virtue of selecting. For, indeed, I have based selection on some set of criteria. There were, of course, many more responses over the term. And as you might expect in open discussion some students spoke up more than others; therefore, some voices are heard from more than once in this chapter.

Alhough I have refrained from any sort of linear form to distinguish a story from any other response, I did select under a kind of operationalized criteria that seemed to emerge even as I began to make selection. For example, I attempted to mix up the pool of stories so that a variety of responses are given and not always in support of the text or the discussion that a response pertains to. I also tried to represent male and female responses about equally (surprisingly, there were more males in this class than are usually in my classes). A third criteria had to do with articulation and the capability of quoting stories verbatim. In other words, because of the nature of transcriptional data, sometimes spoken language does not appear lucid in written form; that is, sometimes words are missing or thoughts seem incomplete. Therefore, in order for me to have used those stories I would have had to fill in the blanks and that would have meant my finishing students' thoughts thus interpreting. So I refrained from using any story that was not complete enough on tape to quote verbatim.

Finally, I did do some categorizing after studying the transcripts at length although I realize that developing categories tends to privilege findings, and such a practice is a hold over from positivism. In this instance categorizing privileged findings by justifying exclusion of some stories, and exclusion is directly related to power. I am complicit then in participating in an exclusionary act not so much perhaps for what I legitimated, but for what I possibly denied—for the "unthought in any thought, the shadow" as Lather suggests (what I might have avoided denying and what might have been apparent had I been willing to select some stories that seemed incomplete).36

Though I didn't devise the categories a priori, I did recognize as I examined the data that a further method for fine tuning selection would be to simply choose stories that seemed to go along with the categories of recovery in the process of currere: looking back, looking forward, and imagining the future. So if stories, worked in those categories and if they satisfied the other criteria, then they were selected.

In Chapter 7 I share my own story of struggle as a teacher. That is, I share some of the questions, fears, conflicts, and anxieties I experience in working toward self-critical reflective practice. And though I've tried not to make selections that privilege my choice of questions, fears, conflicts, and anxieties, it is probably the case that I've done so regardless of my conscious desire not to.

CHAPTER 7

Toward Reflexive/Reflective Practice

Some students say democracy in the classroom doesn't work. I ask them why, and they reply that it is too touchy-feely. I ask what that means, but they can't put their fingers on an answer that they seem to believe. I have to ask myself why they see what I attempt to model as touchy-feely. When we debate tracking issues and I say, "No! We don't need tracking. Tracking is insidious! It's evil, it denies some in favor other others," and then I give examples they can all recognize, I hear a fascist, not someone who is touchy-feely. Anytime I'm shaking my finger and being that directive, I'm also being authoritarian.

For example, when I give my students in composition courses intervention models that I expect them to use in my class and possibly with the students they teach, I am being very directive. The very nature of the word *intervene* suggests I'm intervening in someone's process, which is, in fact, precisely what I am doing. I believe I am teaching students how to help give each other feedback over their writing when the fact is, some students may not benefit from this feedback. Instead, when I provide such concrete suggestions for changing their writing, some students will give up what they thought about the piece and simply follow my well-intended teacherly instructions.

In fact, it seems when I examine the language I use most of the time, even in my course syllabi, for example, I border on authoritarianism. Words like *course requirements* and *due dates* and *participation required* are fairly directive. They replace words like *options* or *student-set agendas,* and so forth. These and other words are used in an attempt to create structure for my students who are both inexperienced and experienced teachers—a structure they seem to want, I seem to need to give, and a structure that may undermine my best attempts at teaching with their best interests in mind.

I am still concerned about students use of the word *touchy-*

feely, however. I want to sort out why they would think this. I want to know what the limitations of democratic classrooms are and why, in general, I consider a more democratic classroom better for students. If I want such a model because it is more egalitarian, more student centered, less authoritarian, are not my very directive intervention strategies and tracking statements evidence of the authoritarianism that still resides within me? It disturbs me that some groups of people call everything progressive touchy-feely. Many of the process reading and writing methods are often referred to in that way, but what is the opposite? For me, the opposite is the drill and skill mentality—the worksheets, diagramming sentences until you're blue in the face, answering the questions at the end of anthologized literature selections, and so forth. Is another opposite, democratic teaching and learning that allows no room for people to be individuals—to learn in individual ways—even while they work collaboratively in learning teams or groups? I'm concerned about these questions and more.

Questioning my own complicity in the practices that keep authoritarianism alive is one part of a self-reflective critique or reflective turn; acting on that recognition is another matter. Finding ways to juggle institutional requirements and teach for freedom is, perhaps, the most difficult part of teacher work. As I struggle to finds ways of working between constraints, on the one hand, and the multiple possibilities that exist for me and my students, on the other, I include this critique as fit material for discussion in methods courses. Discussing my own struggles seems to be one way for teachers-to-be to learn this struggle, as it applies to the particular methodologies of their discipline. These issues surface frequently, sometimes deliberately, and sometimes as a part of a student's agenda. Even after we've recognized the need for social critique as we read and study literature, films, and other artistic media, like advertising, television programming, and MTV, questions of position, authority, and control with respect to the teaching of any curricula are still the hardest questions. And it is through the attempted negotiation of art and experience in the dynamic terrain of classrooms, that self-critical reflection seems to occur most naturally. Being self-critical, raising questions about our own practice is what I think we have to do if we are not to accept blindly such models as the perfect solution in any class. Even the use of the word *model* implies a universal. If we are assuming by the fact that we can use a model of democratic teaching and learning that all human beings within our system or class-room function in very similar ways, we may be suffering false consciousness. And if we set up any one model, use any one approach in each of our classes, still we may be assuming too much. For example, if 150 students are even a tenth of the student body of a school then we may have misread the structure of the society within schools. As a microcosm of the wider society, it is perhaps much more diverse than we have imagined. Perhaps not even a tenth of all peoples within any given community or society function the same, especially with respect to reading, writing, learning, and so forth.

Of course, this is not to suggest that we should teach school the way society teaches us.[1] For in that vast school we often learn the hegemonic ideas thought of as common sense that many of us in education work so hard to derail. Perhaps we might consider, however, that part of the reason common sense is so difficult to derail is the rather privileged status it is often given. In other words, besides its offering a rather tempting way of simplifying that which is complex, it's such a handy phrase—we say so casually that something's just a matter of common sense. Just as it might seem a matter of common sense that those who have adopted philosophies of democratic teaching will be less likely to be control oriented and more likely to interrogate relations of power, unfortunately, this may not necessarily be the case. Through self-critique I have located a number of places in my own teaching where control and domination exist—where my critical feminist/democratic educator principles have failed to help me erase the power/powerless dichotomy.

Specifically, what I mean to question here has to do with how we view difference and particularly in terms of the different needs of students and how they take up schooling in different ways—and perhaps how our common sense perception suggests that we are more alike than different. For example, I perceive that common sense has often led us to think if we but devise lessons with sound democratic philosophies then they will automatically meet the needs of all students, and if we question the effects of power we will somehow remove the threat of power in our own lives and in our work. Because students are different, however, I cannot assume single-minded strategies will improve their situations in my classroom or in the world even if I believe that strategy has sound educational value, even if many before me have valued it as well. I cannot say what others will value.

Though I have often imagined democracy to produce justice; it has been largely that—an imagined democracy. For if having democratic values were enough to truly disengage power, then women and children would not continue to be marginalized, and literacy—the supposed answer to social ills—would not continue to privilege some at the expense of others.[2] I use to imagine that we really did mean we were interested in educating all the children until I noticed children who appeared lost even in democratically organized classrooms. And as I have said of my own classroom, despite my conscious desire, students are perhaps still subjected to unacknowledged forms of domination and control. Yet perhaps it is not the nature of the classroom, but the lack of ongoing critique, especially ongoing self-critique, that leads us down rigid paths narrowly construed, no matter the philosophical underpinning. Perhaps it is both.

We need then to examine when something we do works and when it does not. And we need to examine what we mean when we say something works. For whom does it work? And who has decided that it works? For example, in the hit movie, *Lean on Me*,[3] in which Joe Clarke attempts to rid a high school of drug users and pushers in order to make room for students who want to learn, would a democracy have worked better than his very authoritarian means of handling the situation? Are there times when in order to be fair, we have to be unequal? And are we ever equal anyway? Is it necessary to be unfair to some groups in order to be fair to others, or do some situations warrant the extreme measures employed by Joe Clarke, for example? When is it fair to forcibly require that one member of society give up his or her rights for the good of the many in that society? When an injustice is committed? And who of us should be designated as judge of what is unjust, particularly where schooling is concerned?

As I look at my own teaching, turn the gaze on myself, I know that even as I attempt to be humanitarian and egalitarian, I have an agenda. That agenda may be freedom; nonetheless, I want it heard. I want it so badly that I frequently work in ways that are less than liberatory for students in order that my goals be realized. What I am suggesting here is not that we give up our goals for a more egalitarian classroom, just that we recognize that we are not wholly innocent in our quest for egalitarianism. That is, as I ask students, no *require* that students participate in class discussions so that I do not have to assume the more authoritarian role of lecturer, am I totally innocent in making that requirement? No. I may believe students will have a more positive experience if they participate. I may believe that the teaching-learning relationship will be improved, positioning students for a more active voice in our classroom. Nonetheless, in making such a requirement I may have violated some very important considerations. For example, what of the student who has difficulty speaking so that even within a small group the student becomes nervous and cannot speak without stuttering? Haven't I violated that student's rights? Or am I to operate only in the interest of the entire class as a group? When I have students who do not participate and I penalize them for it, do I often consider that a particular language difficulty may be the problem? Or that they haven't had any sleep, or that they've had a fight with their best friend, or that any number of human situations could keep them from wanting to participate on any given day? Do I see myself as so approachable that I think any student will come to me with any personal concern to rid themselves of responsibility on a particular day?

Additionally, we need to examine our motives and those of our students when what we do seems to work well. Again, whose view tells us it works well? For example, I believe in journals. I assign a journal in one form or another in nearly every class I teach. I tell my students that I want them to raise questions of their readings, that journals are a place to think through these questions on paper, and that we will use them as a springboard for discussion. This from a recent syllabus gives a relative degree of structure, makes my students feel more secure that they *can give me what I want*, and, of course, reproduces the very problems I attempt to work my way out of:

> Responses should show that you have carefully considered the reading material. Responses should not be a summary of the readings; instead, they should be your thoughtful reactions to the materials read in common. You may agree, disagree, raise questions, and so forth. In any case, your journal should reflect a considered response rather than whatever pops into your mind as you read. Critique ideas presented in terms of their validity for classroom practice. Balance this against what you have seen in schools thus far. How might you adapt or extend ideas to use in your own teaching?

Seems innocent enough. However, when occasionally a student writes nothing in his or her journal, I do not consider that perhaps the reading raised no questions. No, I think the student simply has not read.

On the other hand, when students dutifully keep a journal and willingly share entries with class for purposes of beginning our discussions, am I certain that these journals really represent students' thinking or does it simply represent obedient students—students who have learned to play the game well? Do I consider whether or not their playing the game results in a learning experience, or do I simply assume that it does?

Or what about students who seem to agree with all the course material (i.e., take up the party line), can I be sure those students are thinking at all? Is it not, perhaps, more likely that the student who disagrees with everything in the course is thinking, especially when she or he may go to such great lengths to defend a particular stand? Or do I easily pass that student off as resistant to my assignment when I might otherwise think that resistance is healthy? When I myself resist so many things, am I likely to penalize a student for resisting my assignment? If a student resists a suggestion that perhaps he or she takes as a directive, do I ever think that student is resisting power, and have I not encouraged students to interrogate and enjoin political resistances that might work to put an end to domination?

Do I consider how students take up what I intend, what I think seems harmless enough? And why do I think they will value what I value just because I think it's good for them? (Did we value eating spinach or peas as children because our parents said it was good for us?) Can I be so certain that the approach I value is best that I discount the student who may not need to write his or her thoughts in order to help generate discussion? And what of students who write in the margins of their text? Am I operating in the best interest of those students when I require that students turn in their journals at the end of the term, even if it means that margin-writers have mounds of busy work in order to complete course requirements?

Developing the habit of self-critique may be a necessary prelude to reflective practice. However, teachers may not/do not have the luxury of separating perceptual tasks from action in the form of teaching. Therefore, a possible way into reflective practice may be the acceptance that we do not have to know everything in order to proceed—that, indeed, continuing to question, puzzle out, wonder, and so forth may be the kind of reflective thinking needed for reflective action. Being patient with uncertainty may help us be reflective and if we turn that reflection inside ourselves to critique our own thoughts, actions, directions, and so forth then ongoing, reflexive critique may become a natural part of our being and becoming. Thinking and acting may not be quite the simple matter that some have attempted to describe, nonetheless, doing both/and (i.e., thinking, acting, and ongoing self-critique) in the service of teaching for freedom, of practicing freedom as Freire suggests,[4] seems more likely to produce reflective practice. What follows is an example of some of my own struggles to teach reflectively.

THINKING AND ACTING

Where do I go from here? How do I make these issues problematic? And how do I begin to address issues of inequality that affect all our students lives? For example, how do I help prospective teachers to consider/question the diverse nature of learners in the public schools when I have not always considered the different learning needs of the students in my own classes who are going to be teachers? I have often turned to literature for help. But turning to literature alone suggests everyone I teach gets as much out of reading as I do. That's a fairly easy assumption to make since most of my students are going to be English teachers. But is it a fair assumption? Is it not just as likely that some of my prospective English teachers might get as much if not more out of some films as books. A recent example of this hit me squarely over the head.

In an English methods course, one of our topics of inquiry was "What does it mean to be an English teacher in multicultural classrooms?" We read collectively Sylvia Ashton-Warner's *Teacher* pairing that with Cynthia Brown's *Literacy in Thirty Hours*.[5] *Teacher* is the story of Ashton-Warner's teaching experiences with the Maori children of New Zealand. The book challenges traditional teaching methods favoring free imaginative learning instead of rigid patterns of behavior. Brown's book is basically an unpacking of Paulo Freire's early work in Northeast Brazil.[6]

Students immediately made connections between Ashton-Warner's work and Freire's as described by Brown. In particular, students saw connections between the key-word vocabulary and Freire's method of teaching from pictures of ordinary things familiar to Brazilians. Daily Ashton-Warner asked each child what he or she wanted, and she wrote the word on a big card and handed it to the child. For example, one child's word was socks. Words represented real needs the children had. Needs like food, clothing, and shelter were integrally related to literacy learning and my students seemed to understand that against the sociopolitical realities of both the Maori children and the Brazilian adults.

Further, in *Literacy in Thirty Hours*, Cynthia Brown interviews Herb Kohl on the subject of multicultural learners. Kohl suggests that before American teachers approach the subject of language with children of other cultures, they should first discuss with students the conditions and circumstances of the culture from which they come. From these readings students seem to begin to understand both the political nature of literacy and what Elspeth Stuckey has termed the "violence of literacy" or literacy that manages sets of relationships and power.[7]

Next we read an interview with Paulo Freire by the editor of *Language Arts* entitled "Reading the World and Reading the Word" in which Freire raises the problem of teacher-student relationships with respect to reading and writing.[8] Through a discussion of what Freire calls "making Easter" (i.e., the dominator teacher dies everyday to "be born again as the dominated, fighting to overcome oppression" with his or her students, "to be born again as an open mind, a creative mind"), he makes the problematic the issue of "certainties."[9] This particular issue appears in *Teacher* and throughout the next two schooling narratives we examine: Mike Rose's *Lives on the Boundary* and Eliot Wigginton's *Sometimes a Shining Moment*.[10] The issue is raised in Freire's response to this question, "What is your vision of education?"

Freire describes education as politics, art, and knowing, and he says that the dimension of how we do what we do is an artistic dimension and not just a methodological one. Freire says that when we constantly ask questions of ourselves and our students, then we make sure we are uncertain by legitimating uncertainty. If uncertainty becomes a legitimate way of "walking toward" knowledge or knowing as Freire puts it, then being uncertain is one way of challenging reified, privileged forms of knowledge that tend to represent stasis rather than growth (what I perceive is implied in the use of the progressive form "knowing" and "walking toward").[11]

In *Lives on the Boundary*, Rose's own story of schooling and multiculturalism, the problem of teacher as politician, artist, and knower is illuminated.[12] Rose's attempts to get at the needs of students for whom schools have traditionally been lax in serving provides a context for making connections between what Freire names as the "how" dimension of teaching that is different from the more traditional prepackaged, drill and skill, workbook dominated, and impersonal "how to" dimension. Likewise, Wigginton illuminates this "how" dimension as he tells the story of how he and his students turned traditional English study into the study of rural Georgia and its people and began to produce the Foxfire books.[13] Both books catalog the difficulties, uncertainties, and failures on the way to successfully pioneering educational experiences that serve the needs of students not bureaucracies.

The topic of inquiry seemed well served by these readings. Students wrote lucidly in their journals about the need for curricular materials and approaches that are sensitive to students' multicultural histories. They particularly seemed interested in Ashton-Warner's "organic reading" as an appropriate method to be used in classrooms with multicultural students of all ages. Following Freire's idea of systematizing what students do know so they can move on (the image here is of teachers as gatherers and organizers of information instead of dispensers), students suggested the connections between the inside-out approaches of both Ashton-Warner and Freire as a possible means of helping multicultural learners "build bridges to other cultures."[14]

Here, student-teachers' ideas helped me to think through problematic schooling issues that I wrestle with. For example, I'm wondering what happens when our best intentions for creating the conditions for reflection actually result in our leaping ahead to making connections for students. After all we may not be able to teach inquiry and reflection, but we may plan for that to happen by carefully planning a curriculum that invites such activity. But even when I stay far away from how-to approaches do I not in subtle other ways pull students along according to *my plan*? Is my how dimension really an artistic dimension that bubbles up through mutual curiosity over engaging material or is it a politically determined interventive dimension with a new name, a new face, but still teacher directed all the same? And yet how is it possible to do otherwise? And how do I reconcile the tensions between teacherly intentions and students' needs? Perhaps, I cannot, but I can acknowledge that those tensions exist, and I can continue to explore how my intentions are taken up in my classrooms and in those to which my students go on to teach. For example, if by pulling together particular materials students make particular assumptions and/or connections, then it may be more worth examining those assumptions and/or connections than continuing to worry with why they made them. However, if I arrange and show students applications and/or make connections for them (even through a variety of experiences) *that* is quintessentially different from their making those connections themselves— what might amount to "real" sense making. And *that* is often the case in courses that teach us "how to" teach. The "gathering" metaphor (also used by Ann Berthoff as the "gathering hand" metaphor[15]) may offer another way of seeing how the sense-making process tends to work. In other words, the notion of gathering refers to what the mind does as it gathers information through a process of inquiry, sorts and selects, sets one thing against something else to find relationships as it spirals toward meaning—in other words, differentiates between newly gathered information and whatever else is known through previous lived experiences that seem relational.

When students connected the experiences of each of the authors to their own experiences and to the experiences of others they'd observed, they seemed to "grasp the soul" of the text, to create their own meanings.[16] Each story affirmed the love of teaching and that was also positive for students. Each story affirmed the intuitive abilities of children and adults to work with words that are their own, that are familiar, and that seem safe to them. Each story affirmed the incredible amount of unlearning that seems to take place when we believe as teachers that we must "plaster" on rather than "gather" so much information in the service of teaching. In other words, each story seemed to remind us that sometimes the hidden curriculum students understand from our teaching suggests to them that some things are essentially more worth knowing than others, and that, in general, as teachers we think that what we have to teach is more worth knowing than what students might learn without us.

From these readings, prospective teachers seemed also to begin to understand that some of the apathy that plagues school children may be due to a stifling of creativity—to children literally being "plastered" to death.[17] Each story affirmed that sometimes teaching means observing and sometimes it means creating an environment in which learning might occur and sometimes it means simply getting out of the way so that learning might happen organically, spontaneously, and without any help from us. But then, student-teachers almost unanimously were reminded that controlling not guiding is what they had seen in schools and that the absence of control called into question teachers' positions. Prospective teachers believed they might feel threatened, parents would complain to administrators, and soon they would be back to justifying their existence at the expense of what might be for students an especially important learning experience. So when we ask what it means to be a teacher we are also questioning what we call practice.

Because how we see practice seems integral to arguments about student and teacher positioning and whose knowledge seems to be legitimate, it may be reasonable then to push students to think more deliberately about educational systems and how they embed within the larger society. However, connections here between knowledge and power and how valuations of each work within the structures and substructures of a wider context are not easy for students to make themselves. Even when the readings lead me to such connections, I cannot assume that my students will be led to make similar links—they are younger; they have experienced less and their classed, raced, and gendered positions have given them different lenses through which to see this wider context. So, at these moments, interventive or not, I do push my students to ask harder questions, analyze deeper structures; I am more deliberate about critical methodologies.

Here, the obvious arguments occur. Long past conversations about students rising to level of teachers' expectations (to borrow from Dewey[18]), long past conversations about empowered teachers helping students to become empowered, we finally come to the argument that is so complex and yet central to all that we are about. My final "yes, but" is that schools are simply not set up like little laboratories with inquiring teachers and learners running about logging discoveries. And then the seeming simple but hard questions begin. But why not? And could they be? And who will ever help students to be critical inquirers if not teachers? And how will bureaucracies be better served if students and teachers are not more inquisitive? And finally who does the school serve? And why? And why wouldn't a society that espouses democratic principles want citizens who question, challenge, and make intelligent decisions?

I want to return now to where I began in this discussion of diverse learners to make what I believe to be an important point that took me many years to learn. That is, showing films in class may not necessarily be seen as a poor excuse for teaching. Indeed, it can be some of our best teaching if we use the film as we might use literature for the vicarious experience of it and for purposes of deconstruction and social critique. We can ask, in film just as we can in literature, whose lives, whose experiences, are affirmed and through what means? And sometimes, as alluded to earlier, the overwhelming "big screen" may have a stronger visual affect on some learners than on others.[19] This particular example comes to mind.

In the course to which I previously referred, students also gave book talks (including film): Many of their talks were from books in the bibliography of schooling narratives included at the end of this text. Several of the Pat Conroy novels were used: *The Great Santini, The Water Is Wide, The Prince of Tides, The Lords of Discipline*.[20] I remember that the enthusiasm for each of these books was good. However, on seeing the moving version of *The Prince of Tides*,[21] even with all the Hollywood glitz, I can't help wondering whether this medium wouldn't reach some students even more than Conroy's book.

Although the film does not dramatize classroom teaching and learning to the extent that we might imagine it, we see, nonetheless, the passion that is rekindled when Tom Wingo coaches Bernard in football. Bernard is the son of Wingo's sister's therapist; Wingo and the therapist become lovers.

Bernard has been in training to be a concert violinist most of his life, but he wants to play football. His father, an acclaimed violinist, is against the sport for fear Bernard will injure his fingers. (I do not use this example to privilege football over violin lessons but because it is the only well-illustrated teaching scene.) Bernard discovers the joy of learning under the tutelage of Tom, an ex-football coach and English teacher. And Tom remembers the joy of teaching through his experiences with Bernard.

What he seems to learn while in New York (despite the fact that Tom went to New York City to try to help his sister, Savannah) and what the film suggested to me during Tom's interactions with Bernard (here teaching/learning seems to occur during play) is that teaching and learning are acts in which the mysteries of life continue to unfold.

Significant revelations about Tom's past (mysteries about his life) seemed to emerge during conversations when Savannah's therapist was probing for information that she thought would help Savannah (here significant teaching/learning seemed to occur during conversation that involved narrative). What seems significant here is Tom's new understanding of "masculinity" apart from the traditional male stereotype (except with respect to his acting on what appeared to be mutual physical attraction between him and the therapist). Because Tom is forced to remember painful childhood experiences in order to help Savannah, who is hospitalized for attempted suicide, Tom himself experiences a kind of awakening in which the instance of remembering sets him and his sister free. Tom breaks almost all of what he calls "the Southern way" or codes of male behavior—those meanings and practices he has been socialized into, especially by his mother and father—when he deals with his problems by talking about the past instead of making a joke to change the subject. Crippled by a life of denial, Tom finally remembers, talks about, and cries over the rape (his own, Savannah's, and his mother's), the murder (Luke, Tom and Savannah's older brother, shoots two of the rapists, and his mother stabs the third), and the subsequent cover-up of the whole ordeal followed by the attempt to pretend it never happened. New understanding about himself enables Tom's reconnection with those things in his life about which he seems to care most—his family and his teaching. Shortly thereafter, he returns to South Carolina and the Charleston coast to rekindle his relationship with his wife and to resume his teaching.

What struck me about this film was its capacity to help me see the complexities of the private self that has to meld with the teaching self in order to be capable of feeling secure without controlling. Teachers' lives are often mirrored by their students' lives. Predispositions and learned behaviors go with us into any classroom setting and become as much a part of the curriculum (at least, the hidden curriculum) as do the more overtly stated goals and objectives. Films like this one may further open the space for discussion of those social dynamics that are a part of understanding what it means to be a teacher. When examining stories of schooling, we need to look at the schooling that goes on outside of the classroom also if we are to begin to understand teachers as well as students.

Two other films, *Grand Canyon* and *Boyz N the Hood*, give us that window on students' lives, and the frightening, larger-than-life effect of the big screen again seems to add a dimension of understanding.[22] For example, in both films the sort of hopelessness that children feel who grow up in streets where violence is a way of life is made startlingly apparent. When a child laughs and says he never expects to make it to twenty-five, the viewer has to take seriously what is happening in our world today. What the imaginations of white, middle-class teachers and students might be incapable of reproducing, the movie screen reproduces with harsh reality. I agree with Bill Nichols that this harsh reality is more than the effect of holding a mirror up to society (a cultural reproduction theory of movies and films).[23] We are forced to look at and really see (which means perceiving or more than seeing visually) the fear that lives inside many school children, especially those children for whom school seems to make no difference. If the reality is that many children do not believe they will live to be adults because of drive-by shootings that claim victims indiscriminately, then how can they imagine that school will make a difference—school that seems filled with curricula that makes no sense for their lives?

What the particular children whose lives are represented in these films seem to be learning on the streets is a kind of survival of the fittest that school does not address—that money equals power and power equals respect. If they have no money to buy respect, then they buy it with a weapon. Indeed, then, the sort of cultural, social critique of power that we so often omit from our curricula is seen through the street-wise eyes of many children. And I wonder when I see the kinds of social lessons children learn from everyday life, why it is we, in education, believe our so-called legitimate knowledge makes more sense. It seems to only make more sense to targeted audiences, and children who have virtually turned off school seem to recognize this.

Ashton-Warner suggests the "warrior" metaphor for thinking about the sort of pent-up anger and aggressiveness that results in violence by her "little ones."[24] Perhaps, the notion of warriorlike tendencies could be extended to gangs and gang violence. In other words, warriors are protectors who fight. Gang violence also seems to surround the issue of protecting one's turf. Because kids' experiences (some more than others) seem to have been devalued for so long, many have become virtually invisible (to use Sue

Allen's words).[25] Perhaps, then, the strong need to form gangs and act like warriors grows out of the need for some kind of self-identity.

Filmmakers consciously assemble and edit footage to create a collage effect that in itself produces a particular image of reality. If we approach film as we might music that is altered with each conductor's orchestration or each pianist's own expression or as what Eco refers to as an open text, then we might use that moment in film and music (including rap) to begin to create a new social analysis of education.[26]

For example, on the subject of gang violence and the idea of a weapon buying respect/power, a rap musician known as Ice T produces lyrics or "language that functions as a medium of power like a gun" (to use Rashidah Muhammad's words).[27] This particular rap song compares the mind to a "riot gun" and rap to television. It suggests that if we (society) think(s) rap is bad, we should watch TV. The verse concludes by saying that rap music is the stuff of street-life or what's learned in city streets.[28]

The lyrics of this rap tune suggest to me once again Stuckey's notion of "the violence of literacy"—violence that suggests that the dominant culture regulates who can use language to achieve power and who must use a gun. Stuckey writes:

> Lives are defined by language if language is a tool of oppression. . . . The violence of literacy is the violence of the milieu it comes from, promises, and perpetuates. It is attached inextricably to the world of food, shelter, and human equality. . . . To elucidate the violence of literacy is to understand the distance it forces between people and the possibilities for their lives.[29]

The gun replaces the power of one's words if one's words do not measure up or if we as educators have narrowly defined literacy as the ability to read and write privileged texts but not to use language to get things done in the "real" world.

As "Squeeze the Trigger" and *Boyz N the Hood* and *Grand Canyon* tend to show us the harsh realities, I am concerned with how these words and images are taken up in the lives of young people.[30] As the contributors to Giroux and Simon's collection of essays on *Popular Culture, Schooling, and Everyday Life* suggest, we do need to understand and legitimate the stories and traditions that have long been denied as a part of the processes of learning.[31] Particularly when the scope of students popular cultural experiences includes rap music and MTV (especially those children ages ten to fifteen according to recent surveys), we need to help students develop the abilities to produce sensitive readings that critique not only the violence but also the social injustice that both contributes and becomes a part of cultural conflict. All students (our teacher education students and those they will teach) deserve access to the histories and skills that will set them free—that they will need in order to be productive citizens in any community. As the rap song "Too Legit to Quit" by MC Hammer seems to suggest, kids who have been taught to be critical consumers of schooling, in general, may come to understand that they have a right to question, to know, to say No, and to ask harder questions.[32]

But *Grand Canyon*, in particular, suggests something else about educational reform and social change that makes it especially important for my classes in which resistance and revolution are key themes from which to explore topics of inquiry like "What does it take to start a revolution? And once a revolution is begun, how do we keep it going?" The continual reference to the Grand Canyon in the movie and the final scene in which a black family and a white family, who have recently adopted a Hispanic baby, is juxtaposed with the landscape of the Grand Canyon serves as a reminder of how small we are in the scheme of things, but also how vital we are to change.[33] As noted by the Heisenberg principle, one tiny thing changes everything.

For example, a black man from the tow service rescues a white man from gang violence when his car breaks down late at night. The white man feels indebted and from that moment on will not stay out of the black man's life. The white man plays matchmaker with the black man and helps two lonely adults find each other. Additionally, the white man, an immigration lawyer, helps the black man's sister and children move to a street where the threat of gangs and violence is lessened. Meanwhile, a mother, the immigration lawyer's wife, is jogging and hears a baby cry. It turns out the baby is Hispanic and has been abandoned near Carmolena Street. The point I'm trying to establish here, despite the possible racist and classist stereotypes (white middle-class family helps black working-class family and later white family adopts Hispanic baby abandoned by underclass or homeless mother), is that one tiny thing can begin a landslide of activity just like the pebble that is kicked into the Grand Canyon that has the potential to perpetuate continual shifts in the landscape.

I purposefully avoided using the names of the characters to illustrate how in the movie not they (as individuals necessarily) but their actions seemed mysteriously tied to the shifting and changing of the universe. Additionally, I refer to their races because in the movie, though each family is represented by name, the characters seem almost more to represent collective races than individual lives, perhaps to illustrate how small we are individually but how large we are collectively and collectively we may have more of a chance to start a landslide.

Additionally, the black man, who seems to represent the one person in the movie with the most understanding of life and the universe, comments on several occasions that the Grand Canyon is like this big hole through which the earth opens up and releases all its rage and violence. He says repeatedly, "Something's got to change."[34]

Additionally, part of the upheaval of rage suggested by *Grand Canyon* may be seen in the increasing number of music videos on MTV that seem to valorize the negative portrayal of women by musicians such as Motley Crue with songs like "Sticky Sweet" and Van Halen with "Good Enough."[35] The words in both songs make sexual references that seem to suggest that when a woman is "hot," she is finally "good enough." Additionally, violence to women is suggested in lyrics like "Spanked" by Van Halen, "Where There's a Whip There's a Way" by Faster Pussycat, "The Jungle" by Guns 'n Roses, and "Slice of Pie" by Motley Crue.[36] In each case, violent acts of sexuality such as beating and raping occur. In a class project for a course I teach on women and minorities, one student counted the word *kill* fourteen times, *dying* twelve times, *death* seven times, and *slaughter* once all in one album alone—Metallica's "Master of Puppets."[37] Does seeing violent videos on music television suggest that violence has been raised to the status of art?

Gloria Anzaldua suggests art is political when she writes:

> For many of us the acts of writing, painting, performing, and filming are acts of deliberate determination to subvert the status quo. Creative acts are forms of political activism employing definite aesthetic strategies for resisting dominant cultural norms and are not merely aesthetic exercises. We build culture as we inscribe in these forms.[38]

If young people see music videos as an alternative art form, to what do they consider that it protests? They may believe that the

raucous behavior protests sameness or perhaps what they presume to be middle-class values, but if they examined the violence
against women, would they see protest or perpetuation of dominant cultural attitudes about women that perceive that domination is normal and sexism is just a new term invented by angry
feminists (or if protest, then perhaps feminism is what particular
acts of violence against women protest)?

Here the illusion of art may be seductive, but if teachers are
willing to take up such issues, we may be capable of helping students deconstruct such music and music videos in the service of
also teaching about the partiality of that form of cultural representation. If as Anzaldua suggests, we inscribe culture through
such forms, then it seems necessary to help students raise questions about the nature of such a culture.

And if as some students tell me when I show how angry such
violence makes me (all violent acts and especially sexually violent
acts) that kids don't really pay that much attention because they
are so sensitized, I have to ask then if it doesn't affect their conscious awarenesses, what are the effects of violence on the subconscious mind? Could some of the rage depicted in movies like
Grand Canyon, and *Boyz N the Hood* arise from the effects of
violence on the subconscious?[39] Instead of ignoring violence and
rage, we need to examine perhaps its source, but more importantly its effects on individuals and on society. We need to make
problematic the harm such rage and violence brings not just to
women but to all who are uncritical consumers of the particular
version of popular culture packaged in some popular music and
music videos.

And especially important might be an examination of how
such acts signal protest, if indeed they do. Here, however, it seems
less of a concern to me, at least, to ponder the deliberate nature of
protest or perpetuation and more important to ask, who stands to
gain, who stands to lose in either case? In other words, if the particular acts around particular music or music videos protest, how
and to what are they in protest of, and who gains, who loses? On
the other hand, if particular acts around particular music or
music videos perpetuate dominant attitudes and subsequent conditions, how and to what extent do they perpetuate what, and
who gains, who loses?

It is one thing to recognize and accept as part of a cultural
experience all kinds of media texts; it is another to teach students

to be critical consumers of that culture. As we help students question the nature of violence and rage in all forms of art, expose negative stereotypes, and question social and economic/materialistic structures that mediate sets of relations and seem to perpetuate the kind of rage the music videos discussed here sell, we need also to help students recognize "the limits and partialness of specific languages, cultures, and experiences in terms of both the positive and the negative impacts they have had and might have in contributing to the construction of a democratic state."[40]

It is not enough to have educational reform that refines technique or even that attempts to understand what it means to be a teacher in a diverse setting—even if implicit in that goal is the goal of understanding the diverse learner. Educational reforms and social reforms need to be addressed simultaneously. One may not occur without the other! Social and educational change is relational and may only affect those whose lives are most at stake when understood as they apply not just to what is taught and how it is taught, but to particular attitudes and perceptions toward particular phenomena.

What I am learning as I struggle to be self-critical and reflective is that there are no simple solutions to complex problems and most things I think are solutions are really invitations to ask harder questions. A thought for the day is posted everyday in my favorite coffee shop; one day the thought was "Solutions are answers to yesterday's problems."

Perhaps more important, however, than learning that simple solutions are not applicable to complex problems is what I am learning about multiplicity—in other words, that there may be multiple paths to approaching any problem. Actually, I suppose I've always believed this; I had not, however, applied it to teaching. I was never a good test taker or survey taker, and so on because I could not or would not see one right path—one convergent answer—to a problem. I would write in the margins of the answer sheets, but what about this choice or this or this.

And now I think that's how my students must feel when I limit their choices in my ready-made curriculum each term, a curriculum that changes often, but one, nonetheless, that I create prior to meeting my students. I, too, am so socialized with respect to planning my courses, I forget to think about whether what I plan will be right for the particular class of students in a particular term. The fact is I may not even trust that teachers-to-be or experienced teachers will want to tackle hard issues, will want to go beyond a "what to do on Monday" curriculum. So, I don't ask, but not asking may doom my students who are prospective teachers and those who are experienced teachers to a practice that may cripple their attempts to make real change. For example, my negotiating curriculum with students and their negotiating curriculum with students would amount to real change. And change that might mark the beginning of more change.

In other words, I've wanted to say, thought about it a lot, but haven't had the nerve to say, "What do you want to learn this term?" And together we could build the curriculum from there. I really have no excuse other than, if truth be told, I want to teach what I want to teach—I have an agenda. But that is exactly what teachers in schools tell me when I ask why they don't do thus and such that would amount to changed practice—often in terms of both form and content.

The fact of the matter is I haven't been in partnership with my students, and perhaps part of the reason may also be that I'm not sure we could actually have a partnership. Oh, I do think students would tell me what they're interested in, but if I began making suggestions, investing my preferences, then suddenly I believe I'd see authority switch back to me and students yield their preferences in favor of mine. Perhaps I've seen the give-the-teacher-what-the-teacher-wants syndrome too often to believe that students would hold out for what they truly are interested in learning if they think I want to teach something else.

So I can't say we're a partnership, though I do believe I learn from my students. I may not be willing to wait until after the term begins to order books (though I could because of my arrangement with a local bookstore, not the campus bookstore—an issue in preserving tradition unto itself for our campus book orders must go in a full term in advance), but I do, on the other hand, leave space in the course outline for additional readings to be filled in after the course begins. In other words, I've begun asking on the first day of class, after I've handed out and explained the syllabus, what they've learned in other classes and what they would like to learn in my class so that I can pull together additional readings that reflect their concerns. Having tried this much I may eventually have the nerve to try more. But when I think of the problems associated with pulling an entire semester course together at the last minute (even though in my department I have the freedom to do this) or of the million other real not imagined dilemmas that could result, I continue to do the work of planning the bulk of the course ahead, which means planning my agenda. And what a particularly odd message I must send when I talk to student-teachers about teaching/learning relationships/partnerships and then I ask them to write lessons plans, an assignment that is an institutionalized part of a methods class. Indeed, the catch-22 for all teachers may be how much planning is enough and how much is too little.

One of the ways, however, that I have strengthened my teacher as learner and learner as teacher relationships with students has to do with the way I prepare for teaching a course and for each class—something I have no philosophical or practical problems with. In other words, I fully believe in what Gordon Pradl has referred to as teaching from the point of utterance.[41] This approach has strong links to Shor and Freire's dialogical curriculum and affirms the notion that if you teach literature or any text from an authoritative stance—one any teacher of any subject might have who teaches from the same texts all the time, it will be difficult to convince students that you learn from their ideas as they learn from yours.[42] I'm not convinced students believe that even under this approach. But I perceive it is more likely that they're readings will affect my reading of a text if I have not read and studied the text so many times that I am sure I have the most valid if not only valid interpretation. Perhaps my comfort with this approach has to do with a lack of trust in my own ability to let students' interpretations, their voices, count as much as mine if I know the text too well. Perhaps under the latter situation, I would simply lecture instead of trying to convince them that their meanings mattered—something I'm pretty sure would be false on my part and I'd never be able to successfully convey. Perhaps it is my strategy for remaining uncertain before my students so that together we may walk toward knowing as Freire put it.[43] So I let students see me struggle to make sense of a text I've done little more than a cursory reading of prior to reading in-depth with them to prepare for class (and I do not hesitate to let students know this, but of course, I also realize that my in-depth reading may be different from theirs). Nonetheless, when students see me struggle to make sense, it may suggest to them that it's okay not to know every reading of any text prior to teaching it, that students' voices offer valid perspectives/readings, and that within the multiplicity of perspectives we may carve meanings that make some sense to all of us. I perceive that, at least, such practice may encourage uncertainty that may have the potential to yield inquiry and reflection.

This, of course, is all much to the chagrin of many of my colleagues who see my excitement as books frequently arrive in my mailbox. Occasionally someone will ask me how I have time to read so many books, and I tell them they are for a course I'm teaching. The next question is almost always, "How can you teach a book you haven't studied for years?" With this opening I explain how I do it and to what justification knowing that they read many of the same theorists I read, and what follows is usually a smile and a rapid exit from the mailbox area in the English Department main office (this approach is really a reward for me because I possibly get to read many more new books than they do since I read new books with my students nearly every term).

Another way I have worked around the tensions associated with a completely negotiated curriculum but also the dilemma I feel for being able to bring myself to negotiating more of it is to use more literature and other aesthetic media than what students see as "real texts." Textbooks provide "controlled" information, but literature or a literary text (film, television, music, etc.) is more open-ended, especially if it is not what students consider canonical literature that they (and I because we've all studied the same literature) have come to see as having a particular interpretation. Although the text may intend to present one view of the world, critical readers and writers do not have to reproduce that view, especially if, as Brown suggests, teachers are willing to have their students see reading as an act of political participation[44] or as more than walking on words as Freire put it.[45] Students may produce new meanings which represent their classed, raced, and gendered views of the world. Though I prefer the open-ended nature of literature and film because this is where students have the opportunity to take over the agenda of any class, but because I want their readings of aesthetic texts to at least entertain my agenda, I generally pair literature and other artistic materials with brief critical readings (sometimes passages, sometimes whole articles, rarely an entire book-length critical text, and even sometimes newspaper editorials and frequently from alternative publications). Helping students walk toward a critical reading, which is more than walking on the words, is the goal of my pairing disparate texts.

Though my agenda is there and they know it, the open-ended nature of aesthetic texts still lends itself to multiple interpretations, and students still tend to react to issues that resonate most with their personal and collective experiences. Sometimes the critical readings may do little more than plant seeds of thought that students may come back to later. Regardless, such endeavors do seem to loosen the controls and give students more room to play with ideas and more space to think globally about teaching and locally about what they might do in specific situations without reducing their efforts and mine to a lesson plan. Our talk usually gets to issues within the literary text that are spelled out in the critical text and that relate on some level to the classroom and to teaching/learning.

Relative to some of the kinds of issues I build courses around that I perceive extend our classroom beyond its four walls are topics of critical inquiry that have to do with revolution. For example, Lloyd Alexander has written a particularly fine collection of children's books around this theme.[46] The stories blend Welsh legend and mythology to unfold in a kind of giving of directions for building a revolution, winning a revolution, and holding on to revolution.

Westmark helps us examine questions related to how to build a revolution; that is, how to plan for change.[47]

The story centers around the fact that the kingdom of Westmark is a dangerous place to live because the villainous Chief Minister Cabbarus is in power. Theo is forced to leave the country and live like a fugitive. With friends, Theo plots his return to save Westmark. The story provides a medium for discussing issues of power and control related to the larger society and to schooling structures; that is, What does power imply? Who has it? How can it be decentralized, particularly in classrooms? When it is decentralized, how much power do students really have? Experienced teachers talk about the possibility that questioning authority might mean that students lose respect for teachers. Here we make problematic the notion of certain forms of respect—for example, teachers ask if respect that is commanded through control is "real" respect. One thing most students, prospective and experienced teachers seem to realize from reading *Westmark* is that people have to join together if they want to effect change.

The Kestrel is the sequel to *Westmark*; it helps us examine the question, How to win a revolution?[48] In this book Mickle, or

Princess Augusta, ascends the throne just as war breaks out. Theo and friends remain joined in their efforts to save the throne. What the book illustrates so poignantly is that change occurs slowly and not easily. This creates the space to question some of the educational reform proposals that suggest solutions that seem to reduce very complex problems into what appears simple.

How to hold on to revolution is the subject of *The Beggar Queen*.[49] In this book Theo, Luther, Mickle, and the others are trying to determine the best way to dismantle the monarchy and distribute its riches among the poor in the countryside. Equality is held up as the key to holding on to revolution—freedom for every man, woman, and child in the kingdom of Westmark. Readers seem to recognize commonalities between the storybook kingdom of Westmark and any society in which materialism tends to create centralized power and wealth and is available to only a few. Toppling the system, as in these books, meant decentralizing power and distributing the riches of the kingdom. Freedom meant freedom from hunger as well as freedom to vote. A new constitution was formed that made such freedoms the legitimate right of every human.

In this fantasy representation of revolt, the masses, and the new beggar queen were joined. However, as Raymond Williams has suggested, in the real world the dominant culture seems to "at once produce and limit its own forms of counterculture."[50] In other words, what Alexander leaves for us to examine further is the particular ideological mechanism that is articulated in any social movement (i.e., How did Theo organize and mobilize his troops? Who decided that Theo was in charge? Through what process did revolt become collective action? How did it become a class movement? and so forth).

Those questions became more important as we pushed on the boundaries of fantasy and sociopolitical reality to extend our critique to embedded issues that lay just beneath the surface of the literary experience. We brought in newspaper clippings of current events around the world (e.g., democratization and the subsequent dismantling of the Soviet Union, language debates in Quebec, Canadian government and the possible suspension of socialized medicine, anti-abortionists, election issues, Middle East peace conference talks, etc.). I brought in clippings from a newspaper that is not distributed on the local news-stands and that represents the voice of the people (e.g., issues related to Wichita pro-choice activists, Thomas's attack on right to raise issues of sexual harassment, 60,000 marching in New York against Haiti Coup, farmers holding protests across Canada, the debate over the "right to die with dignity," whether sanction on Yugoslavia is in workers' interests, challenges to labor movement posed by Duke vote). We compared versions of particular events reported in different news media. And we examined reform documents like *A Nation at Risk*, *The Paideia Proposal*, and several working papers for the *Schools for Tomorrow* proposal.[51] And we examined Kathleen Weiler's book *Women Teaching for Change*.[52] We compared versions of school reform reported in each of these documents as well as Weiler's feminist analysis of women teachers and administrators working for change. We examined the topics of inquiry for the course against the particular topics that fell out of our reading both the literary selections and the professional selections. Students immediately noted that issues of power and what is valued materially were key topics in all the texts. Students seemed to make connections between the way knowledge is valued and the way material possessions are valued.

We examined one final source briefly, Philip Wexler's discussion of "the commodification of education."[53] Here Wexler describes the revaluation of education in terms of valuable commodities such as "minimum-competency tests," "teacher effectiveness," and "performance objectives," a process that drains the content of any cultural or historical relevance and reduces learning to narrowly defined technical skills.[54] Again, this process of school reorganization is linked more with job placement than with raising the intellect or stirring the imagination—the latter being abilities that would allow individuals and groups of individuals to pose solutions to problems in this society rather than to function simply as workers.

This brief passage along with Weiler's study, school reform proposals, and the variety of newspaper clippings that are offered up as curriculum read against the imaginative literature of Lloyd Alexander suggests that, perhaps, one thing needed for a revolution is the "reconstruction of social imagination in the service of human freedom."[55] The move to technologize education seems to reproduce slaves not masters, workers not thinkers, and seems to assure a particular segment of society that there will be no revolution or that if revolt is attempted it will have limited effect. If schools can train workers to make whatever meager salaries are available then there is no need to redistribute the wealth as Mickle, the beggar queen, sought to do in the kingdom of Westmark.

Both the movie *Grand Canyon* and Alexander's books seem to suggest the vital role of social action as the key to structural change in society.[56] The kind of change alluded to in all the works discussed in this chapter thus far is the kind of social change that does not simply create structural differences, though some argue that even here a class analysis limits the overall effect of change. I would argue, however, that global change is not, nor should it be, an either/or proposition—that is, either we change structures or we change everyday perceptions. Change, it seems then needs to include both a change in structure and a change in everyday perception and action (including the language through which perception is interpreted) and it occurs slowly over time. My thinking relative to this issue is perhaps why this book could be neither a matter of theory nor a matter of practice, but an attempt to blend both throughout (it may also explain why it took so many years to write).

Another grouping illustrates this point and are books I use under a thematic emphasis called "Novels of Resistance."[57] We examine these books against a series of newsworthy events related to social change. Many of the same clippings noted previously in this section work also to enhance discussion and analysis of these books. What is of particular interest about all of the books is the way in which they show how slow and deliberate change is.

Margaret Sacks's *Beyond Safe Boundaries* is set in South Africa and portrays the blatant injustices due to apartheid.[58] The story begins during the early years of the anti-apartheid movement with the portrayal of class and race differences as illustrated by Elizabeth's family's privileged way of life—a life of tennis clubs, servants, and private schools. Until Elizabeth's sister, Evie, joins the movement, Elizabeth knows little about other ways of life in South Africa. When she learns about police brutality, false arrests, phone tappings, Elizabeth can no longer ignore the injustices in her country. Finding a voice to speak out and in an arena where she will be heard when so many others are silenced, then, becomes the focal point of the remainder of the book.

Following this portrait of a white South African girl's struggle to find an arena where she can make a difference is the story of the other people in South Africa, those who know people do not listen when you are weak, only when you are strong. *Chain of Fire* by Beverly Naidoo is the story of working-class people in South Africa (but could be anywhere) who know they must form a chain—a collective—in order to be strong.[59]

The story is told from the perspective of a fifteen-year-old girl, Naledi, who with her friends and other residents of the village of Bophelong form a chain to resist being forcibly made to leave their homes. As Naledi and her friends and family refuse to retreat, the school is closed, the church is bulldozed, and the water supply is shut off. What follows is an evocative portrait of apartheid in its most malignant forms. As buildings fall and bodies weaken, new links in the chain of fiery resistance are forged.

Articles like "South African Political Parties Set Negotiations," "South Africa Shut Down 2 Days as Millions Strike," and an article on Nelson Mandela as he addresses the issue of burned houses and refugees who flee violence in Natal, South Africa, provide a nonfictional account of the action described in both books.[60] In the same way that literature seems to illumine problems that professional texts raise, examining current newspaper clippings brings social issues closer and provides historical links as well as additional information. Current events pairings also help to establish a sense of time, perspective, lived-through experiences, and they immediately add a range of knowing that helps us see that the experiences illuminated in the novels are a part of a wider cultural struggle.

The dedication page to *The Forty-Third War* by Louise Moeri is written "to all children everywhere trapped in war."[61] The novel chronicles eight days in the life of a young Central American boy. The story begins when Uno Ramirez becomes a soldier in his country's forty-third revolution. Details and events are presented realistically, but what readers seem to be left with is the understanding that if the revolution is not won in forty-three wars then there will be more. There will always be more. A country in need of change will always be in revolution because the need is great.

Rice without Rain by Minfong Ho is the story of a people learning that century-old traditions are outdated and need to change in order for people to survive.[62] Jinda, the seventeen-year-old protagonist, learns to trust outsiders who bring hope of taking charge of one's own destiny. However, at the same time that Jinda and her family find hope from these strangers, they struggle to preserve their rapidly declining culture. *Rice without Rain* is a book about hope that change can engender, but it is also a book about fear of the unknown through loss of tradition.

Neal Shusterman's novel, *Dissidents*, is about one young man's attempt to be his own person in Moscow.[63] Derek moved to Moscow to live with his mother, the U.S. Ambassador to the Soviet Union, after his father's untimely death in Chicago. Set in contemporary Russia, Derek becomes friends with the daughter of an exiled dissident. Like Derek, Anna is also an outsider. After Anna's mother dies, the story centers around Derek's attempt to reunite Anna with her father across the thousands of miles that separate them. During this adventure Derek learns the painful truth about his own father.

Each novel can be analyzed for the particular structures that mediate against human agency, but they can also be examined for what Greene called "fields of possibility" [quoting Sartre].[64] Using this Sartrean perspective along with Greene's like notion of one who has a "consciousness of possibility," we (my students and I—in this course some teaching majors and some not) read and examine the textual material, focusing on the particular obstacles that seem to block social change. We raise possibilities for alternative paths in order to both meet and beat the obstacle or circumvent it and move on; we also discuss possible arenas for exploring those paths with other interested people. Then we turn our discussion to the particular constraints and obstacles that block pathways to freedom. We attempt to name our obstacles as problems, and then we consider various possible solutions that might get us around perceived obstacles. We discuss alternative solutions and continue to explore public arenas of debate in which we might expect to have our voices heard.

Going through this process, again and again, with each of the novels, students may begin to understand the role having a consciousness of possibility seems to play in helping to make change; they may begin to understand the need for thinking and debating in an open forum; and they may begin to understand the need to extend their voices to a wider audience, taking up individual problems then as a part of a cultural struggle—thinking and acting; seeing individual capacities and collective responsibilities.

Working to help teachers-to-be and experienced teachers understand the roles we all have in change tends to be the subject of much that I do. How we see ourselves in relation to others, what we value, and how it is we come to value what we value seems important. And finally how we understand the particular sets of beliefs we have and the affect those beliefs can have on our abilities to act in any given situation may be crucial to our participation in any project of possibility.

BELIEFS THAT LIMIT AND ENHANCE

Questions about teachers' beliefs and how teachers see the practice of schooling may be integral to curriculum reform, especially in teacher preparation. As students are called on to explore their own personal histories, their social, political, economic, and cultural realities through a curriculum of multiple voices, their predispositions tend to become more apparent. Recognizing what one believes is important, how those beliefs impinge on future practices is another matter and may depend on how we approach teacher education.

Cultural studies with particular emphasis on pairing a variety of texts, including books, films, television, music, and so on may arouse tensions to a point where students willingly question the nature of specific schooling practices—practices that tend to marginalize, practices that tend to reduce teaching to implementation and learning to the mastery of discrete skills, and practices that tend to limit human potential. With professional readings that form a social critique of meanings and practices, literature, film and television stories can provide another lens for seeing issues of power, ideology, and culture. In this way stories examined in concert with professional readings become more than a literary or pop cultural experience. Stories can, indeed, illumine our past, help us rediscover truths about ourselves, and lead the way for making culture.

In *Growing Minds and Becoming a Teacher* Herb Kohl iterates the importance of hearing each other's stories.[65] This idea is echoed in Robert Coles's *The Call of Stories*.[66] Yet as Landon Beyer suggests in "Aesthetic Experience for Teacher Preparation and Social Change," the general public including many educators usually consider aesthetic experiences in any form as "frills" or nonacademic and "play-full."[67] Part of the work of autobiography is to "uncover" the story—the story that has concealed ideological meaning. That, of course, makes narrative practice not only a "frill," it tends to make it relatively dangerous work in that part of any uncovering (or "unearthing of something previously sealed" as Beyer states) suggests critical inquiry into relationships "that were formerly hidden by the dominant traditions in social and educational theory."[68] Bruce Springsteen emphatically sings in "War,"[69] however, that not questioning our leaders can get us killed.

Not questioning, not pursuing education as inquiry into both the knower and the known may also get us killed, metaphorically speaking if not otherwise. We need a new vision, and I believe as others that part of that vision can occur through the systematic use of aesthetic materials—materials that allow for an opening onto educational theory, social theory, and critical practice, materials that allow for imagining our world as if could be otherwise. Beyer says that part of the way in which aesthetic practice makes possible alternative practice is through metaphor or seeing connections between things not usually united.[70] And Victor Nell sums up my thoughts this way (I extend Nell's commentary to include the reading of films, television, and the several media):

> Reading envelops us in "alternative realities. . . . Like dreaming, [aesthetic practice] performs the prodigious task of carrying us off to other worlds . . . [made of] dreams we would most like to have, and, like dreams, [aesthetic experiences] have the power to change consciousness."[71]

Within the pages of this text I have tried not to suggest methodology, yet at the same time I have tried to theorize the particulars of my own practice through self-critique and explanation/illustration. I have attempted to provoke thought, invite discussion, and suggest possible paths to the question of school reform. Although I have discussed possibilities for framing narrative practice, I wish to reiterate here that I perceive narrative as but one path. That is, I perceive that we need to consider educational reform and social reform in terms of multiple possibilities—a stance basic to the notion of both/and.

Historically, school reorganization is seen as the move or swing to one particular path over another. For example, as stated earlier, we consider the restructuring of schools either along the lines of everyday perceptions and actions or we consider it from the perspective of structural reorganization. We do not generally consider both ways at once. However, perhaps it is time we began to examine the embeddedness of both as a network of interrelated systems that do not work in lock-step sequence but side-by-side together—thought and action, structure and agency, constraint and possibility, educational reform and social change.

NOTES

PREFACE

1. Gloria Anzaldua, "Tlilli, Tlapalli: The Path of the Red and Black Ink," in *The Graywolf Annual Five: Multicultural Literacy*, Rick Simonson and Scott Walker, eds. (Saint Paul: Graywolf Press, 1988), 30–32.

2. Ibid., 30, 40.

3. Ibid., 30.

4. Ibid., 30, 37.

5. Clare Juncker, "Writing (with) Cixous," *College English* 50 (1988): 424.

6. Dale M. Bauer, "The Other 'F' Word: The Feminist in the Classroom," *College English* 52 (1990): 388.

7. Roland Barthes, *Image-Music-Text*, Stephen Heath, trans. (New York: Hill & Wang, 1977), 142.

8. Barbara Eckstein, *The Language of Fiction in a World of Pain* (Philadelphia: University of Pennsylvania Press, 1990), 25.

9. Barbara Johnson, *A World of Difference* (Baltimore: Johns Hopkins University Press, 1987), 15.

10. Eckstein, *The Language of Fiction in a World of Pain*, 26.

11. Alan Bass, Introduction to *Writing and Difference* by Jacques Derrida, Alan Bass, trans. (Chicago: University of Chicago Press, 1978), xv. Though I make some attempt to situate my notions of difference and uncertainty within the context of Derrida's work, I want to make clear that this by no means represents a thorough examination of what he might mean by "difference" and/or "differance." That discussion is not within the scope of this book. Furthermore, I see his work as only one among many contributions to that particular philosophical stream of thought.

12. Eckstein, *The Language of Fiction in a World of Pain*, 25–26.

13. Janet Miller, "Breaking Forms: (Re)Writing and (Re)Reading Power and Authority in Academic and Feminist Discourse." A paper given at the Bergamo Conference on Curriculum Theory and Practice, Dayton, OH, October, 1990.

14. Eckstein, *The Language of Fiction in a World of Pain*, 181.

15. Ibid., 29.

16. Ibid., 34.

17. Ibid., 28.

18. Anzaldua, "Tlilli, Tlapalli: The Path of the Red and Black Ink," 30.

19. Jo Anne Pagano, *Exiles and Communities: Teaching in the Patriarchal Wilderness* (Albany: State University of New York Press, 1990), 81.

CHAPTER 1. INTRODUCTION: NARRATIVE FRAMES

1. Rosemary Sutcliff, *Blue Remembered Hills* (Toronto: The Bodley Head, 1983); Alice Childress, *A Hero Ain't Nothing but a Sandwich* (New York: Avon Books, 1973); Robert Cormier, *The Chocolate War* (New York: Dell, 1974); John Williams, *Stoner* (New York: Viking, 1965).

2. Cormier, *The Chocolate War*.

3. Louise Rosenblatt, *The Reader, the Text, the Poem* (Carbondale and Edwardsville: Southern Illinois University Press, 1978).

4. Ann Berthoff used the term "dialectical notebook" in a seminar she gave for the Michigan Quadrangle Coalition on Literacy in May, 1988. She refers to this same notebook, what she also calls a "double-entry" notebook, in *Forming/Thinking/Writing* (Rochelle Park, NJ: Hayden, 1978).

5. Inspired by Rachel Carson's *Silent Spring* (Boston: Houghton Mifflin, 1962), Flo Krall's presentation at the Bergamo Conference on Curriculum Theory and Practice at Dayton, Ohio, 1988, began with her own growing-up story as she suggested the relationship between her past experiences and her present teaching life. Her story made me want to remember and focus on my childhood especially in relation to educational experiences. Professor Krall's willingness to engage the personal suggested for me its importance respective to teaching and learning. Thinking about the personal/public connections became a strong impetus for beginning this project.

6. Ken Kantor, Ann Trousdale, Sue Jungck, Ann Bennison, and Dan Marshall, "Images of Schooling in the Arts," presented at the Bergamo Conference on Curriculum Theory and Practice at Dayton, Ohio, 1988. This presentation also emphasized personal connections.

7. Delese Wear, "Medicine and Literature," presented at the Bergamo Conference on Curriculum Theory and Practice at Dayton, Ohio, 1988. Though this presentation dealt primarily with the teaching of literature to medical school students, dimensions of the personal and the public were very much a focus.

8. In Rosenblatt, *The Reader, the Text, the Poem*, 16, 46–47 transactional theory is described as the "live-circuit set up between the reader and the text." This theory assumes the reader's role is active not passive and that there is a transaction between the reader and the text because the reader brings prior experiences to the text and the text offers the reader new insights, ideas, and experiences. Both change as a result of the transaction. The reader has grown and the text has been (re)written in the reader's mind reflecting his or her own understanding/interpretation from background of experience. Each time a reader reads the text is (re)created. Rosenblatt's transactional theory, often referred to as a reader-response theory, suggests that primary or personal responses to texts lead the way for more critical analyses or evaluations.

9. Sylvia Ashton-Warner, *Spinster* (New York: Simon & Schuster, 1963).

10. Sylvia Ashton-Warner, *Teacher* (New York: Simon & Schuster, 1963).

11. Cynthia Brown, *Literacy in Thirty Hours* (Chicago: Center for Open Learning and Teaching, 1978).

12. Paulo Freire, *Pedagogy of the Oppressed* (New York: Continuum, 1970).

13. Ashton-Warner, *Spinster*, 158.

14. Ibid., 103.

15. Brown, *Literacy in Thirty Hours*, 5.

16. Ashton-Warner, *Spinster*, 40.

17. Rosenblatt, *The Reader, the Text, the Poem*, 16, 46–47.

18. Ashton-Warner, *Teacher*, 34.

19. Ashton-Warner, *Spinster*, 158.

20. This particular passage from Freire, *Pedagogy of the Oppressed*,

67, explicitly articulates the student-teacher partnership: "Through dialogue, the teacher-of-the-students and the students-of-the-teacher cease to exist and a new term emerges: teacher-student with students-teachers. The teacher is no longer merely the one-who-teaches, but one who is himself taught in dialogue with the students, who in turn while being taught also teaches."

21. Robert Scholes, *Textual Power* (New Haven: Yale University Press, 1985), 24.

22. Many of the sources for this bibliography were suggested in I. M. Tiedt and S. W. Tiedt, *Unrequired Reading* (Corvallis: Oregon State University Press, 1963).

23. Locating ideological codes through which meaning is produced is a method of semiotic analysis discussed in Umberto Eco, *The Role of the Reader: Explorations in the Semiotics of Texts* (Bloomington: Indiana University Press, 1979); J. Frow, "Discourse and Power," *Economy and Society* 14 (1985): 193–214; Stuart Hall, "The Problem of Ideology—Marxism without Guarantees," in *Marx: 100 Years On* (London: Lawrence and Wishart, 1983), 57–85; Julia Kristeva, ed., *Desire in Language: A Semiotic Approach to Literature and Art*, Thomas Gora, Alice Jardine, and Leon S. Roudiez, trans. (New York: Columbia University Press, 1980); Bill Nichols, *Ideology and the Image: Social Representations in the Cinema and other Media* (Bloomington: Indiana University Press, 1981).

24. See, for example, Louis Althusser, "Ideology and Ideological State Apparatuses," in *Lenin and Philosophy and Other Essays* (New York: New Left Books, 1971); Jean Anyon, "Social Class and the Hidden Curriculum of Work," *Journal of Education* 62 (1980): 67–92; Michael Apple, *Ideology and Curriculum* (Boston: Routledge & Kegan Paul, 1974); Apple, *Education and Power* (Boston: Ark Paperbacks, 1982); Mikhail Bakhtin, *The Dialogic Imagination: Four Essays*, Michael Holquist, ed., Caryl Emerson and Michael Holquist, trans. (Austin: University of Texas Press, 1981); Terry Eagleton, *Criticism and Ideology* (London: Humanities Press, 1976); Eagleton, *Marxism and Literary Criticism* (Los Angeles: University of California Press, 1976); Michel Foucault, *The Archaeology of Knowledge*, Alan Sheridan, trans. (New York: Pantheon Books, 1972); Foucault, *Discipline and Punish: The Birth of the Prison*, Alan Sheridan, trans. (New York: Vintage Books, 1979); Foucault, *Power and Knowledge: Selected Interviews and Other Writings, 1972–1977*, Colin Gordon, ed., Colin Gordon, Leo Marshall, John Mepham, Kate Soper, trans. (New York: Pantheon, 1980); Paulo Freire, *Pedagogy of the Oppressed*; Freire, *Education for a Critical Consciousness* (New York: Continuum, 1973); Freire, *The Poli-

tics of Education (South Hadley, MA: Bergin & Garvey, 1985); Henry Giroux, *Theory and Resistance in Education: A Pedagogy for Opposition* (London: Heinemann Educational Books, 1983); Antonio Gramsci, *Selections from the Prison Notebooks*, Q. Hoare and G. Norwell-Smith, eds. and trans. (New York: International Publishers, 1971); Carol Gould, "Philosophy of Liberation and the Liberation of Philosophy," in *Women and Philosophy: Toward a Theory of Liberation*, C. C. Gould and M. W. Wartofsky, eds. (New York: Capricorn Books, 1976); Maxine Greene, *Teacher as Stranger* (Belmont, CA: Wadsworth Publishing, 1973); Greene, *Landscapes of Learning*, (New York: Teachers College Press, 1978); Greene, "Sense-Making through Story: An Autobiographical Inquiry," *Teaching Education* 2 (1987): 9–14; Greene, *The Dialectic of Freedom* (New York: Teachers College Press, 1988); Madeleine Grumet, *Bitter Milk: Women and Teaching* (Amherst: University of Massachusetts Press, 1988); Julia Kristeva, *Revolution in Poetic Language*, Margaret Waller, trans. (New York: Columbia University Press, 1984); Nel Noddings, *Caring: A Feminine Approach to Ethics and Moral Education* (Berkeley: University of California Press, 1984); Pagano, *Exiles and Communities*; Raymond Williams, *The Long Revolution*, (New York: Columbia University Press, 1961); Williams, *Television and the Working Class* (Lexington, MA: D. C. Heath, 1975); Williams, *Technology and Cultural Form* (New York: Schocken Books, 1975); Williams, *Marxism and Literature* (New York: Oxford University Press, 1977); Williams, *Problems in Materialism and Culture* (London: Verso Editions, 1980); Williams, *The Year 2000* (New York: Pantheon Books, 1983); Virginia Woolf, *A Room of One's Own* (New York: Harcourt Brace Jovanovich, 1929).

25. Noddings, *Caring*, 101.

26. Apple, *Education and Power*; Freire, *Pedagogy of the Oppressed*; Henry Giroux, ed., *Teachers as Intellectuals* (South Hadley, MA: Bergin & Garvey, 1988); Pagano, *Exiles and Communities*; Janet Miller, *Creating Spaces and Finding Voices: Teachers Collaborating for Empowerment* (Albany: State University of New York Press, 1990).

27. Michael Apple, *Teachers and Texts: A Political Economy of Class and Gender Relations* (New York: Routledge & Kegan Paul, 1986); Freire, *Pedagogy of the Oppressed*.

28. Giroux, *Theory and Resistance in Education*.

29. Apple, *Education and Power*, 182.

30. Giroux, *Teachers as Intellectuals*, 162.

31. Miller, *Creating Spaces and Finding Voices*.

32. Freire, *Pedagogy of the Oppressed*, 70–71.

33. Giroux, *Teachers as Intellectual*, 51.

34. Bakhtin, *The Dialogic Imagination*; Foucault, *The Archaeology of Knowledge, Discipline and Punish, Power and Knowledge*; Gramsci, *Selections from Prison Notebooks*.

35. Williams, *The Long Revolution*, 355.

36. Henry Giroux and Peter McLaren, "Teacher Education as a Counter Public Sphere: Notes Toward a Redefinition," in *Critical Studies in Teacher Education: Its Folklore, Theory, and Practice*. Thomas Popkewitz, ed. (New York: The Falmer Press, 1987), 266–297.

37. Williams, *The Long Revolution*, 355.

38. Pagano, *Exiles and Communities*.

39. Miller, *Creating Spaces and Finding Voices*.

40. Jesse Goodman, *Elementary Schooling for Critical Democracy* (Albany: State University of New York Press, 1992).

41. James Schwoch, Mimi White, and Jack Reilly, *Media Knowledge* (Albany: State University of New York Press, 1992).

42. Henry Giroux and Roger Simon, *Popular Culture, Schooling, and Everyday Life* (Westport, CT: Bergin & Garvey, 1989).

43. Evan Watkins, *Work Time* (Palo Alto, CA: Stanford University Press, 1989).

44. I refer to aesthetic texts here in much the same sense that Madeleine Grumet does in her essay, "The Politics of Personal Knowledge," in *Stories Lives Tell: Narrative and Dialogue in Education*, Carol Witherell and Nel Noddings, eds. (New York: Teachers College Press, 1991); 67–77. Reaching beyond traditional literary form, Grumet describes "aesthetic form [as] a resymbolization of experience distinguished from other markings, account books, shopping lists, even letters, by its freedom from instrumentalism." (68) The latter is especially important to my notion of embodied narrative that is both personal and public.

45. For a good discussion of Marxist literary criticism, see Eagleton, *Marxism and Literary Criticism*; Williams, *Marxism and Literature*.

46. For a discussion of psychoanalysis as it relates to embodied narrative, see Kristeva, *Revolution in Poetic Language*; and Jacques Lacan, "The Mirror Stage as Formative of the Function of the I," and "The

Subversion of the Subject and the Dialectic of Desire in the Freudian Unconscious," in *Ecrits: A Selection*, Alan Sheridan, trans. (New York: Norton, 1977), 2, 319.

47. For discussions of semiotics and its relation to psychoanalysis, see Jeffrey Mehlman, "The Floating Signifier: From Levi-Strauss to Lacan," *Yale French Studies* 48 (1972): 37; Claude Levi-Strauss, "The Effectiveness of Symbols," in *Structural Anthropology*, vol. 1, Claire Jacobson and Brooke Grundfest Schoepf, trans. (New York: Basic Books, 1963), 203. For a discussion of the phenomenological bases of modern linguistics, see Jacques Derrida, "The Supplement of Copula: Philosophy Before Linguistics," in *Textual Strategies*, Josue V. Harari, trans. and ed. (Ithaca, NY: Cornell University Press, 1979), 82–120; also Derrida, *Speech and Phenomena, and Other Essays on Husserl's Theory of Signs*, David B. Allison, intro. and trans. (Evanston, IL: Northwestern University Press, 1973). For a different but related perspective on language, one that speaks to the overlap in theories, philosophies, and methods of inquiry when the goal is to discuss how each works with and against the other in embodied narrative—in Husserl, narrative in which the subject is a subject of intuition, conscious of his or her own essence or experience—is offered in Edmond Husserl's theory of signs and in his introduction to the study of phenomena or the recovery of phenomena that allows one to know one's essence, particularly through linguistic tracings. See Husserl, *Ideas: General Introduction to Pure Phenomenology*, W. R. Boyce Gibson, trans. (London: Allen and Unwin, 1969). On the nature of reconceptualizing the self through narrative, see Madeleine Grumet, "Autobiography and Reconceptualization," in *Journal of Curriculum Theorizing* 2 (1980): 155–158; and William Pinar, "Autobiography and the Architecture of Self," presented at the annual conference of the American Educational Research Association, San Francisco, April, 1986. The use of and/or reference to phenomenological and/or reconceptualist methods has not necessarily been for purposes of seeing if something begins in a particular place or at a particular time nor even for what might be called the whole picture (I do not assume a complete picture exists); rather, it has been more to examine phenomena historically (to get a sense of its history), perhaps, simply to see what I can see and as much of it as I am capable of seeing at any particular moment in time with the idea that the closer one gets to an object/image/construct, the more one can entertain the possibilities for other constructs.

48. Foucault, *Power and Knowledge*, 99, 114–115, 145.

49. Jacques Derrida, *Of Grammatology*, Gayatri Spivak, trans. (Boston: Johns Hopkins University Press, 1976), 86–87. In this discussion Derrida considers our "beginning to write without the line . . . also

to reread past writing according to a different organization of space . . . to read what wrote itself between the lines." (86) This, for me, perhaps best exemplifies the notion of erasures.

50. Eckstein eloquently presents several descriptions of deconstruction in *The Language of Fiction in a World of Pain*, 33–34. Specifically, she contrasts her own thinking with J. Hillis Miller's approach; Miller's method seems to be more of a disentangling of a web with the impression that you can disentangle to the point of nothingness. The deconstructive interrogation I describe more closely follows Eckstein's approach.

51. Jacques Derrida, *The Ear of the Other: Texts and Discussions with J. Derrida*, Peggy Kamuf, trans., Christi V. McDonald, ed. (New York: Schocken Books, 1985), 84.

52. Gloria Anzaldua, "Haciendo caras, una entrada (An Introduction)," in *Making Face, Making Soul: Creative and Critical Perspectives by Women of Color*, Gloria Anzaldua, ed. (San Francisco: Aunt Lute Foundation Books, 1990), xxv–xxvi.

53. Michel Foucault, "The Political Function of the Intellectual," *Radical Philosophy* 17 (1977): 12–14.

54. Michael Ryan, *Marxism and Deconstruction: A Critical Articulation* (Baltimore: Johns Hopkins University Press, 1982), 1.

55. Gloria Anzaldua, *Borderlands: La Frontera* (San Francisco: Aunt Lute Foundation Books, 1987).

56. Eckstein, *The Language of Fiction in a World of Pain*, 17.

57. Barbara Johnson, *The Critical Difference: Essays in the Contemporary Rhetoric of Reading* (Baltimore: Johns Hopkins University Press, 1980), x–xi.

58. Gayatri Spivak, trans., "Draupadi" by Mahasveta Devi, *Critical Inquiry* 8 (1981): 382.

59. For excellent discussions of "otherness," see Kristeva, *Revolution in Poetic Language*; and Stuart Charme's, *Vulgarity and Authenticity: Dimensions of Otherness in the World of Jean-Paul Sartre*, (Amherst: University of Massachusetts Press, 1991).

60. Kristeva, *Revolution in Poetic Language*, 47–49.

61. Anzaldua, *Making Face, Making Soul*, xvi.

62. Simone de Beauvoir, *Memoirs of a Dutiful Daughter* (New York: Harper & Row, 1959), 179, 182.

63. Kristeva, *Revolution in Poetic Language*, 48; see also Mehlman, "The Floating Signifier: From Levi-Strauss to Lacan," 37; and Lacan, *Ecrits*, 299.

64. Kristeva, *Revolution in Poetic Language*, 48–49, 147–148. Kristeva defines rupture as "scission and separation . . . when it is considered from the point of view of the subject and already constituted in meaning . . . and because [scission and separation] emphasize the underlying unity which withdraws and is reconstituted in . . . rejection." (147–148) Rejection in this sense references a prelinguistic phase, according to Kristeva.

65. Fredrich Nietzche, *On the Genealogy of Morals*, (New York: New Vintage Books, 1969), 27.

66. Derrida, *Of Grammatology*, 27–73. In this critique of phenomenology, Derrida posits the indeterminacy of meaning.

67. Kristeva, *Revolution in Poetic Language*, 41, 88, 195–197. As a signifying practice Kristeva adds "narrative, meta-language, contemplation, and text-practice" to Lacan's four discourse types: "the hysteric, the academic, the master, and the analyst." (88) For a further rendering of the place of the body in narrative as social practice, see Marilyn Edelstein, "Metaphor, Meta-Narrative, and Mater-Narrative in Kristeva's 'Stabat Mater,'" in *Body/Text in Julia Kristeva*, David Crownfield, ed., (Albany: State University of New York Press, 1992), 27–52. In Crownfield's book, Kristeva is referred to both as a border crosser (from Bulgaria to Paris) and as a boundary crosser because she, as Edelstein writes: "[moves] fluidly . . . between structuralism and poststructuralism, modernism and postmodernism, philosophy and literature, religion and psychoanalysis." (27–28) And in "Inter-Text 7" Crownfield writes that her work marks "a more positive possibility. . . . Through knowledge and technique we acquire some mastery of the symbolic and awareness of its limits, and through play and practice we live and move through it." [I read play and practice as narrative so fully embodied that it upends the symbolic. I read symbolic here as a representation such as when narrative is considered only as a representation of experience. I perceive within Kristeva's body/text a fully cognizant and present subject at play constructing self and world.]

68. Alfred Schutz, "On Multiple Realities," in *The Problem of Social Reality*, Collected Papers I, Maurice Natanson, ed. (The Hague: Martinus Nijhoff, 1967), 213.

69. Greene, *Landscapes of learning*, 22–23.

70. Bakhtin, *The Dialogic Imagination*, 341–344.

71. For a thorough discussion of residual and emergent meanings and practices, see Williams, *Marxism and Literature*, 121–127. For a clear example of how Williams both critiques society and speaks of possibility see, *The Long Revolution*, 101–122.

72. For a discussion of the ways in which humans continually make themselves up—reconstruct, reorganize—within the articulated frames of discourse, power, and knowledge, see Foucault, *Power and Knowledge*, 211.

73. Alice Jardine, *Gynesis: Configurations of Women and Modernity* (Ithaca: Cornell University Press, 1985), 18.

74. Foucault, *Power and Knowledge*, 114–115.

75. Bakhtin, *The Dialogic Imagination*, 344.

76. Kristeva, *Revolution in Poetic Language*, 49.

77. Barthes, "Introduction to the Structuralist Analysis of Narratives," in *Image, Music, Text*, 123–124.

78. Jerome Bruner, *Actual Minds, Possible Worlds.* (Cambridge: Harvard University Press, 1986); Kenneth Bruffee, "Social Construction, Language, and the Authority of Knowledge: A Bibliographic Essay," *College English* 48 (1986): 773–790; see also Harold Rosen, "The Autobiographical Impulse," in *Linguistics in Context: Connecting Observation with Understanding*, Deborah Tannen, ed. (Norwood, NJ: Ablex Publishing, 1988), 69–88.

79. Stephen Greenblatt, *Shakespearean Negotiations: The Circulation of Social Energy in Renaissance England* (Los Angeles: University of California Press, 1988), 4.

80. Foucault, *Power and Knowledge*, 113, 131, 198–199.

81. See, for example, Williams, *Marxism and Literature* and *Problems in Materialism and Culture*; Eagleton, *Criticism and Ideology* and *Marxism and Literary Criticism*; Gramsci, *Selection from Prison Notebooks*.

82. Freire, *Education for a Critical Consciousness*, 57–58.

83. Foucault, *Power and Knowledge*, 113.

84. Chandra Mohanty, "On Race and Voice: Challenges for Liberal Education in the 1990s," *Cultural Critique* 0882–4371 (1990): 179–208.

85. Anzaldua, *Making Face, Making Soul*, xxiv.

CHAPTER 2. REFLECTION AND TEACHING

1. John Dewey, *How We Think* (Carbondale: Southern Illinois University Press, 1933), 120, 175.

2. Annie Dillard, "Spring," in *Pilgrim at Tinker Creek* (New York: Quality Paperback Book Club, 1990/1974), 104–122.

3. Ibid., 105.

4. Dewey, *How We Think*, 120.

5. Dillard, "Spring."

6. Foucault, *Power and Knowledge*, 211.

7. Ibid., 212.

8. Dillard, "Spring," 105.

9. Ibid.

10. See, for example, Valerie Walkerdine, *Counting Girls Out* (London: Virago Press, 1989).

11. Adrienne Rich, *Of Woman Born* (New York: w. W. Norton, 1986), 64, 67.

12. Derrida, *Writing and Difference*, 8.

13. Sander Gilman, *Difference and Pathology: Stereotypes of Sexuality, Race, and Madness* (Ithaca, NY: Cornell University Press, 1985), 17.

14. Johnson, *The Critical Difference*, x–xi.

15. Greene, *Landscapes of Learning*, 122.

16. Jacques Derrida, *Positions* (Chicago: University of Chicago Press, 1981), 27.

17. Ira Shor, *Culture Wars: School and Society in the Conservative Restoration 1969–1984* (New York: Routledge & Kegan Paul, 1986), 59–103.

18. Jerome Harste, Virginia Woodward, and Carolyn Burke, *Language Stories and Literacy Lessons* (Portsmouth, NH: Heinemann Educational Books, 1984), xiii.

19. Bauer, "The Other 'F' Word: The Feminist in the Classroom," 385.

20. Anzaldua, "Tlilli, Tlapalli: The Path of the Red and Black Ink," 30.

21. Juncker, *Writing (with) Cixous*, 424.

22. Patti Lather, *Getting Smart: Feminist Research and Pedagogy with/in the Postmodern* (New York: Routledge, 1991), 163.

23. Kristeva, *Revolution in Poetic Language*, 49.

24. Foucault, "The Political Function of the Intellectual," 14.

25. Dillard, "Spring," 105.

26. Kristeva, *Revolution in Poetic Language*, 49.

27. Foucault, *Power and Knowledge*, 212.

28. Spivak, "Draupadi," 382.

29. Johnson, *A World of Difference*, 15.

30. Derrida, *Positions*, 27.

31. Foucault, *Power and Knowledge*, 211; Williams, *The Long Revolution*, 121–122.

32. Eckstein, *The Language of Fiction in a World of Pain*, 17.

33. Stephen North, *The Making of Knowledge in Composition* (Upper Montclair, NJ: Boynton/Cook, 1987).

34. Stanley Aronowitz and Henry Giroux, *Postmodern Education* (Minneapolis: University of Minnesota Press, 1991), 92–93.

35. Ibid.

36. See Pierre Bourdieu and Jean-Claude Passeron, *Reproduction in Education, Society, and Culture* (London: Sage, 1977); see also David Swartz, "Pierre Bourdieu: The Cultural Transmission of Social Inequality," *Harvard Educational Review* 47 (1977): 545–555.

37. Bruffee, "Social Construction, Language, and the Authority of Knowledge," 773–790.

38. Bakhtin, *The Dialogic Imagination*; Foucault, *The Archaeology of Knowledge*.

39. Bourdieu and Passeron, *Reproduction in Education, Society, and Culture*.

40. Bakhtin, *The Dialogic Imagination*, 294.

41. See Kristeva, *Revolution in Poetic Language* and Bakhtin, *The Dialogical Imagination*.

42. Bourdieu and Passeron, *Reproduction in Education, Society, and Culture*.

43. Giroux, *Teachers as Intellectuals*, 51.

44. Derrida, *Writing and Difference*, 8.

45. See Foucault, *Power and Knowledge*, 109–133.

46. Rudine Sims, *Shadow and Substance: Afro-American Experience in Contemporary Children's Fiction* (Urbana, IL: National Council of Teachers of English, 1982).

47. Rudine Sims, "Words by Heart: A Black Perspective," *Interracial Books for Children Bulletin* 12 (1980): 12–15, 17.

48. Forrest Carter, *The Education of Little Tree* (Albuquerque: University of New Mexico Press, 1976).

49. See Henry Louis Gates, Jr., "'Authenticity,' or the Lesson of Little Tree," *New York Times Book Review* (November 24, 1991), 9, 26–30; Rick Hampson, "Indian Author Unmasked as KKK Leader," *Detroit Free Press* (October 5, 1991); John Leland and Marc Peyser, "New Age Fable from an Old School Bigot? The Murky History of the Best-selling 'Little Tree'," *Newsweek* (October 14, 1991), 62; Diane McWhorter, "Little Tree, Big Lies," *People Magazine* (October 28, 1991), 119–121.

50. For an excellent discussion on this subject, see Lather, *Getting Smart*, 162–164.

51. Donald Schon, *Educating the Reflective Practitioner* (San Francisco: Jossey-Bass, 1987).

52. Sheila Rowbotham, "What Do Women Want? Woman Centered Values and the World as It Is," *Dalhousie Review* 64 (Winter, 1984–1985): 650.

53. For a complete discussion of the concept of teachers as "transformative intellectuals," see Giroux, *Teachers as Intellectuals*, 121–128. I am also using the notion of an intellectual in the Foucauldian sense as the intellectual who is both positionally linked to an "apparatus of truth" and simultaneously engaged in a struggle to detach the "power of truth from the forms of hegemony, social, economic and cultural, within which it operates." See *Power and Knowledge*, 132–133. John Dewey's philosophies have also addressed the need for teachers to have a space to grow and become otherwise. He writes, "We are free in so far as we are becoming different from what we have been." See "Philosophies of Freedom," in *On Experience, Nature, and Freedom*, R. Bernstein, ed. (New York: Liberal Arts Press, 1960/1928), 280.

54. For an excellent and comprehensible study of the patriarchal nature of language see, Dale Spender, *Man Made Language* (Boston: Routledge & Kegan Paul, 1980).

55. Greene, *Teacher as Stranger*.

56. Bakhtin, *The Dialogic Imagination*. 341–342.

57. Greene, *The Dialectic of Freedom*, 4.

58. George Wood told me this story in December, 1986.

59. Marie Nelson and I discussed this concept at a colloquium on literacy and democracy in November, 1990.

60. Rich, *Of Woman Born*, 64, 67.

61. Refer to Foucault, *Power and Knowledge*, 113–131 for a more political discussion on this subject.

62. Dewey, *How We Think*, 172.

63. For a more complete discussion of dialogical processes, see Bakhtin, *The Dialogic Imagination*.

64. Mohanty, *On Race and Voice*, 195.

65. I had a conversation with Jennifer Gore on this subject at the American Educational Research Association Annual Meeting, Chicago, April, 1991.

66. Anzaldua, *Borderlands*, 195.

67. See, for example, Ruth Bleier, "Lab Coat: Robe of Innocence or Klansman's Sheet?" in *Feminist Studies Critical Studies*, Teresa de Lauretis, ed. (Bloomington: Indiana University Press, 1986) 55–66; Ruth Hubbard, *The Politics of Women's Biology* (New Brunswick: Rutgers University Press, 1990); Evelyn Fox Keller, *Feeling for the Organism: The Life and Work of Barbara McClintock* (San Francisco: Freeman, 1983); Fox Keller, "Making Gender Visible in the Pursuit of Nature's Secrets," in *Feminist Studies Critical Studies*, Teresa de Lauretis, ed. (Bloomington: Indiana University Press, 1986), 67–77; Carolyn Merchant, *The Death of Nature: Women, Ecology, and the Scientific Revolution* (San Francisco: Harper & Row, 1980).

68. Hubbard, *The Politics of Women's Biology*, 8.

69. Ibid.

70. Bleier, "Lab Coat," 55–66.

71. Woolf, *A Room of One's Own*.

72. Ibid., 54.

73. On the importance of story in meaning-making, see Bruner, *Actual Minds, Possible Worlds*; Gordon Wells, *The Meaning Makers:*

Children Learning Language and Using Language to Learn (Portsmouth, NH: Heinemann, 1986).

74. Williams, *The Long Revolution*, 353–354; for a more complete discussion of Williams notion of progress as a process see pages 344–355.

75. Ibid., 353.

76. Ibid., 353–354.

77. A version of this text on the plight of children living in pain and poverty is printed in a flier published by the Potter Park Outreach Ministries and distributed to social organizations in the hopes of receiving donations to help children.

78. Eckstein, *The Language of Fiction in a World of Pain*, 181.

79. Pagano, *Exiles and Communities*, 13.

80. Gramsci, *Selections from the Prison Notebooks*, 324.

81. Louis D. Rubin, Jr. ed., *An Apple for My Teacher* (Chapel Hill, NC: Algonquin Books, 1987).

82. Greene, *Teacher as Stranger*, 268.

83. Torey Hayden, *One Child* (New York: Avon Books, 1980).

84. This statement references Dillard's bird watcher in "Spring," 105.

85. Greene, *Teacher as Stranger*, 269.

86. Schon, *Educating the Reflective Practitioner.*

87. Gene Maeroff, *The Empowerment of Teachers: Overcoming the Crisis of Confidence* (New York: Teachers College Press, 1988).

88. Dillard, "Spring."

89. Greene, *Teacher as Stranger.*

90. Ibid., 268.

91. Herbert Marcuse, *The Aesthetic Dimension* (Boston: Beacon, 1978), 72.

92. Greene, *Teacher as Stranger.*

93. Greene, *Teacher as Stranger*, 267.

94. Dewey, *Experience and Education*, 55.

95. Dewey, *How We Think*, 118.

96. Ibid., 118.

97. Greene, *Landscapes of Learning*, 22–23.

98. This quote from a student's journal references the following books: J. D. Salinger, *The Catcher in the Rye* (New York: Bantam, 1964); Alice Walker, *The Color Purple* (New York: Simon & Schuster, 1985); Sylvia Plath, *The Bell Jar* (New York: Harper & Row, 1971).

99. Henry David Thoreau, *Walden* (New York: Washington Square Press, 1963).

100. Schutz, "On Multiple Realities," 213.

101. Greene, *Teacher as Stranger*, 269.

102. Greene, *Landscapes of Learning*, 223.

103. Dewey, *Experience and Education*, 36.

104. Thoreau, *Walden*, 16.

105. Greene, *Teacher as Stranger*, 270.

106. Gould, "Philosophy of Liberation and the Liberation of Philosophy," 38.

107. Greene, *Landscapes of Learning*.

108. Williams, *Marxism and Literature*, 132–133.

109. Marilyn Frye, *The Politics of Reality: Essays in Feminist Theory* (New York: The Crossing Press, 1983), 5.

110. Williams, *Marxism and Literature*, 131.

111. Williams, *The Year 2000*, 250.

112. Personal communication with Andrew Gitlin, April, 1991. For further reading on the subject, see Andrew Gitlin, "Power and Method," paper presented at the American Educational Research Association Annual Meeting, Chicago, April, 1991.

113. Eudora Welty, *One Writer's Beginning* (New York: Warner, 1983), 16.

114. Robert Coles, *The Call of Stories* (Boston: Houghton Mifflin, 1989), 30.

115. Ibid.

116. Daphne Patai, "Who Should Eat the Last Piece of Cake?" *International Journal of Oral History* 8 (1987): 5–27: 6–7.

117. Ibid., 7.

118. Coles, *The Call of Stories*, 7.

119. Personal communication with I. E. Seidman, March, 1991.

120. Coles, *The Call of Stories*, 8.

121. Gitlin, "Power and Method."

122. Patai, "Who Should Eat the Last Piece of Cake?," 6–7.

123. Quoted from the Division K Newsletter/AERA, 1991, 2.

124. Michael Polanyi, *Personal Knowledge* (Chicago: University of Chicago Press, 1958).

125. Richard Butt and Danielle Raymond, "Studying the Nature and Development of Teachers' Knowledge Using Collective Autobiography," *International Journal of Educational Research* 13 (1989): 403–419.

126. Pinar, "Autobiography and the Architecture of Self."

127. Greene, *Landscapes of Learning*.

128. Margaret Buchman, "Argument and Contemplation in Teaching," *Oxford Review of Education* 14 (1988): 201–214: 203.

129. Greene, *Landscapes of Learning*, 22–23.

130. Gustave Flaubert, *Madame Bovary*, Joan Charles, trans. (New York: International Collectors Library, 1949), 3.

131. Freire, *Pedagogy of the Oppressed*.

132. *Dead Poets' Society*. Peter Wier, dir., with Robin Williams (Hollywood: Touchstone, 1989).

133. See Apple, *Ideology and Curriculum*; Bourdieu and Passeron, *Reproduction in Education, Society, and Culture*; Henry Giroux, *Ideology, Culture and the Process of Schooling* (Philadelphia: Temple University Press, 1981).

134. Mike Rose, *Lives on the Boundary* (New York: Penguin, 1989).

135. Bakhtin, *The Dialogic Imagination*.

136. Greene, *Landscapes of Learning*, 22–23.

137. *Dead Poets' Society*, Wier; *Lean on Me*, John G. Avildsen, dir., with Morgan Freeman (Warner Bros., 1989); *Teachers*, Arthur Hiller, dir., with Nick Nolte and Judd Hirsch (United Artists, 1984); *Educating*

Rita, Lewis Gilbert, dir., with Michael Caine and Julie Walters (Columbia, 1984); "Head of the Class," (Lansing: Fox, 1989); "Parker Lewis Can't Lose," (Lansing, Fox, 1991).

138. Freire, *Pedagogy of the Oppressed*; Paulo Freire and Donaldo Macedo, *Literacy: Reading the Word and the World* (South Hadley, MA: Bergin & Garvey, 1987).

CHAPTER 3. EDUCATION AS A LIBERAL ART

1. Landon Beyer, *Knowing and Acting: Inquiry, Ideology, and Educational Studies* (New York: Routledge, 1988), 40–41.

2. Henry Giroux and Peter McLaren, "Teacher Education as a Counter Public Sphere: Notes toward a Redefinition," in *Critical Studies in Teacher Education: Its Folklore, Theory and Practice*, Thomas Popkewitz, ed. (New York: The Falmer Press, 1987), 266–297.

3. Beyer, *Knowing and Acting*.

4. Ibid., 41.

5. E. D. Hirsch, Jr., *Cultural Literacy: What Every American Needs to Know* (Boston: Houghton, 1987).

6. Williams, *Marxism and Literature* and *The Long Revolution*.

7. Schutz, "On Multiple Realities," 213.

8. Christopher Lasch, *The Minimal Self* (New York: Norton, 1984), 59.

9. Beyer, *Knowing and Acting*, 40.

10. Joseph Campbell, *The Power of Myth* (New York: Doubleday, 1988), 99.

11. *Dead Poets' Society*, Weir.

12. Mark Collins, "Make-Believe in *Dead Poets' Society*," *English Journal* 78 (1989): 74–75: 74.

13. Hirsch, *Cultural Literacy*.

14. Stanley Aronowitz and Henry Giroux, "Schooling, Culture, and Literacy in the Age of Broken Dreams: A Review of Bloom and Hirsch," *Harvard Educational Review* 58 (1988): 80–102.

15. Ibid., 91.

16. Hirsch, *Cultural Literacy*; Allan Bloom, *The Closing of the American Mind* (New York: Simon & Schuster), 1987.

17. *Dead Poets' Society*, Weir; Aronowitz and Giroux, "Schooling, Culture, and Literacy in the Age of Broken Dreams."

18. Henry Giroux, "Critical Literacy and Student Experience: Donald Graves' Approach to Literacy," *Language Arts* 64 (1987): 175–181.

19. *Dead Poets' Society*, Weir.

20. Bloom, *The Closing of the American Mind*; Hirsch, *Cultural Literacy*.

21. Giroux, "Critical Literacy and Student Experience."

22. Bel Kaufman, *Up the Down Staircase* (Englewood Cliffs: Prentice Hall, 1964).

23. Muriel Sparks, *The Prime of Miss Jean Brodie* (New York: Plume, 1984).

24. Pink Floyd, *The Wall* (Hollywood: Warner Bros., 1979).

25. Paulo Freire and Henry Giroux, "Pedagogy, Popular Culture, and Public Life," Foreword to Henry Giroux and Roger Simon, *Popular Culture, Schooling, and Everyday Life* (Westport, CT: Bergin & Garvey, 1989), ix.

26. Mohanty, "On Race and Voice," 195.

27. Henry Giroux, David Shumway, Paul Smith, and James Sosnoski, "The Need for Cultural Studies," in *Teachers as Intellectuals*, Henry Giroux, ed. (South Hadley, MA: Bergin & Garvey, 1988), 143–157.

28. Greene, *Landscapes of Learning*; see also, Kantor, Trousdale, Jungck, Bennison, and Marshall, "Images of Schooling in the Arts;" and Buchman, "Argument and Contemplation in Teaching."

29. Williams, *Television and the Working Class*, 57.

30. Greenblatt, *Shakespearean Negotiations*, 4.

31. See, for example, Bourdieu and Passeron, *Reproduction in Education, Society, and Culture*.

32. Greenblatt, *Shakespearean Negotiations*, 5.

33. Ibid.; see also Mohanty, "On Race and Voice."

34. Watkins, *Work Time*.

35. Scholes, *Protocols of Reading*, 1.

36. Williams, *Television and the Working Class* and *Marxism and*

Literature; Eagleton, *Criticism and Ideology* and *Marxism and Literary Criticism*.

37. Judith Fetterly, *The Resisting Reader: A Feminist Approach to American Fiction* (Bloomington: Indiana University Press, 1978).

38. Ibid.; Todd Gitlin, "Television's Screens: Hegemony in Transition," in *Cultural and Economic Reproduction in Education: Essays on Class, Ideology, and the State*, Michael Apple, ed. (Boston: Routledge & Kegan Paul, 1982), 202–246; Watkins, *Work Time*. Ira Shor and Paul Freire also refer to students suggesting "problem-themes" out of their own cultural experiences when engaging in dialogue. See *A Pedagogy for Liberation: Dialogues on Transforming Education* (South Hadley, MA: Bergin & Garvey, 1987).

39. Greene, *Landscapes of Learning*, 219.

40. Pagano, *Exiles and Communities* and Grumet, *Bitter Milk*.

41. Gordon Kelly, Introduction to "Mother Was a Lady: Strategy and Order in Selected American Children's Periodicals, 1865–1890." (Diss., University of Iowa, 1970), 1–32; Lenore Weitzman, "Sex-role Socialization in Picture Books for Preschool Children," *American Journal of Sociology* 77 (1973): 1125–1151; Marcia Lieberman, "Someday My Prince Will Come: Female Acculturation Through the Fairy Tale," *College English* 5 (1972): 382–395.

42. Kate Chopin, *The Awakening* (New York: Churchill International Corporation, 1978).

43. Ibid., 79.

44. Goodman, *Elementary Schooling for Critical Democracy*.

45. Grumet, *Bitter Milk*.

46. Helene Cixous, "The Laugh of the Medusa," *Signs* 1 (1976): 875–893.

47. Toni Morrison, *Beloved* (New York: New American Library, 1987), 164.

48. Schutz, "On Multiple Realities," 213.

49. Gramsci, *Selections from the Prison Notebooks*.

50. Morrison, *Beloved*, 273.

51. Joel Taxel, "The American Revolution in Children's Fiction: An Analysis of Historical Meanings and Narrative Structure," *Curriculum Inquiry* 14 (1984): 7.

52. Marcuse, *The Aesthetic Dimension*, 72.

53. Gould, "Philosophy of Liberation and the Liberation of Philosophy," 38.

54. Chopin, *The Awakening*, 168.

55. Nichols, *Ideology and the Image*.

56. Ibid., 57.

57. Kristeva, *Desire in Language*; Gilles Deleuze, *Cinema 2: The Time-Image*, Hugh Tomlinson and Robert Galeta, trans. (London: The Athlone Press, 1985).

58. Nichols, *Ideology and the Image*, 57.

59. Rosenblatt, *Literature as Exploration*.

60. Gilles Deleuze, *Cinema 1: The Movement-Image*, Hugh Tomlinson and Barbara Habberjam, trans. (London: The Athlone Press, 1985).

61. Rosenblatt, *The Reader, the Text, the Poem*.

62. Virginia Woolf, "The Movies and Reality," in *Film and/as Literature*, John Harrington, ed. (Englewood Cliffs, NJ: Prentice-Hall, 1977), 267.

63. Georg Lukacs, *Studies in European Realism* (London: Hillway, 1950).

64. Watkins, *Work Time*.

65. Gitlin, "Television's Screens," 202.

66. Ibid.

67. Evan Watkins, "Television Programming and Household Flow: Critical Analysis of Mass Culture in a Politics of Change," *The Centennial Review* 34 (1990): 34.

68. Woolf, "Movies and Reality."

69. For more in-depth discussions of the political economy of texts and publishing, see Michael Apple, "Regulating the Text: The Socio-Historical Roots of State Control," *Educational Policy* 3 (1989): 107–123; Michael Apple and Linda Christian-Smith, eds., *The Politics of the Textbook* (New York: Routledge & Kegan Paul, 1991).

70. James L. Collins and Michael Williamson, "Spoken Language and Semantic Abbreviation in Writing," *Research in the Teaching of English* 15 (1981): 23–35.

71. Mohanty, "On Race and Voice," 195

72. Frederic Jameson, *The Political Unconscious* (Ithaca, NY: Cornell University Press, 1981).

73. Bakhtin, *The Dialogic Imagination*, 294.

74. Ibid., 295.

75. Ibid., 341–344.

76. George Kelly, *The Psychology of Personal Constructs* vol. 1 (New York: Norton, 1955).

77. Jameson, *The Political Unconscious*.

78. Ira Shor and Paulo Freire, *A Pedagogy for Liberation: Dialogues on Transforming Education* (South Hadley, MA: Bergin & Garvey, 1987).

79. Barbara Hardy, "Narrative as a Primary Act of Mind," in *The Cool Web: The Patterns of Children's Reading*, M. Meek, A. Warlow, and G. Barton, eds. (Great Britain: Atheneum, 1977), 12.

80. Anzaldua, "Tlilli Tlapalli: The Path of the Red and Black Ink," 30.

81. Eckstein, *The Language of Fiction in a World of Pain*, 181.

82. Apple, *Teachers and Texts*, 6.

83. *Dead Poets' Society*, Weir.

84. Lasch, *The Minimal Self*, 59.

85. Linda McNeil, *Contradictions of Control* (New York: Routledge & Kegan Paul, 1988), xiii.

86. "Parker Lewis Can't Lose," (Lansing: Fox, 1991); also see, for example, the principal's response to Gabe Kotter's role in the sitcom "Welcome Back Kotter," (Jacksonville: CBS, 1969).

87. *Ferris Beuller's Day Off*, John Hughes, dir., with Matthew Brokerick and Allen Ruck (Hollywood: Paramount Pictures, 1986).

88. *Dead Poets' Society*, Weir; *Teachers*, Arthur Hiller, dir., with Nick Nolte and Judd Hirsch (Hollywood: United Artists, 1984).

89. Bakhtin, *The Dialogic Imagination*.

90. Greene, *Landscapes of Learning*, 169.

91. Scholes, *Protocols of Reading*.

92. Williams, *Marxism and Literature*; Eagleton, *Marxism and Literary Criticism*.

93. Shor and Freire, *A Pedagogy for Liberation*.

94. Williams, *Television and the Working Class*.

95. *Dead Poets' Society*, Weir.

96. See Williams, *Television and the Working Class* and Shor and Freire, *A Pedagogy for Liberation* for a comparison of and complete discussion of the role of dialogue in making sense of the world from television and other texts.

97. Philip Wexler, *Social Analysis of Education* (New York: Routledge & Kegan Paul, 1987), 110.

98. See Wolfgang Iser, *The Art of Reading: A Theory of Aesthetic Response* (Baltimore: Johns Hopkins University Press, 1978); Eco, *The Role of the Reader*.

99. Roland Barthes, *S/Z* (New York: Wang & Hill, 1974), 5.

100. See Grumet, "Autobiography and Reconceptualization," and William Pinar, "Life History and Educational Experience: Part I," *Journal of Curriculum Theorizing* 2 (1980): 159–212.

101. Personal communication with Stanley Straw, February, 1989, Chicago, Illinois.

102. Rosenblatt, *The Reader, the Text, the Poem*.

103. Ibid.

104. Lukacs, *Studies in European Realism*; Rosenblatt, *Literature as Exploration*.

105. Grumet, *Bitter Milk*; Michael Apple, "Gendered Teaching, Gendered Labor," in *Critical Studies in Teacher Education: Its Folklore, Theory and Practice*, Thomas Popkewitz, ed. (New York: Falmer, 1987), 57–83.

106. "Our Miss Brooks," Perry Clark, prod. (Jacksonville: CBS, 1950); Kaufman, *Up the Down Staircase*; Sparks, *The Prime of Miss Jean Brodie*.

107. For an excellent discussion, see Freire, *Education for a Critical Consciousness*, 1–58.

108. For a thorough discussion of how tracking reproduces social forms, see Henry Giroux and Peter McLaren, "Reproducing Reproduction: The Politics of Tracking," in *Teachers as Intellectuals*, Henry Giroux, ed. (South Hadley, MA: Bergin & Garvey, 1988), 186–195.

109. McNeil, *Contradictions of Control*.

110. Schon, *Educating the Reflective Practitioner*, xi.

111. Freire, *Education for Critical Consciousness*, 1–58.

112. Giroux and McLaren, "Reproducing Reproduction: The Politics of Tracking," 186–195.

113. Childress, *A Hero Ain't Nothing but a Sandwich*.

114. Bruner, *Actual Minds, Possible Worlds*.

115. Hardy, "Narrative as a Primary Act of Mind," 12.

116. Annie Dillard, *An American Childhood* (New York: Harper & Row, 1987), 178–184.

117. Ibid., 183.

118. Ibid., 178–184.

119. Victor Nell, *Lost in a Book* (London: Yale University Press, 1988).

120. *Lean on Me*, John G. Avildsen, dir., with Morgan Freeman (Hollywood: Warner Bros., 1989).

121. Suzanne Langer, *Philosophy in a New Key* (Cambridge, MA: Harvard University Press, 1957).

122. Berthoff, *Forming/Thinking/Writing*.

123. *Stand and Deliver*, Ramon Menendez, dir., with Edward James Olmos and Lou Diamond Phillips (Hollywood: Warner Bros., 1988).

124. Rose, *Lives on the Boundary*.

125. Giroux, *Theory and Resistance in Education*.

126. Shor and Freire, *A Pedagogy for Liberation*.

127. Wells, *The Meaning Makers*.

128. Janet Miller, "Generative Criticism in Curriculum Theory and Professional Practice." A paper given at the Annual Meeting of American Educational Research Association, Chicago, IL, April, 1991.

129. Ibid., 2.

130. Ibid.

131. Ibid.

CHAPTER 4. TEACHING AND TEACHERS
IN STORIES OF SCHOOLING

1. "Our Miss Brooks," Clark; "Leave it to Beaver," (Jacksonville: CBS, 1950).

2. *Teachers*, Hiller.

3. Dorothy Heathcote, "How Does Drama Serve Thinking, Talking, and Writing?" *Elementary English* 47 (1970): 177–80, 177.

4. Linda Christiansen, "Unlearning Myths That Bind Us: Students Critique Stereotypes in Children's Stories and Films," *Rethinking Schools*, special ed. (1991), 53–55, 53.

5. The Brothers Grimm, "Cinderella," in *Grimms' Fairy Tales*, E. V. Lucas, Lucy Crane, and Marian Edwardes, trans. (New York: Grosset & Dunlap, 1945), 155–165.

6. David Dillon, ed. "Reading the World and Reading the Word: An Interview with Paulo Freire," *Language Arts* 62 (1985): 15–21.

7. Ariel Dorfman, *The Empire's Old Clothes: What the Lone Ranger, Babar, and Other Innocent Heroes do to our Minds* (New York: Pantheon, 1983), ix.

8. "Parker Louis Can't Lose," Fox.

9. Washington Irving, "The Legend of Sleepy Hollow," in *The Complete Tales of Washington Irving*, Charles Neider, ed. (New York: International Collectors Library, 1975), 31–56.

10. Eliot Wigginton, *Sometimes a Shining Moment* (New York: Doubleday, 1986), 291.

11. Pat Conroy, *The Water is Wide* (New York: Bantam, 1986).

12. *The Class of Miss MacMichael*, George Barrie, prod. as adaptation of the novel by Sandy Hutson (Columbia, 1975).

13. McNeil, *Contradictions of Control*.

14. Ibid., 157–158.

15. Ibid., 158.

16. Ibid., 158–159.

17. "Little House on the Praire," (Lansing: Fox, 1991).

18. Henry Giroux and Paulo Freire, "Introduction," to Kathleen Weiler, *Women Teaching for Change* (New York: Bergin & Garvey, 1988), x.

19. Cormier, *The Chocolate War*.

20. This definition of hegemonic control is offered for more thorough discussion throughout Gramsci, *Selections from the Prison Notebooks*.

21. Charles Dickens, *Nicholas Nickleby* (London: Chapman & Hall, 1839).

22. Williams, *Marxism and Literature*, 108–114.

23. Foucault, *Discipline and Punish*.

24. See, especially, Williams, *Marxism and Literature*, 121–135.

25. Evan Hunter, *The Blackboard Jungle* (New York: Simon & Schuster, 1954).

26. *Lean on Me*, Avildsen.

27. Alan Peshkin, "Whom Shall the Schools Serve?" in *Justice, Ideology, and Education*, Edward Stevens and George Wood, eds. (New York: Random House, 1987), pp. 291–310.

28. Ibid., 294.

29. See Gramsci, *Selections from the Prison Notebooks*; Williams, *Marxism and Literature*.

30. Williams, *Marxism and Literature*, 87, 110.

31. Joseph Heller, *Catch 22* (New York: Simon & Schuster, 1961).

32. Gramsci, *Selections from the Prison Notebooks*, 25.

33. Ibid., 40.

34. See also Williams, *Problems in Materialism and Culture*.

35. Williams, *Marxism and Literature*, 113–114.

36. *Lean on Me*, Avildsen.

37. John Williams, *Stoner: A Novel* (New York: Viking, 1965).

38. Freire, *Education for Critical Consciousness*, 1–58.

39. William Raspberry, "School and Business Partnerships," *The New York Times* (October 23, 1990).

40. John Dewey, "Democracy in Education," *The Elementary School Teacher* 4 (1903): 193–204.

41. Arthur Bestor, *The Restoration of Learning* (New York: Alfred A. Knopf, 1955).

42. For a more thorough treatment of this topic, see Paul Willis,

Learning to Labour: How Working Class Kids Get Working Class Jobs (Westmead: Saxon House Press, 1977).

43. For an excellent discussion of sexist language patterns, see Spender, *Man Made Language.*

44. Ashton-Warner, *Spinster*, 41, 61.

45. For an excellent and thoroughgoing discussion of 'valuation,' see Barbara Herrnstein Smith, *Contingencies of Value: Alternative Perspectives for Critical Theory* (Cambridge: Harvard University Press, 1988).

46. See, for example, recent studies by Michael Apple, "Curricular Form and the Logic of Technical Control: Building the Possessive Individual," in *Cultural and Economic Reproduction in Education*, Michael Apple, ed. (Boston: Routledge & Kegan Paul, 1982); Madeleine Arnot, "Male Hegemony, Social Class, and Women's Education," *Journal of Education* (1984): 64–89; Stanley Aronowitz and Henry Giroux, *Education under Siege: The Conservative, Liberal, and Radical Debate over Schooling* (South Hadley, MA: Bergin & Garvey, 1985); David Cohen, "Greater Expectations," *The Nation* (May 25, 1985): 615–622; Sara Freedman, "Master Teacher/Merit Pay—Weeding out Women from Women's 'True' Profession," *Radical Teacher* 25 (1985): 24–29.

47. Weiler, *Women Teaching for Change.*

48. Giroux and Freire, Intro. to Weiler, *Women Teaching for Change*, xiii.

49. Ibid., 151.

50. Grumet, *Bitter Milk*, 43.

51. Pagano, *Exiles and Communities*, xiii.

52. Ibid.

53. Mary Field Belenky, Blythe McVicker Clinchy, Nancy Rule Goldberger, Jill Mattuck Tarule, *Womens Ways of Knowing: The Development of Self, Voice, and Mind* (New York: Basic Books, 1986).

54. Noddings, *Caring.*

55. Pagano, *Exiles and Communities*, 81.

56. Ashton-Warner, *Spinster.*

57. Ibid., 103, 117.

58. Ibid., 58–61.

59. Grumet, *Bitter Milk*, 54.

60. Weiler, *Women Teaching for Change*, 85.

61. Ibid., 84.

62. Weiler, *Women Teaching for Change*, 83.

63. Frye, *The Politics of Reality*, 5.

64. For an excellent discussion of mathematics education and female socialization, see Walkerdine, *Counting Girls Out*.

65. E. Abrams, *A Curriculum Guide to Women's Studies for Middle School, Grades 5–9* (New York: The Feminist Press, 1981).

66. Grumet, *Bitter Milk*, 55.

67. Dan C. Lortie, *Schoolteacher: A Sociological Study* (Chicago: University of Chicago Press, 1975), 54.

68. Kenneth Zeichner, "Alternative Paradigms on Teacher Education," *Journal of Teacher Education* 34 (1983): 7

69. Ashton-Warner, *Spinster*, 101.

70. For a thorough treatment of this topic, see Arnot, "Male Hegemony, Social Class, and Women's Education."

71. Weiler, *Women Teaching for Change*.

72. Belenky et al., *Women's Ways of Knowing*.

73. Weiler, *Women Teaching for Change*, 118–119.

74. Apple, "Gendered Teaching, Gendered Labor," 73.

75. Sherwood Anderson, "The Teacher," in *Winesburg, Ohio: A Group of Tales of Ohio Small-Town Life* (New York: Huebsch, 1919).

76. Ashton-Warner, *Spinster*.

77. Kathleen Kranida, *One Year in Autumn* (Philadelphia: Lippincott, 1965).

78. Lillian Hellman, *The Children's Hour* in *Twenty Best Plays*, John Gassner, ed. (New York: Crown, 1939).

79. Nancy Garden, *Annie on My Mind* (New York: Farrar, Straus & Giroux, 1982).

80. Mildred Taylor, *Roll of Thunder, Hear My Cry* (New York: Bantam Books, 1976).

81. Ibid., 139–140.

82. See Williams, *Marxism and Literature* and Kranida, *One Year in Autumn*.

83. Gramsci, *Selection from the Prison Notebooks*.

84. Apple, "Gendered Teaching, Gendered Labor," 76–78.

85. Taylor, *Roll of Thunder, Hear My Cry*.

86. *Separate but Equal*, a General Motors Mark of Excellence production, George Stevens, Jr. prod. (Lansing: Lifetime, 1991).

87. Walter Feinberg and Jonas Soltis, *School and Society* (New York: Teachers College Press, 1985), 123.

88. James Hilton, *Good-bye Mr. Chips* (Boston: Little, 1934).

89. Ibid., 81.

90. Taylor, *Roll of Thunder, Hear My Cry*.

91. Hilton, *Good-bye Mr. Chips*.

92. Freire, *Education for Critical Consciousness*, 57.

93. Brown, *Literacy in Thirty Hours*, 5.

94. For a discussion of the importance of reading the word/world critically, see Paulo Freire, "The Importance of the Act of Reading," in *Rewriting Literacy: Culture and the Discourse of the Other*, Candace Mitchell and Kathleen Weiler, eds. (New York: Bergin & Garvey, 1991), 139–146.

95. Judy Mitchell and Don Sakers, *Another Country* (a play) in *Leaves of October* (New York: Baen, 1988).

96. Freire, *Education for Critical Consciousness*, 57.

97. Weiler, *Women Teaching for Change*, 151.

98. See, for example, Anthony Giddens, *Central Problems in Social Theory* (Berkeley: University of California Press, 1983); Giroux, *Theory and Resistance in Education*; Giroux and McLaren, "Teacher Education as a Counter Public Sphere"; and Weiler, *Women Teaching for Change*, 151–153.

99. Weiler, *Women Teaching For Change*, 151.

100. Williams, *Marxism and Literature*, 121–127.

CHAPTER 5. TURNING THE GAZE

1. From the movie *Pump up the Volume*, Allan Mogledi, dir., with Christian Slater and Ellen Greene (Burbank: New Line Cinema, 1990). This quote not only suggests the theme of the movie, but also perhaps

the theme of this chapter; that is, students have to talk hard if they want their voices to be heard given the constraints of their positioning.

2. "Welcome Back Kotter," CBS.

3. Carol Gilligan, *In a Different Voice* (Cambridge, MA: Harvard University Press, 1982), 61–63.

4. Greene, *The Dialectic of Freedom*, 4.

5. Ruth Vinz, "Silences," in *Vital Signs 1: Bringing Together Reading and Writing*, James L. Collins, ed. (Portsmouth, NH: Heinemann & Boynton/Cook, 1990), 52.

6. Bakhtin, *The Dialogic Imagination.*

7. See Derrida, *Of Grammatology*; and *Writing and Difference.*

8. See the interview with Paulo Freire by the editor of *Language Arts*, David Dillon, "Reading the World and Reading the Word," 15.

9. Buchman, "Argument and Contemplation in Teaching."

10. Greene, *The Dialectic of Freedom*, 3.

11. Ibid.

12. Nicholas Burbules and Suzanne Rice, "Dialogue across Differences: Continuing the Conversation," *Harvard Educational Review* 61 (1991): 393–346.

13. Williams, *Marxism and Literature*, 108.

14. Burbules and Rice, "Dialogue across Differences," 402.

15. *Pump up the Volume*, Mogledie.

16. Rosemary Sutcliff, *Blue Remembered Hills* (Toronto: The Bodley Head, 1983).

17. Williams, *Marxism and Literature*, 48–52.

18. Sutcliff, *Blue Remembered Hills*, 95–97.

19. Ibid., 31–32, 53–54.

20. Lisa Delpit, "The Silenced Dialogue: Power and Pedagogy in Educating Other People's Children," *Harvard Educational Review* 58 (1988): 280–298.

21. Mina Shaughnessy, *Errors and Expectations* (New York: Oxford University Press, 1977).

22. Delpit, "The Silenced Dialogue," 283–284.

23. Sutcliff, *Blue Remembered Hills*, 53–54, 63.

24. *Children of a Lesser God*, Burt Sugarman, dir., with William Hurt and Marlie Maitlin (Hollywood: Paramount, 1986).

25. For a more complete discussion of the notion of teacher-as-colonizers and for a discussion of the potential of autobiographical narrative to combat such behaviors, see, Jo Anne Pagano, "Moral Fictions: The Dilemma of Theory and Practice," in Witherell and Noddings, eds., *Stories Lives Tell*; 202–205.

26. Gilligan, *In a Different Voice*, 62.

27. Williams, *Marxism and Literature*, 23.

28. Louise Rosenblatt, "The Reading Transaction," a paper given at the Fall Conference of the National Council of Teachers of English, November, 1984, Philadelphia.

29. *Children of a Lesser God*, Sugarman.

30. Cormier, *The Chocolate War*.

31. In *Teachers as Intellectual*, Giroux distinguishes between resistance that is personal and that which is political, 160–163.

32. Taylor, *Roll of Thunder, Hear My Cry*; Cormier, *The Chocolate War*.

33. Giroux, *Teachers as Intellectuals*, 160–163.

34. Jamaica Kincaid, *Annie John* (New York: Farrar, Strauss, & Giroux, 1983), 120.

35. *Pump up the Volume*, Mogledie.

36. For similar issues in other films, see, for example, *Stand and Deliver*, Menendez; and *Lean on Me*, Avildsen.

37. Miriam Cohen, *First Grade Takes a Test* (New York: Dell, 1980).

38. For excellent discussions of ideological regulation in curricular materials and other literature, see Apple, *Ideology and Curriculum* and "Regulating the Text"; also Apple and Christian-Smith, eds., *The Politics of the Textbook*.

39. Greene, *Teacher as Stranger*, 16.

40. Feinberg and Soltis, *School and Society*.

41. Ibid., 121–122.

42. Jesse Stuart, *To Teach, To Love* (New York: The World Publishing Co., 1936).

43. Wigginton, *Sometimes a Shining Moment.*

44. Mohanty, "On Race and Voice," 180.

45. The English painter, Ford Maddox Brown's famous painting, "Work," is on display in the Manchester Art Gallery.

46. A reprint of Brown's painting "Work" is also featured in a number of common reference books.

47. Mohanty, "On Race and Voice."

48. Ibid., 181.

49. Foucault, *The Archaeology of Knowledge*, 120–122.

50. Barthes, *Image-Music-Text*, 142.

51. Freire, *Pedagogy of the Oppressed.*

52. Derrida, *Positions*, 27.

53. Barthes, *Image-Music-Text*, 142.

54. Williams, *Marxism and Literature*, 35.

55. Freire, *Pedagogy of the Oppressed*, 67.

56. Ibid.

57. Freire, *Education for Critical Consciousness*, 38.

58. Ibid.

59. Ibid., 58.

60. Ibid., 57.

61. See Pagano, *Exiles and Communities* and in the essay "Moral Fictions," in Witherell and Noddings, eds., *Stories Lives Tell*; and Grumet, *Bitter Milk* and especially the chapter, "Where the Line is Drawn" (in *Bitter Milk*).

62. Freire, *Education for Critical Consciousness*, 57.

63. Ibid., 56.

64. Ibid., 57–58.

65. Pagano, *Exiles and Communities*, 80.

66. Kristeva, *Revolution in Poetic Language*, 49.

67. Pagano, *Exiles and Communities*, 81.

68. Anderson, "The Teacher," 163.

69. Childress, *A Hero Ain't Nothing but a Sandwich*.

70. Ibid., 90.

71. Freire, *Education for Critical Consciousness*, 1–58.

72. See Berthoff, *Forming/Thinking/Writing*; and my discussion of her "double-entry" notebook in Chapter 1 of this book.

73. Willis, *Learning to Labour*.

74. Childress, *A Hero Ain't Nothing but a Sandwich*.

75. John Ogbu, "Class Stratification, Racial Stratification, and Schooling," in *Class, Race, and Gender in American Education*, Lois Weis, ed. (Albany: State University of New York Press, 1988), 163–182.

76. Ibid., 170.

77. Ibid.

78. Lois Weis, *Between Two Worlds: Black Students in an Urban Community College* (Boston: Routledge & Kegan Paul, 1985).

79. Childress, *A Hero Ain't Nothing but a Sandwich*.

80. *Teachers*, Hiller.

81. Wexler, *Social Analysis of Education*, 70.

82. *Teachers*, Hiller.

83. Williams, *Stoner*.

84. Freire, *Pedagogy of the Oppressed*.

85. *Educating Rita*, Lewis Gilbert, dir., with Michael Caine and Julie Walters (Hollywood: Columbia, 1984).

86. Freire, *Pedagogy of the Oppressed*, 67.

87. The film text of *My Fair Lady* or Bernard Shaw's *Pygmalion: A Romance in Five Acts* (New York: Penguin, 1957) may be read in contrast to *Educating Rita* for a more in-depth examination of literacy narratives. Subsequently, incorporating the article by Janet Carey Elred and Peter Mortensen, "Reading Literacy Narratives," *College English* 54 (1992): 512–539 may enhance discussion of each of the imaginative texts.

88. Ethel Ross Oliver, *Journal of an Aleutian Year* (Seattle: University of Washington Press, 1988).

89. *To Sir with Love*, James Clavell, dir., with Sidney Portier and Lulu (Burbank: Columbia Pictures, 1966).

90. *Making History* is reprinted by permission in *The Democracy and Education Bulletin*; the excerpt is from a larger volume entitled *Taking Part, Making History* (Boston: Educators for Social Responsibility, 1986).

91. Ibid., 12–13.

92. For a more in-depth discussion of the notion and usage of "cultural capital," see Basil Bernstein, *Class, Codes, and Control* (London, Routledge & Kegan Paul, 1977); Bourdieu and Passeron, *Reproduction in Education, Society, and Culture*; Giroux, *Teachers as Intellectuals*.

93. *To Sir with Love*, Clavell.

94. Ibid.

95. June Jordan, "Nobody Mean More to Me Than You and the Future Life of Willie Jordan," *Harvard Educational Review* 58 (1988): 363–374.

96. Ibid., 366–367.

97. Walker, *The Color Purple*.

98. Jordan, "Nobody Mean More to Me Than You and the Future Life of Willie Jordan," 368

99. Bruce Springsteen, "War," on *Live/1975–85* (New York: Columbia Records, 1986).

100. Freire, *Pedagogy of the Oppressed*, 67.

101. Nichols, *Ideology and the Image*, 57.

102. Jordan, "Nobody Mean More to Me Than You and the Future Life of Willie Jordan," 374.

CHAPTER 6. MORE STORIES

1. *Henny Penny*, Golden Book Classic.

2. Louisa May Alcott, *Little Women* (New York: Dent, 1948); and *Little Men* (London: Blackie, 1964).

3. Welty, *One Writer's Beginning*, 16.

4. On the process of recovering or taking stock of one's life his-

tory—a process referred to as *currere*, meaning to look backward, to look forward, and after reflection for the purpose of sense making to project oneself into the future—see, Grumet, "Autobiography and Reconceptualization"; Madeleine Grumet, "The Politics of Personal Knowledge," *Curriculum Inquiry* 17 (1987): 319–329; Pinar, "Life History and Educational Experience: Part I"; William Pinar, "Life History and Educational Experience: Part II," *Journal of Curriculum Theorizing* 3 (1980): 259–286; Pinar, "Autobiography and the Architecture of Self."

5. Shor and Freire, *A Pedagogy for Liberation*, 135.

6. Ulric Neisser, *Memory Observed: Remembering in Natural Contexts* (New York: W. H. Freeman, 1982).

7. Quoted in Ashton-Warner, *Teacher*, 26–27.

8. Dickens, *Nicholas Nickleby*.

9. Weiler, *Women Teaching for Change*, 73–100.

10. McNeil, *Contradictions of Control*, xiii, 180.

11. Cormier, *The Chocolate War*; Childress, *A Hero Ain't Nothing but a Sandwich*.

12. Rose, *Lives on the Boundary*; *Stand and Deliver*, Menendez.

13. Wigginton, *Sometimes a Shining Moment*; *To Sir with Love*, Clavell; *Making History*.

14. Jesse Stuart, *Mr. Gallion's School* (New York: McGraw Hill, 1967).

15. Wigginton, *Sometimes a Shining Moment*; Stuart, *To Teach, To Love* and *Mr. Gallion's School*; *To Sir with Love*, Clavell; *Lean on Me*, Avildsen; *Stand and Deliver*, Menendez.

16. *To Sir with Love*, Clavell; Jordan, "Nobody Mean More to Me Than You and the Future Life of Willie Jordan."

17. Ashton-Warner, *Teacher*.

18. Ibid.

19. Freire, *Pedagogy of the Oppressed*, 67; *Educating Rita*, Gilbert.

20. Weiler, *Women Teaching for Change*.

21. *Teachers*, Hiller.

22. *Stand and Deliver*, Menendez; Rose, *Lives on the Boundary*.

23. Ibid.

24. Herbert Kohl, *Growing Minds and Becoming a Teacher* (New York: Harper & Row, 1984).

25. Ibid.

26. Pagano, *Exiles and Communities*, 13; Weitzman, "Sex-role Socialization in Picture Books for Preschool Children."

27. Conroy, *The Water Is Wide*.

28. *Lean on Me*, Avildsen.

29. *Dead Poets' Society*, Weir.

30. Giroux and McLaren, "Reproducing Reproduction"; Childress, *A Hero Ain't Nothing but a Sandwich*.

31. Giroux and McLaren, "Reproducing Reproduction"; Cohen, *First Grade Takes a Test*.

32. Dewey, *Experience and Education*.

33. John Dewey, *Art as Experience* (New York: Minton, Balch, 1934).

34. *Stand and Deliver*, Menendez; *Pump up the Volume*, Mogledie.

35. Weiler, *Women Teaching for Change*.

36 Lather, *Getting Smart*, 125.

CHAPTER 7.
TOWARD REFLEXIVE/REFLECTIVE PRACTICE

1. Gramsci, *Selections from the Prison Notebooks*, 5–27.

2. Elspeth Stuckey, *The Violence of Literacy* (Portsmouth, NH: Heinemann & Boynton/Cook, 1991).

3. *Lean on Me*, Avildsen.

4. Freire, *Education for Critical Conscious*, 57.

5. Ashton-Warner, *Teacher*; Brown, *Literacy in Thirty Hours*.

6. Freire, *Pedagogy of the Oppressed*.

7. Stuckey, *The Violence of Literacy*.

8. Dillon (interview with Freire), "Reading the World and Reading the Word."

9. Ibid., 18, 21.

10. Ashton-Warner, *Teacher*; Rose, *Lives on the Boundary*; Wigginton, *Sometimes a Shining Moment*.

11. Dillon (interview with Freire), "Reading the World and Reading the Word," 17.

12. Rose, *Lives on the Boundary*.

13. Wigginton, *Sometimes a Shining Moment*.

14. Ashton-Warner, *Teacher*; Dillon (interview with Freire), "Reading the World and Reading the Word"; the quote is from a student in class.

15. Berthoff, *Forming/Thinking/Writing*.

16. Dillon (interview with Freire), "Reading the World and Reading the Word," 19.

17. Refers to Ashton-Warner, *Teacher*.

18. Dewey, *Experience and Education*.

19. Woolf, "Movies and Reality."

20. Pat Conroy, *The Great Santini* (New York: Bantam, 1987); Conroy, *The Water Is Wide*; Conroy, *The Prince of Tides* (Boston: Houghton Mifflin, 1986); Conroy, *The Lords of Discipline* (Boston: Houghton Mifflin, 1980).

21. *The Prince of Tides*, Barbara Streisand, dir., with Nick Nolte and Barbara Streisand (Burbank: Columbia Tristar, 1992).

22. *Grand Canyon*, Lawrence Kasden, dir., with Danny Glover, Steve Martin, and Mary McDonnell (Beverly Hills: Fox, 1992); *Boyz N the Hood*, John Singleton, dir., with Morris Chestnut and Larry Fishburne (Burbank: Columbia Tristar, 1991).

23. Nichols, *Ideology and the Image*.

24. Ashton-Warner, *Teacher*, 98–100.

25. Sue Allen is a graduate student in the English Department.

26. Eco, *The Role of the Reader*. See also Wexler, *Social Analysis of Education*, 110.

27. Rashidah Muhammad is a graduate student in the English Department and was my research assistant on this project.

28. Ice T, "Squeeze the Trigger," on *Rhyme Pays* (Universal City: MCA, 1992).

29. Stuckey, *The Violence of Literacy*, 92–94.

30. Ice T, "Squeeze the Trigger," on *Rhyme Pays*; *Boyz N the Hood*, Singleton; *Grand Canyon*, Kasden.

31. Giroux and Simon, *Popular Culture, Schooling, and Everyday Life*.

32. Hammer, "Too Legit to Quit," on *Too Legit to Quit* (New York: Capitol Records, 1991).

33. *Grand Canyon*, Kasden.

34. Ibid.

35. Motley Crue, "Sticky Sweet," MTV; Van Halen, "Good Enough," MTV;

36. Van Halen, "Spanked," on *Buy Now, Pay Later* (Burbank: Warner, 1993); Faster Pussycat, "Where There's a Whip There's a Way," on *Smashes, Thrashes & Hits* (New York: Polygram); Guns and Roses, "The Jungle," on *Appetite for Destruction* (New York: Asylum Records, 1985); Motley Crue, "Slice of Pie," MTV.

37. Metallica, *Master of Puppets* (Los Angeles: Asylum Records, 1986).

38. Anzaldua, *Making Face, Making Soul*, xxiv.

39. *Grand Canyon*, Lawrence Kasden; *Boyz N the Hood*, John Singleton.

40. Giroux and Simon, *Popular Culture, Schooling, and Everyday Life*, xi.

41. Gordon Pradl, "Close Encounters of the First Kind: Teaching the Poem at the Point of Utterance," *English Journal* 66 (1987): 66–69.

42. Shor and Freire, *A Pedagogy for Liberation*.

43. Dillon (interview with Freire), "Reading the World and Reading the Word," 21.

44. Brown, *Literacy in Thirty Hours*, 5.

45. Dillon (interview with Freire), "Reading the World and Reading the Word," 16.

46. Mimi Cecil, a seventh-grade English teacher, introduced me to these books and suggested this theme.

47. Lloyd Alexander, *Westmark* (New York: Dell, 1981).

48. Lloyd Alexander, *The Kestral* (New York: Dell, 1982).

49. Lloyd Alexander, *The Beggar Queen* (New York: Dell, 1985).

50. Williams, *Marxism and Literature*, 114.

51. The Reagan National Commission on Excellence, *A Nation at Risk* (Washington, D.C.: United States Government Printing Office, 1983); Mortimer Adler, *The Paideia Proposal* (New York: McMillan, 1982); The Holmes' Group, *Schools for Tomorrow* (Working Papers, Michigan State University, 1987–88).

52. Weiler, *Women Teaching for Change.*

53. Wexler, *Social Analysis of Education.*

54. Ibid., 70.

55. Giroux and Simon, *Popular Culture, Schooling, and Everyday Life.* x.

56. *Grand Canyon*, Lawrence Kasden; Alexander, *Westmark*; *The Kestral*; *The Beggar Queen.*

57. Mimi Cecil introduced me to these books also and to this thematic emphasis.

58. Margaret Sacks, *Beyond Safe Boundaries* (New York: Penguin, 1989).

59. Beverly Naidoo, *Chain of Fire* (New York: Harper Collins, 1989).

60. Derek Bracey and Greg McCartan, "South African Political Parties Set Negotiations," in *The Militant* 55 (December 20, 1991): 1, 9; August Nimtz, "South Africa Shut Down 2 Days as Millions Strike," in *The Militant* 55 (November 27, 1991): 1, 6; Greg McCartan, "Mandela: South Africa Violence Caused by Apartheid Regime," in *The Militant* 55 (November 1, 1991): 1, 11.

61. Louise Moeri, *The Forty-Third War* (New York: Houghton Mifflin, 1989).

62. Minfong Ho, *Rice without Rain* (New York: Lothrop, Lee & Shepard Books, 1990).

62. Neal Shusterman, *Dissidents* (Boston: Little, Brown, 1989).

64. Greene, *The Dialectic of Freedom*, 4.

65. Kohl, *Growing Minds and Becoming a Teacher.*

66. Coles, *The Call of Stories.*

67. Landon Beyer, "Aesthetic Experience for Teacher Preparation and Social Change," *Educational Theory* 35 (1985): 385–397.

68. Ibid., 387.

69. Springsteen, "War."

70. Beyer, "Aesthetic Experience for Teacher Preparation and Social Change," 393.

71. Nell, *Lost in a Book*, 2.

ANNOTATED BIBLIOGRAPHY
OF SCHOOLING NARRATIVES

Anderson, Sherwood. "The Teacher," in *Winesburg, Ohio: A Group of Tales of Ohio Small-Town Life*. New York: Huebsch, 1919, 303 pp.

Insight into the life of Kate Swift, a small town teacher—her frustrations and her desires.

Ashton-Warner, Sylvia. *Spinster*. New York: Simon & Schuster, 1963, 242 pp.

Anna Vorontosov, an unorthodox teacher of small children, describes her experiences with the Maori children of New Zealand.

Ashton-Warner, Sylvia. *Teacher*. New York: Simon & Schuster, 1963, 224 pp.

A detailed account of the organic reading process—a process that draws on the child's thoughts, ideas, and words.

Barlow, James. *Term of Trial*. New York: Simon & Schuster, 1962, 316 pp.

The story of Graham Wier's experiences as an English teacher. Set in an industrial area in England.

Barth, John. *End of the Road*. Garden City, New York: Doubleday, 1958, 230 pp.

Jacob Horner's experiences as an English teacher at a state teacher's college.

Beith, John H. *The Lighter Side of School Life*. Boston: Foulis, 1914, 226 pp.

A collection of sketches of teachers in English public schools.

Boyce, Burke. *Miss Mallett*. New York: Harper, 1948, 247 pp.

The story of Emily Mallett, a dedicated high school teacher, whose enthusiasm for teaching is felt by every student whom she considers equally important.

Buchan, Laura, and Jerry Buchan. *Hearth in the Snow*. New York: Funk, 1952, 306 pp.

A story of schooling in Alaska.

Cadigan, Robert J., ed. *Stories of School and College Life; September to June*. New York: Appleton, 1942, 424 pp.

A collection of short stories about young people of school age. The book is designed for use by students or by teachers. Stories are grouped by topics; for example, "The Home and the School," "Students in Trouble," "Students and Teachers."

Caldwell, Erskine. *Episode in Palmetto*. New York: Duell, 1950, 252 pp.

A story of a student's feelings toward his teacher and the difficulties those emotions can bring both to the student and the teacher. The complexities of student-teacher relationships is the theme.

Carleton, Jetta. *The Moonflower Vine*. New York: Simon & Schuster, 1962, 352 pp.

A story of Matthew, teacher and superintendent of schools and father of four girls.

Childress, Alice. *A Hero Ain't Nothing but a Sandwich*. New York: Avon Books, 1973, 127 pp. (YA)

A story of a teen-age junkie set in Harlem. Insightful view of school's attitude toward troubled kids.

Cohen, Barbara. *Fat Jack*. New York: Atheneum, 1980, 182 pp. (young adult)

Judy befriends a new student and learns the meaning of true friendship during the senior production of *Henry IV, Part One*.

Cohen, Miriam. *First Grade Takes a Test*. New York: Dell Publishing, 1980, pp.

The story of Anna Maria's first experience with standardized tests and how she responds to the results.

Cormier, Robert. *The Chocolate War*. New York: Dell Publishing 1974, 191 pp. (young adult)

This story is about life in a Catholic high school. Ruled by gangs and teachers who seem almost evil, one student in the school tries to live by a motto even he doesn't understand—Do I dare disturb the universe?

Delima, Agnes. *The Little Red Schoolhouse*. New York: Macmillan, 1942, 355 pp.

This story has an introduction by John Dewey.

Deuel, Leo, ed. *The Teacher's Treasure Chest*. Englewood Cliffs, New Jersey: Prentice-Hall, 1956, 372 pp.

A collection of fiction and nonfiction about teachers and teaching.

Engstrand, Stuart. *Miss Munday.* New York: Dial, 1940, 340 pp.

The story of Helen Munday; it typifies the teacher of another day. Frightened by her principal, she lives a life enmeshed by the demands of her profession, which allow her no freedom of thought or action.

Erskine, John. *My Life as a Teacher.* New York: J. B. Lippincott Co., 1948, 246 pp.

A personal narrative cataloging a notable half-century in American education. Erskine gives his views on teacher education and what he considers differences in teachers and educators.

Fleming, Berry. *The Lightwood Tree.* Philadelphia: Lippincott, 1947, 378 pp.

The story of a high school history teacher who champions a cause. Set in Georgia in 1943.

Fuess, Claude M., and Emory S. Basford. *Unseen Harvests: A Treasury of Teaching.* New York: Macmillan, 1947, 678 pp.

Fictional and nonfictional writings about education.

Gary, Romain. *A European Education.* New York: Simon & Schuster, 1960, 248 pp.

The story of Polish Janek, who said, "They have put us in a *good* school. . . . We're receiving a good education . . . a European education. That's something you receive when they shoot your father, or when you kill somebody, or when you die of hunger."

Hellman, Lillian. *The Children's Hour,* in John Gassner, ed., *Twenty Best Plays.* New York: Crown, 1939, 874 pp.

A false tale of lesbianism is told at the Wright-Dobie School Girls, and a teacher's career and her marriage is ruined.

Hentoff, Nat. *Does This School Have Capital Punishment?* New York: Delacorte Press, 1981, 170 pp. (young adult)

A sequel to *This School Is Driving Me Crazy,* the story of Sam Davidson is that of a likable character with a stormy academic career. While trying to stay out of trouble in his new school, Sam is framed for possession of marijuana.

Hickok, Lorena A. *The Touch of Magic: The Story of Helen Keller's Great Teacher, Anne Sullivan Macy.* New York: Dodd, Mead, 1961, 184 pp.

A famous story of great teaching.

Hilton, James. *Good-bye, Mr. Chips.* Boston: Little, 1934, 125 pp.

The classic tale of an English schoolmaster.

Hughes, Thomas. *Tom Brown's School Days.* New York: Bowman, 1908, 350 pp.

The famous story of school life in the English public school during the nineteenth century. The familiar spirits of boyhood, student-teacher relationships, the reaction to the death of a loved one—all are topics in this book.

Hunter, Evan. *The Blackboard Jungle.* New York: Simon & Schuster, 1954, 309 pp.

Deals with teaching problems in a large city high school.

Irving, Washington. *The Legend of Sleepy Hollow.* New York: Putnam, 1899, 191 pp.

Another classic schoolmaster. Teacher-student relationships are a big topic.

Kaufman, Bel. *Up the Down Staircase.* Englewood Cliffs, New Jersey: Prentice-Hall, 1964, 340 pp.

An in-depth look at a teacher of minutiae.

Kranida, Kathleen. *One Year in Autumn.* Philadelphia: Lippincott, 1965, 218 pp.

A Seattle high school English teacher's story. Student-teacher relationships.

Levitin, Sonia. *Smile Like a Plastic Daisy.* New York: Atheneum, 1984, 182 pp. (young adult)

Story of Claudia's quest for personal freedom. Mr. Xavier, Claudia's journalism teacher, and Glenda French, a lawyer, play an integral role.

Lin Yutang. *Chinatown Family.* New York: John Day, 1948, 307 pp.

Young Tom Fong, born in China, helps his family succeed in New York City. Miss Cartwright and Mr. Watson, Tom's teachers, are instrumental to Tom's development.

Lutes, Della T. *Country Schoolma'am.* Boston: Little, 1941, 328 pp.

The autobiography of a young country school teacher and how she conquers even the toughest boys.

Malamud, Bernard. *A New Life.* New York: Farrar, Straus, 1961, 336 pp.

An urban-oriented Jewish instructor asks, "What is wrong with higher education?"

Mann, R. J., and Perry Clark. *Our Miss Brooks.* New York: Dramatic, 1950, 95 pp.

A humorous story of the life of an English teacher.

Moeri, Louise. *First the Egg.* New York: E. P. Dutton, 1982, 99 pp. (young adult)

Students in a marriage and family class are asked to carry around an egg and treat it like a newborn baby keeping a baby book on its progress. During this project students learn to work with peers, develop a trusting relationship, and share responsibility.

Oliver, Ethel Ross. *Journal of an Aleutian Year.* Seattle: University of Washington Press, 1988, 248 pp.

The account of a teacher's year-long experience on Atka, a tiny island in the Aleutian chain.

Peterson, Houston, ed. *Great Teachers, Protrayed by Those Who Studied Under Them.* New Brunswick, New Jersey: Rutgers, 1946, 351 pp.

Firsthand accounts of teachers as remembered by former students. Selections by well-known authors.

Reece, Bryon H. *The Hawk and the Son.* New York: Dutton, 1955, 192 pp.

An English and history professor comes to the aid of a student who is accused of rape.

Summers, James L. *The Long Ride Home.* Philadelphia: The Westminster Press, 1966, 170 pp. (young adult)

Story shows two teenagers' problems coping with their alcoholic father. Also shows the school and classmates as a strong support system.

Sutcliff, Rosemary. *Blue Remembered Hills.* Toronto: The Bodley Head, 1983, 141 pp.

The memoirs of Rosemary Sutcliff, an autobiographical story of informal schooling, tells of her childhood in which stricken with juvenile arthritis she kept much to books and bed.

Stuart, Jesse. *To Teach, To Love.* New York: The World Publishing Company, 1936, 315 pp.

What teaching means to a famous American teacher-writer. He describes the teachers who inspired him, and those who did not, and tells what made the difference.

Stuart, Jesse. *Mr. Gallion's School.* New York: McGraw-Hill Publishing, 1967, 337 pp.

Story of a teacher for whom teaching was more than a job; it was his life. This thought-provoking novel, though fictionalized, is based on Stuart's personal experiences as a school principal. His views on teaching, delinquincy, parental responsibilities, as well as his assessment of school boards comes through.

Taylor, Mildred. *Roll of Thunder, Hear My Cry.* New York: Bantam Books, 1976, 210 pp. (young adult)

The passionate struggle of a black family determined to survive against all odds. Important school scene in which teacher (who is the mother in this family) is fired for teaching more history of slavery than the textbook represents.

Wallant, Edward L. *The Children at the Gate.* New York: Harcourt, 1964, 184 pp.

The story of an education, but not the education received in school. A story of informal schooling and community between central protagonist, Angelo, and his friend, Sammy.

Ward, Mary Jane. *The Professor's Umbrella.* New York: Random, 1948, 313 pp.

An English professor is fired on a moral's charge. Later we learn that his discharge had to due with the president's prejudice toward Jews.

Warren, Robert Penn. "The Unvexed Isles," in *Circus in the Attic.* New York: Harcourt, 1931, 276 pp.

An English professor is caught in a web of dullness from which he cannot find a means of escaping.

Wells, H. G. *Joan and Peter: The Story of an Education.* New York: Macmillan, 1918, 594 pp.

Joan and Peter, cousins, do not attend formal schools until they are teenagers when suddenly they are into strange situations. The theme: education is the task of everyone; it can unify the world.

Williams, John. *Stoner; a Novel.* New York: Viking, 1965, 278 pp.

The story of a dedicated scholar.

Wolfe, Thomas. *Look Homeward Angel.* New York: Scribner, 1929, 626 pp.

A complete case history of Eugene Gant, including his home environment, early education, experiences at the university, and a follow-up of later life.

Wolfe, Thomas, *Of Time and the River.* New York: Scribner, 1935, 912 pp.

The story of Eugene Gant's playwriting instructor who is influential in Eugene's development. Eugene becomes an English instructor.

Wolfe, Thomas. *The Web and the Rock.* New York: Harper, 1939, 695 pp.

The story of Thomas Wolfe's college days and his trip abroad.

INDEX